The Dynamic Choral Conductor

by

Royal Stanton

Shawnee Press inc.

Delaware Water Gap, Pa. 18327

Library of Congress Catalog Card No. 79-143878
(M-337)

PREFACE

The poet Trowbridge wrote, "Of nothing comes nothing: Springs rise not above their source. . . ." Translated into choral terms this might read "Of the Conductor comes everything: His choir rises no higher than he lifts them".

Choral conducting literature has exhaustively explored the skills, techniques, knowledge, training, and performance practices essential to the conductor's function. Authors have dealt with the "art" of conducting, recognizing that much more than technique is involved. But what of the conductor himself? Are techniques part of the lengthening shadow of the person? How personal is the "art"?

There is persuasive evidence that the personality — the image — of the conductor is important to choir singers and audience members in today's culture. We hear of the Fred Waring Glee Club, the Robert Shaw, Harry Simeone, and Roger Wagner Chorales, the Norman Luboff Choir, the Gregg Smith and Robert DeCormier Singers, and others whose musical contributions are identified *first* by the name and image of the conductor. Other choirs whose achievements are not tagged by a conductor's name still reflect a towering figure, such as F. Melius Christiansen of the St. Olaf Choir and John Finley Williamson of the Westminister Choir. Several European choirs with traditions longer than the span of a lifetime continue to identify strongly with outstanding conductors who have led them. While watching the 132-year-old Huddersfield Choral Society in rehearsal, the author was told with obvious pride by one of the officers of the organization, "This was Sir Malcolm Sargent's choir, you know!"

This book examines the function of the choral conductor in this light. It will construct an idealized image of the conductor laboring in "average" realms: schools, colleges, churches, and community organizations. How does his environment affect what he does, who he is, and what he must strive to become? How does he communicate to his choir and his audiences? What values in addition to the obvious technical materials of his craft must he embody and convey? Most basic of all, *why* are these values, and his activities which stem from them, vital to his function and the continuing health of the choral art?

Judged on a numerical basis alone, choirs represent an abundantly healthy segment of the total musical activity of America today. Professional organizations, community functions, schools, colleges, churches, commercial enterprises, folk and popular music interests all rejoice in some sort of choral activity. Yet it is ironically and glaringly apparent that with few outstanding exceptions the status and impact of such endeavors is far below that of comparable instrumental and solo-performance activities in public esteem.

Why? Choral singing has at least as long a history and tradition as other styles of performance. Scriptural reference to "heavenly choirs" suggests that the concept of group singing was already firmly established in the minds of the ancient prophets who produced the sacred texts. Is there something about the contemporary scene, or the modern practice of the art, which produces this loss of esteem?

Tides of change have risen higher in the past half-century than in any comparable period in history, and are eroding the foundations of many long-established concepts. Certainly the bases of "traditional" choral art are feeling the ebb and flow of such currents to an increasing and potentially devastating degree. It seems time again to assess the strengths and weaknesses of those bases, because the temper of our times more and more forces choral activity to justify itself, either by pitting its strengths squarely against the exigencies of its time, or by adapting to and building upon them. In either case, the restless ebullience of modern society demands that the action be vigorous and the justification dynamically asserted.

This can be done only by individuals who are motivated and equipped to reveal anew to our times the inner core of dynamic urgency which has always enlivened great choral singing. Their efforts must marshal again, and prove once more in the performance of modern choirs, the demonstrated ability of choral music to move, inspire, and demand the best. It is, lamentably, too easy to find choral organizations who evidently are content to base their activity on opposing motivations: tradition, habit, complacency, or the pursuit of the miniscule. They seem to believe that the honored old choral tradition will forever provide them sanctuary to go on doing what they have always done, in the same comfortable way.

Ever since conducting has been recognized as a distinct function, conductors and writers have engaged in two rather consistent activities: first, documenting their experiences and ideas to show how they felt effective conducting is achieved, and second, lamenting the low state to which the art had fallen in their day. In suggesting that much modern choral conducting suffers from a lack of dynamic urgency, inadequate or outmoded preparation, or simple inept performance, this book may seem to be concerned principally with lamentation. But its complaints spring from a desire to perpetuate effective conducting, and take heart from the presence of many outstanding, dynamic, and effective conductors who, though they are probably a minority of the total, still grace and invigorate the present scene. It is hoped that their efforts and example will be seen as confirmation of the book's tenets.

What is the role of the choral conductor today? What must he be, and do, and act like, if he is to influence the music of his era dynamically? Can he understand why it may well be by the very dynamism of his efforts that the continued viability of choral music may stand or fall?

It is to such broad questions that this book addresses itself. It is presumed that the reader will consult the literature of choral conducting for detailed accounts of skills, factual information, and specific techniques he may need. The present work views techniques in enough detail to suggest how the choral conductor in the "average" situation in America – roughly 99% of the total! – can supply a dynamic response to his specific challenges. Technical devices are considered in the light of a philosophy which says that to be effective in this age of speed, competition, and challenge, choral conducting must be a dynamic, dramatically attractive endeavor which commands the respect, holds the attention, and involves the best effort of busy people. If it fails to assert this place with sufficient vigor, it may well become obsolescent, as the choral art which sustains it loses relevancy to its times.

While the tone of most of the book is frankly idealistic, its specific usefulness will be enhanced by a group of Practical Projects, included in the Appendix after Chapter 9. These are structured to illustrate the principles discussed in several different chapters, and provide means by which the conductor may explore the relevance of those principles to his own situation in an organized way. It is hoped that this may commend the book to the training of new conductors, and also assist the established conductor in re-evaluating his problems and skills.

The author expresses his deep appreciation to his wife, Norine, for her encouragement and patience well beyond the call of duty during the long evolution of this book; to Robert G. Olson for competent advice and counsel; to Mrs. Marjorie Farmer for her expert, good-humored guidance; to the memory of the late John Smallman and Arthur Leslie Jacobs for early encouragement given in hope and faith; to all the skilled conductors from whom the author has had the privilege of learning; and to each member of his choirs during thirty years of conducting, who through either endurance or generosity have continued to come back for one more rehearsal.

Contents

3 | The Conductor's Communicative Techniques (II): Non-Verbal

4 | The Conductor and Choral Tone

7 | The Conductor's Many Jobs

8 | The Conductor's Attitudes about Styles and Repertoire

9 | The Impact of the Conductor's Image

1|Changing Conditions of Choral Conducting

The changing job of the conductor

The nature of the choral conductor's job in America is changing. Its characteristic traditional outlines are being redrawn by the pressures of today's evolving musical scene. Music has mushroomed into Big Business, and its use as a profitable resource by commercially-oriented communications media has altered most phases of musical life. Choral music is no exception; as a result, the choral conductor serves a changeable master.

It is pertinent to re-examine the scope and challenge of the job in the context of these changing conditions. While it has always been necessary to keep choral conducting abreast of its times, today's ever-widening gap between what is "traditional" and what is "new" makes the present mandate particularly urgent. Choral training which is entirely traditional in orientation increasingly exposes conductors to the embarrassment of finding themselves unprepared for crucial challenges which confront them in trying to build choirs that are relevant to modern conditions.

Conditioning of singers and audiences

This growing disparity is part of the fabric of rapid change which clothes most contemporary life. Daily living has been completely reshaped in the last fifty years by a revolution in communication. The principal channels of this revolution — radio, recording, motion picture, and television — have brought both opportunity and frustration to the choral art, and are radically modifying some of its most basic concepts and values. Americans have become musical spectators to a degree unparalleled in history. Whether or not they ever try active participation in music-making for themselves, they are overwhelmed with an omnipresent atmosphere of musical sound, the polished attractiveness of which makes it very easy for them to sit back and listen. In many cases they have to be shown by dynamic and attractive leadership that rewards meaningful to them personally will flow from the effort needed to make the musical sounds for themselves. Once this has been forcefully demonstrated, of course, the power of music to stimulate and satisfy is found to be as great as ever. Nowhere is this situation more relevant than in choral singing.

From the cradle on, potential singers have been nurtured on background musical sounds to an extent which would have been incomprehensible to their great-grandparents. Some of these sounds involved more or less musical productions of the human voice, either singly or in groups. It is logical to assume that the individual's subconscious ideas of what singing sounds like are pretty well structured by his environment long before he receives any conscious training in the matter. This means that the conductor meeting a group of potential choir singers for the first time can hardly hope to write on a clean slate in their minds. He finds it scribbled over with haphazard, widely divergent concepts about tone, musical styles, vocal expressiveness, and musical values generally. His options are limited at the outset: either try to erase vigorously — a dubious procedure at best — or seek to bring order into, and build upon, concepts already present.

A more demanding role today

In the midst of all this diversity, the position of the conductor remains virtually the only — certainly the strongest — hope for the continuing growth, adaptability, and relevance of the choral function. Institutional or traditional reasons for choral activity, such as the liturgy of an established church or a tradition of choral folk-singing, are no longer strong enough to stimulate and justify the periodic renewal of choral effort. While choirs have proliferated in connection with a wide variety of activities and institutions — schools, colleges, churches, recreational functions, commercial enterprises — that very connection often provides the only real reason for their existence, and it is basically a non-musical motivation.

The most basic realization needed in reassessing the conductor's job is that where choral music is continuing to lose influence it is because of *the complacent, uninformed, unskilled manner in which too many choral conductors face today's challenges.* Only where sufficiently dynamic, musical conducting motivates the situation does choral music continue to assert its time-honored, most-valid reason for being: that it is a vital, expressive, satisfying form of human endeavor in its own right. When it glows with this inner fire it has no trouble being heard and accorded the honor due.

The increasing complexity of modern culture has forced upon the conductor a greatly widened spectrum of things he is expected to know, to be, and to do. The more forcefully dynamic his leadership, the larger the realm of these expectations becomes. No longer is he charged merely with directing musical performance within a sheltered, well-ordered artistic environment. He may now be called on to be the catalyst which will move singers away from their television screens and into a rehearsal hall. He must enthuse them about singing, teach voice to the majority who will never study privately, know and select music of interest and variety, provide training in fundamental musicianly skills which will make performance possible, and be proficient in such non-musical skills as organization, publicity, money management, and "public relations". He must know his singers as persons, and be conversant enough with the non-musical world to be regarded as knowledgeable and current. Through and above all he must strive to be a thorough musician, whose musical integrity shines brightly in everything he does.

Modern choirs, nature and purpose

Choirs in other-than-professional settings are comprised primarily of musical laymen, young and old. They participate for many reasons: as part of a learning process, for recreation, musical satisfaction, personal accomplishment, to be of service, in response to their inner need to be part of a group, or from mere curiosity. In welcoming them as they come in, the conductor needs to answer for himself such questions as: What do they expect? What do they need? What can they do? In what ways do they look to the conductor to fulfill their desires and needs and help them realize their potential?

Answers to these questions actually define the job of the dynamic conductor if they are realistic and positive. They also reveal a great deal about the purpose and function of the choir itself which must be understood clearly by the conductor. The reasons for its existence should be clearly defined and generally understood at the outset, so that effort will not be dissipated in the fruitless pursuit of cross-purposes. The available variety of such reasons has multiplied with the complexities of our culture, and it is certain that singers coming into a choir situation bring with them widely varied understandings of what a "choir" is and does.

Even where the environment seems to predetermine the choir's purpose and the nature of its activity, confusion may exist. Does the church choir do "programs" or sing secular music in addition to its liturgical duties? If so, for what purpose? To raise money, build morale, or for "fun" — thus implying that their regular repertoire is not? Shall the school or college choir do masterworks exclusively, or sacred literature, or pop styles, or avant garde works, or some combination? Are choirs in educational institutions aimed chiefly at the education and growth of the singers themselves, or at a select concert audience, or at the Rotary Club? Does the community choir seek to be the non-professional counterpart of the Shaw and Wagner Chorales, an expanded church choir, or some new and unique entity that reflects its community? How aware is *any* choir of its fundamental motivations and most promising opportunities? Answers to these questions will take as many forms as there are choir members, and the conductor is the only one in a position to set a unified course for the whole group. Faced with this need to bring order out of diversity, he may cast covetous looks at many European cathedral choirs, who carry on established traditions which dictate the music to be sung, the time and place of rehearsals and performances (services), and often the qualification and training of singers. But such glances are idle; few, if any, American choirs are graced by equivalent surety of purpose and structure.

Group singing — choral music, if you will — is no longer the exclusive treasure of church and academe, occasionally enjoying professional status in a few established concert organizations. It now thrives in the service of television, radio, recording, and motion picture, both to entertain and to sell everything from Abrasives to Zippers. Fairy-tale success stories of pop groups achieving overnight fame and fortune have cast a new and alluring light on certain types of group singing in the public mind. That this "success" is basically pecuniary only enhances its seductive power, tending to obscure the fact that musical values have been forced to take second place to the mandate for instant, wide-spread acceptance.

It is simply a fact that the common understanding of "choir" is changing from that of a group of singers in robes performing serious (dull?) music to one that includes practically any combination of more than two or three singers performing almost anything. Demands for new flexibility have subdivided the term into "combo", "group", "chorale", "ensemble", "singers", and a host of more graphic appellations. The lure of this "new" and far-ranging orbit of entertaining-glamorous-profitable singing is tremendous, and the gulf between it and more traditional practices is widening.

Relevance of traditional training

It is the traditional viewpoint, however, which still trains most choral conductors. Because this approach has been firmly established, it tends to assume that interest in the choral art as it has always been will continue under its own momentum, and that its rich repertoire and tradition will continue to attract new recruits as in the past. In its most reactionary forms, it refuses to admit that the times may call for a fresh, dynamic approach based on current needs, which will both exploit new resources and preserve the riches of tradition. It is content to regard the large numbers of performing choirs and the large volume of sheet music sold as ample confirmation of present choral health.

Choral music has long been a part of school curricula, and the church choir has its roots in the very earliest American traditions. Yet is lamentably true that a disquietingly large proportion of school and church music is largely a statistical entity which is mechanical, flaccid, and completely devoid of vital meaning. Often it is continued chiefly because it has become traditional in its environment to have it around. That it is bad technically, limp expressively, and in flagrant cases, an outright offense to the ear, fails to deter it. That far too often these faults can be traced directly to demonstrably incompetent direction leads to very little change. American audiences and congregations, a docile, long-suffering, (and diminishing) breed, have evidently learned to close their ears, endure the singing in grim patience, biding their time until they can get back to their TV, where the singing even in the commercials will be more attractive and accurate.

Audiences have had the same early conditioning to music as singers, so that their reactions in the long run cannot be expected to differ sharply. Since choral singing is by nature a social activity, simple public acceptance will always play some part in determining its effectiveness. This fact is crucial for the new chorus singer who is tentatively venturing out of his comfortable audience status, and for whom loftier vistas of the art have yet to unfold their wonders. Indeed, his hesitant explorations may stand or fall primarily on what he feels his peers think about what he is doing. If he finds himself surrounded by sounds which even his inexpert but media-trained ears tell him are dull or bad, unrelated to anything else he knows about, and certainly devoid of challenge, interest, or excitement — and then in addition his friends tell him he is wasting his time — why should he continue?

The problem of diminishing interest, even in the best of traditional choirs, was graphically illustrated in the situations of several leading European choral organizations visited by the author in the fall of 1968. Choirs with up to 150 years of continuous tradition, who were still doing creditable performances of the traditional repertoire, all admitted to increasing difficulty in recruiting new young singers, particularly men. At the same time the streets outside their rehearsals were alive with groups of teenagers and young adults, restively seeking excitement and satisfaction, and carrying portable radios which blared forth the music of the currently popular rock group or protest singer. One could only reflect that it must have been easier for the older generation to decry the irresponsibility of the young than to set about communicating the excitement of choral singing to them.

As a result of this changing climate, *every* choral conductor, novice and old hand, and regardless of the musical style involved, faces a stern challenge every time he meets his choir. What he asks them to do *must* be sufficiently vital and meaningful, and have at least some of its more obvious satisfactions showing clearly, so that it actually commands the full attention and participation of the singers. This is no mean feat in an era in which the human psyche swims in floods of attention-demanding "communication". It may be easier for the individual simply to shut it all off — "drop out" —, and take refuge in inner silence.

Challenge of modern communication

It is ironically true that some of the most effective "music education" takes place quite apart from educational circles. Commercial and communications-media music which the public encounters in every-day social settings is brightly attractive, and communicates forcefully for a very simple reason: It *works!* Effective communication is its principal strength; its economic motivation decrees sudden death for the obscure. Its musical product must be attractive, viable, and completely understandable at once. The overtly bad sounds and tedious repertoire heard in some schools and churches simply are not tolerated.

In defense of church and school, it is obvious that to the extent such sounds and pieces represent processes of growth, learning-by-mistakes, broadening of horizons and development of skills, they are proper and defensible. Church music which actually achieves and imparts genuine spiritual meaning and inspiration must certainly be allowed some technical shortcomings. Commercial interests, after all, don't have to teach their performers anything, nor inspire their audiences to deeds more lofty than accellerated buying.

When, however, choral cacophony results from lack-luster conducting, fumbling communication, arid thought, deficient imagination, tepid enthusiasm, inadequate preparation, or poor technique on the part of the conductor, it cannot be defended at all. School and church music doesn't need to sell a product, and should traffic in a far more precious commodity: rewarding musical experience with which to enrich the inner lives of its singers. Dynamic choral performance is just such experience; tepid, faulty singing is not.

Vital singing is bought with devotion and effort, and the novice chorister may be reluctant at the outset to pay the price. He has absorbed surface musical ideas from his environment so easily that he may fail to see why he should put out the greater effort and time needed to attain the more technical skills of choral singing. The conductor must be prepared to show him challenging reasons, and by the power of dynamic leadership get him so involved in the activity that the singer scarcely has time to be intimidated by its difficulties.

Impatience quickly displaces interest for the novice when drill is tedious and technical explanations drag on. He has come there to *sing,* and although it may not be entirely possible from the viewpoint of the disciplined training needed to accomplish truly artistic performance, he expects to achieve reasonable proficiency by the most direct and pleasant route possible. Perhaps his view of "reasonable" is colored by the limitations of his layman's interest, but in any event he confidently expects the conductor to lead him along that path. If such progress is not forthcoming, he either loses interest and drops out, or contents himself with the non-musical satisfactions of membership, such as status and pleasant social intercourse.

It is thus not sufficient that the conductor have completely adequate technical training, know the score thoroughly, and be led by sensitive artistic insight. He must also become expert in communication, *and uniquely skilled in precisely those methods of teaching which will work in the instant.* In such a realm of mandates, tedium and mediocrity are most undesirable aliens.

The purpose of this book

Hopefully this book will speak to the old hand as well as the beginner. The demands of successive year-in-year-out rehearsal and performance take an inevitable toll of sparkle, inventiveness, drive, and the capacity to be meaningfully unpredictable. If the ensuing discussions can pump new sap into the branches of method or rekindle a spark of excitement in making the old choir produce new sounds, they will be of value. If they can hold out to the budding conductor the assurance that choir building, in the words of the familiar hymn, is "a path, though thorny, *bright*", they will have served well.

The aim here will be to examine *why* the dynamic conductor must act in certain consistent ways, and what he actually *does* to lead his singers into the joys of conquering their musical challenges. Why must he be a master of communication? What should he expect of them? What will he have to teach them about making tone and using their voices? Why is his control in such matters so crucial? How will he woo their tentative interests? How sustain their faltering, imperfect efforts? How does he organize their diverse potentials into one group entity? How will he lead them into the presence of the ancient non-verbal truths of great choral sound? Why and how will he convey the great choral tradition to minds culturally conditioned to equate "new" with "good", and "old" with "inferior"? Why must he treasure, as his ultimate personal challenge, those fleeting, precious moments of intensity when he has at last captured that rare essence: the complete and undivided attention of his singers?

In such moments music is made or turned away. They are his opportunity to tint his singers indelibly with the richest hues of choral meaning. They can also leave the equally indelible mark which forever says to the singer that choral singing is dull, tedious, and forbidding — certainly not for him. The temper of American culture is making such moments harder to come by, and thus increasingly urgent. More than ever before the success of an ongoing choral tradition demands dynamic and comprehensive leadership which is prepared to use them wisely.

Great choral singing needs no defense, whatever its musical style. Poor choral singing can no longer be afforded any defense, whatever *its* style. No more can it be allowed the sanctuary of "Oh, well — it's only school (church, amateur, community) music!" Only, indeed! Some of the greatest composers wrote their most exalted works for precisely this kind of "only" situation. It is doubtful if they would accept such a weak apology as justification for mangling their music. Robert Shaw once remarked that a person who would dump garbage on a church altar would be branded an impious desecrator. Yet how many choirs lay the trash of bad sound, poor technique, and inferior repertoire on religious and educational altars primarily because the conductor's leadership has somehow failed in skill, knowledge, insight, or dynamic vitality!

2|The Conductor's Communicative Techniques (I): Verbal

Communication in conducting

To conduct is to communicate. A principal justification for the role of the conductor is that he communicate a steady flow of musical ideas, cues, nuances, moods, and interpretive concepts to his singers. When this flow is interrupted the conductor's function becomes largely redundant, forcing the choir to rely on its own musicianly empathy to continue, or simply to stop performing as an entity.

Professional musicians know from experience that it is possible to perform without a conductor, and that if the man up in front is glaringly inept they may be called on to make creditable music by themselves, in spite of what happens on the podium. Relying on personal skills of musicianship, they compensate for the conductor's lack of coordination and impetus. When the singers' skills are of a high order, the resulting performance may be technically competent, but is rarely inspired or vibrantly expressive. It lacks the creative leadership which only a conductor can supply.

Amateur singers in school, church, and community choirs are less expert in musicianly skills and must rely even more completely on the conductor's communicative guidance. If he fails to communicate, his choir has no effective means of drawing together as a productive unit. Or if, after the down beat, he withdraws his communicative control because he has to pay more attention to the score than to the singers or shrinks from maintaining the productive tension of constant contact with them, the resulting performance will inevitably be mechanical, uncoordinated, and probably lethargic. Such constant contact requires poise and courage. It is the mark of the truly effective, dynamic conductor at any level of musical endeavor. The communicative control needed to inspire and lead a group of restless adolescents, or to stir the inertia of adult laymen to musical accomplishment differs only in the nature of the musical product from the demands facing the conductor of professional singers. The failure of many conductors to meet this challenge of creative leadership accounts for much indifferent, unsatisfying choral sound.

Amateur singers are primarily concerned with their individual problems in finding the right notes. The professional has had extensive training which prepares him to sing right notes *as the starting point of the rehearsal.* For amateurs and students, however, *learning the right notes constitutes the reason for the rehearsal.* This means that the very nature of the amateur choir rehearsal focuses much attention away from the conductor, so that the demands made of him for forceful, inventive efforts to keep communicative channels open are actually greater than with a professional choir.

A festival performance often exhibits the effects of either the presence or the absence of this kind of leadership. Choirs that sing vitally, with tangible expression and control, invariably are in obvious communication with their conductors. They watch him, and respond instantly; their posture, body motion, facial expression, and rhythmic-tonal product clearly reflect his subtlest indications. Conversely, choirs which sing apathetically or badly seem out of touch with their conductors. Either they do not watch him at all, having found that what he does is meaningless, or at best fail to get much commanding impetus from his activity, which rarely is anything more subtle than mechanical time-beating. Too often it is distressingly clear that such choirs are simply being allowed to "do what comes naturally", with little or no control by the conductor, no conveying of reminders or cues and, most importantly, no inspiration to govern their efforts.

Showmanship

A successful showman develops acute awareness of audience reaction. He bases much of his "act" on the minute-by-minute quality and intensity of the response it evokes. This is pure communication: instant correspondence of mind with minds. As such communication becomes more sensitive it employs an ever-broadening range of devices, — words, gestures, inflections, subtle implications, moods, timing, and an infinite number of visual signs.

The dynamic conductor uses many of these showmanlike skills. His job is to evoke intense public response, and his primary "public" is his choir. His impact is in good part charismatic, founded on the ability to touch subconscious moods and reactions as well as to channel conscious efforts and responses. And, going beyond the showman, he must move his public to concerted, overt expression far more complex than reflex applause or laughter.

Use of such showmanlike communication lends flexibility to the conductor's efforts and excitement to his performances. It imparts an air of inspired improvisation to his conducting which cloaks the structural bones of technique with the living flesh of artistic meaning. The best choral performance at any level reflects the inner personalities of the singers themselves, and is a living, fresh reality at the moment of its creation. The conductor's communicative skill must reach out for this inner response from each singer, exhorting it to come forth, and channeling it into a composite, meaningful group expression.

FIVE LEVELS OF CONDUCTING

How effective his communicative contact with his singers is depends on the conductor's sensitivity to the *level of conducting activity* called for by each situation. Confusion and frustration result from asking singers to achieve technical comprehension completely beyond their grasp. To expect a newly-formed high school choir to conquer Bach's *Singet dem Herrn,* or a volunteer church choir to accomplish a symphonic popular setting created for the Fred Waring or Norman Luboff organizations is simply unrealistic. On the other hand, boredom quickly engulfs a group's efforts when materials are too simple to challenge the choir's capability.

Beyond the degree of difficulty of the materials themselves, the conductor should realize that his communication about a work must carry the choir through normal stages of development, or levels of conducting. Successful leadership makes this forward momentum continuous, not allowing effort to be deflected into dead-ends of stagnant drill or meaningless repetition. To achieve continuous progress in the learning of a work the conductor must communicate with his choir in different ways, according to the requirements of the level on which they are working at any given moment. In one rehearsal he probably works at some time on each level, as he deals with music in varying stages of preparation.

Five meaningful levels of conducting are suggested by the diagram in Example 2:1. The accomplishment of any new work goes through all of these, although the speed with which the transition from level to level is made varies greatly according to the style and difficulty of the music and the choir's capability and readiness. At each level there are specific hazards which can slow down group momentum unless skillfully overcome.

Example 2.1: Five Levels of Conducting

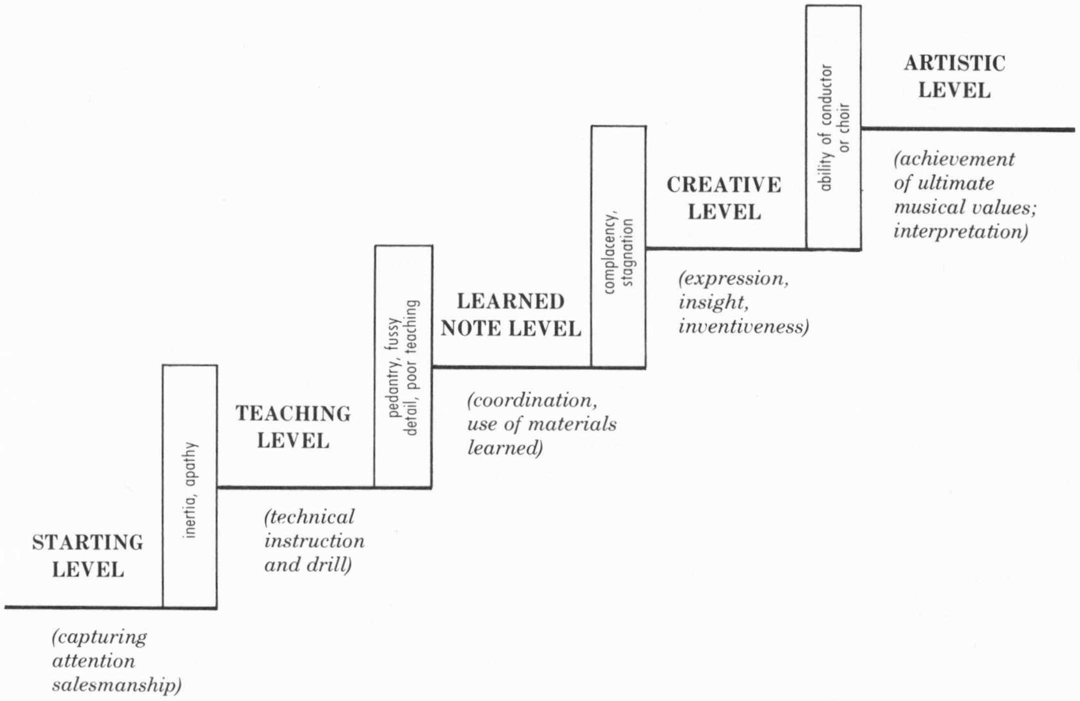

The starting level

The starting level assumes attention and moderate curiosity on the part of the singers. An expert choir virtually by-passes this, since they have developed habits of readiness. For beginning, or poorly-knit choirs, however, considerable effort by the conductor may be needed just to "get them ready to begin to start." Disorganization, talking, and lack of interest or purpose may call for forceful command at the outset, followed by what actually amounts to overt salesmanship. The choir may need to be shown just *why* they should become involved with a new style or work. Their resistance may be largely subconscious, but no effective progress will begin until it is overcome. The barrier of inertia and apathy between this level and the next can be overcome by conducting which embodies persuasion and the example of infectious enthusiasm. If the conductor mistakenly assumes that his singers are above the need for such communication, he compounds his future troubles. The attitudes and facts about the music which they will need on future levels will have to be made up during the activities on those levels, making progress slow and continually frustrating.

The teaching level

The teaching level conveys knowledge about the structure of the music, and develops technical skills in performing it. Communication here is largely a matter of pedagogical skill: knowing *what* is needed, and *how* to convey it. The mood of communication changes from persuasion to forceful exposition. As singers become increasingly involved with the music, the conductor's communication should stimulate and take advantage of added momentum and interest. Barriers which separate this from the next level are ineffective teaching methods or a tendency to get bogged down in fussy pedagogical minutia, forgetting that these are only means to progress. *Every* choir is concerned with this level, even though increasing skill allows more refined methods and a shorter learning time. A new choir of 10th-grade singers in school or church may need to be taught slowly and carefully to sing a triad in tune, while a professional choir can be taught quickly the conductor's understanding of Beethoven's concept of the *Agnus Dei* in the *Missa Solemnis.* But without communicative teaching neither group is liable to enjoy accomplishment commensurate with their capabilities.

The learned-note level

The learned note level is reached when teaching has been successful. Unfortunately, it is a plateau on which too many choirs make their final encampment. Technical matters have been learned: they "know the notes". What more? Even the conductor's guidance becomes less noticed if he doesn't make it increasingly forceful. His communicative activity must depart from the pedagogical and become coordinative, exhortative, and more commanding. He puts it all together. He draws on the accumulated learnings, and produces one composite result.

Real barriers of an insidious sort stand between this level and the next. These are complacency, the stagnation of mechanical reproduction, and vacuity of thought. During the learning process, forward progress was goaded on by the continued presence of wrong notes. Once those have been conquered, singers must be confronted with the challenge, "Now we have the notes; what will we do with them?", and then forcefully led to find answers.

Conducting at this level may become mechanical and pointless in itself. If one conducts a juke-box, the sounds come out the same, regardless of the contortions of the conductor, so why conduct? If a choir is allowed to make juke-box responses to the conductor's efforts, what good is his conducting? The sounds will be mechanical, loud, banal, and essentially meaningless. He must renew and revitalize the challenge of his conducting so that the group sees their accomplishments of learning not merely as achieved resting-places, but as paving stones to further progress.

The creative level

The creative level begins to make music instead of merely reproducing formulas of sound. Here the conductor reaches out to the innermost expressiveness of his singers and inspires them to make music together, by using what they have learned about the meaning of the notes. This should happen in any choir. Children can be led to produce music of ethereal beauty at this level; high school pop combos can sweep everything before them with the overwhelming vitality of a performance which "swings". The "average" church choir can inject moments of awesome spiritual impact into its service when this coordination of creative effort is achieved. But it is the conductor who must make it happen. In his capacities as focal point and impetus, to be discused in Chapter 7, he and he only is in a position to do so.

Achieving this level calls for communication of a direct, personal, and usually emotional sort. The entire battery of nonverbal techniques discussed in Chapter 3 comes into action, and must be used with the acute sensitivity of a showman to moment-by-moment responses. Music, in short, is *created in the instant.*

The artistic level

The creative level may be the highest to which a majority of choirs can aspire, but there is one higher. It is holy ground, to be trod only by musical saints. There is consolation in the historical fact that saints have sometimes emerged from ordinary backgrounds; there may be hope for conductors and choirs determined to strive for this goal. The barriers which stand before it are awesome: limitations of innate capacity, the need for supreme skill, and a high price in devotion and patience. Whether or not a choir ever reaches this exalted state, they should be aware of its existence, to give perspective to their efforts and urge them continually upward. As John Smallman, Robert Shaw, and others have said in so many ways: There is no such thing as "good enough"; there is always a higher plane.

This exalted ground is the artistic level. Here choral singing escapes worldly bounds and soars freely into the realm of the spirit. All the learnings, habits, and accomplishments of lower levels are realized and justified. The music goes beyond being created in the instant, taking on an inspiration and identity which transcends human limitations. That this power of choral sound remains unaltered by changing conditions is confirmed by great choral performances all over the world. One of the brightest hopes for the choral tradition is the fact that in spite of a changed environment and the tendency of many choirs to be swept away by lesser reasons for producing choral sound, true artistry is still the one ultimate and unchangeable value in choral music. This level of performance is harder to come by these days, art being so readily compromised by its surroundings, but fortunate is the conductor who can hold fast to this ideal and convey to his singers his vision of the ultimate good. Even more fortunate is he whose innate capacities give him the means to lead his singers into that promised land.

Regrettably, this level too has hazards of a deceptive sort. The very beauty of music performed with true artistry poses a danger: that choirs will attempt such performance without adequate preparation. The result is either bad performance bred of insufficient skill or mere "gimmickry" of tasteless over-styling. Successful accomplishment of more modest goals is far preferable to either alternative.

What techniques of communication must the conductor command? Many are very explicit, and easily documented. Others are intangible, and like music itself, must be understood in the fleeting instant, or hardly at all. Analysis by reflection or anticipation accounts for only part of their real meaning and impact. As has been said of kissing, true meaning in communication is discovered in the moment of contact. If that moment communicates, understanding happens, and analytical explanations only comment on the fact.

These moments involve choices and decisions, usually made subconsciously or by reflex because there is not time for conscious thought. An example is the conductor's reaction under pressure of deadlines and limited rehearsal time to the frustration of slow learning and sluggish response by his singers. If these universal problems evoke an angry, temperamental outburst, this represents a subconscious choice by the conductor, which instantly communicates to the choir many things in addition to those related to the music. The conductor may reflect later whether or not this was the particular kind of communication he wished to make; but it has been done, and the future relationship of choir and conductor has been affected by it. Great conductors *do* explode in anger and seem to get away with it, for the aura of their "greatness" absorbs such action in a way the average conductor would be foolish to expect for himself. It would be far more productive, and undoubtedly safer, for him to train his reflexes to respond in more constructive ways: the use of humor, a momentary relaxation of tension, or the introduction of an inventive technical device which will correct the fault, dispel the frustration, and communicate only the specific meanings the conductor desires.

A philosophy of rehearsal devices

Rehearsal devices *and the ability to invent them* are the dynamic conductor's stock in trade. While they are technically oriented toward specific faults, they are also fruitful means of communication, for they are most pertinent in moments when singers urgently look to their conductor for communicative guidance in matters of immediate concern. A viable philosophy governing the use of such devices is stated in the definition:

A rehearsal device is a specific communicative technique designed to solve a particular problem quickly, and thus make its own future use unnecessary.

To be most effective, it must *never* become a mechanical exercise, applied as a routine for general welfare, to fill time, or because it is felt rather vaguely to be the thing to do. The practice of opening rehearsals with a mechanical set of "warm-ups" is often only a convenient cover for latecomers to scamper to their seats or for the conductor to finish taking roll. If it is merely a series of vocal calisthenics, memorized and sung in sequence with a minimum of conscious thought, it has little relation to any possible benefits of genuinely preparatory vocalization. Unless this kind of activity is forcefully led by the conductor himself, as an integral part of the rehearsal, with purposes that are pertinent and clearly understood to be so by all the singers, it is an utter waste of time.

The ensuing discussion of verbal techniques of communication, and of the non-verbal methods dealt with in Chapter 3, views them as rehearsal devices in terms of the philosophy stated. They should not be regarded as rigid formulas or "methods" in the sense that one event must inevitably proceed from another. Their virtue is in their evanescense. Their greatest value will be to stimulate the dynamic conductor to reshape their content to suit his own challenges, and to stir him to invent others suited uniquely to his needs.

TECHNIQUES OF VERBAL COMMUNICATION

The most overt form of communication is the spoken word. With Job, the conductor may well reflect, "How forcible are right words!"[1], and heed Joseph Joubert's wry comment, "Words, like glasses, obscure everything they do not make clear."[2] Words can be efficient, swift, colorful vehicles of communication, or cluttered, bumbling, dreary omnibuses. A capacity for using more of the former than the latter in the stresses of rehearsal is an asset beyond price.

The dynamic conductor's verbal techniques — his command of language — ideally should include the following:

Vocabulary

A rich, meaningful, ever-growing vocabulary must be graced by accuracy and variety, replete with synonyms and colorful

1 : VI, 25

2 : Jacob Braude : *Second Encyclopedia of Quotations,* p. 398

ways of expressing ideas. It must be precise both in words and semantics. Use of the wrong word ("assimilate" for "simulate", "appraise" for "apprise", "noisome" for "noisy", and so on) blurs the intended meaning and conveys the least-desirable thing: that the conductor's knowledge is flawed and imprecise.

Terminology

In addition to an accurate knowledge of what the terms are, the conductor needs the ability to use them in ways which convey the meaning without sounding affected. The author admired this process at work in rehearsals of the Kings College Chapel Choir of Cambridge and the Choristers of Canterbury Cathedral. The boys were aged nine to thirteen, but were already accustomed to receiving explicit, technically phrased instructions just once, and acting upon them. Such detailed directions as "The mezzo-forte is followed by a decrescendo on the last two beats of bar 46, reaching the cadence with a fermata on the first half-note of bar 47, pianissimo," produced immediate results, and evidently seemed quite normal to all concerned. The more precise such terminology, the more efficient its communicative power, and thus the faster the pace of the rehearsal.

Idiomatic expressiveness

The conductor must talk the singers' language. It may be complicated, or even made hazardous by the presence in the choir of persons with widely divergent backgrounds, each with its own particular idiom. Yet showing some comprehension of these specialized expressions establishes an immediate bond between the conductor and their users. Great care is needed in the use of such idioms, for a glaringly misused colloquial expression conveys the wrong thing: that the conductor is either talking down to the singers, or making a fumbling attempt to avoid appearing "square".

Phraseology

Command of colorful, humorous, pungent phraseology is a valuable skill most effective when it seems to spring from the inventiveness of the moment. Respighi's *Laud to the Nativity* combines voices with a small instrumental ensemble. On more than one occasion the instruments remain tacet for extended periods, and amateur singers usually have trouble maintaining accurate intonation. As a result, when the instruments re-enter a glaring difference of pitch is obvious and painful. At this point it does little good for the conductor to get angry, scold, or loudly bemoan poor work. At least two very specific things are needed: a better group tone based on improved individual production, and a sharpened awareness by each individual of his personal responsibility for keeping the pitch secure. These add up to increased vitality of performance, devoid of either excessive tension or lethargy. A light touch, such as the remark, "Well, let's all pray for a flat oboe!" has been found effective, because it established rapport in the face of a commonly-felt problem, and eased tensions with a smile. The specific problem could then be attacked with a device aimed at the tonal faults which the conductor would certainly have heard in specific voices or sections. If this device too can be graced by humor, and infused with the excitement of finally disposing of an annoying problem, it will achieve far more than a "drill" applied as a grim punitive necessity.

Informed Commentary

Interest in the music will be heightened by comprehension. When a text or style is obscure or difficult for singers, the conductor must make it clear. Apparently spur-of-the-moment background commentary about a work (which of course is based on thorough preparation by the conductor) may ignite enough interest at the outset to sustain the singer past initially forbidding difficulties. Correct pronunciation and translation of foreign texts is mandatory; simple explanations of stylistic or interpretive demands can convert apathy into curiosity. It hardly needs to be said that a tight rein must be held on one's mere ebullient love of talking, which lets rehearsal time trickle away in words, but well-timed, pertinent commentary can be invaluable.

Emotional expression

Music *is* emotionally expressive; choral music especially so. The conductor must hold before his singers the need to produce sounds which are, after all technical matters have been accomplished, essentially emotional in meaning. It may be virtually impossible to convey this concept in technical terms, being forced to rely, rather, on the piquancy of a nicely-turned colloquial or emotional phrase which may be frankly non-technical in nature. This may be closely related to gesture and facial expression, to be discussed in Chapter 3; it is a principal interpretive tool for the dynamic conductor. George Solti, rehearsing the Royal Choral Society of London in Verdi's *Requiem*[1], suddenly demanded of them ". . . .as much legato as you have never sung in your life yet!" — and got what he wanted at once. The apt phrase, coupled with the right gesture or look, is often the most direct route to a desired response.

Inflection

Public speakers know that the meaning of a word or phrase is completely at the mercy of the tone and inflection with which it is spoken. It can come as a shock to a conductor to discover that although he had scrupulously chosen just the right words of instruction, his choir responded as though he had asked them to do exactly the opposite. When this happens, the conductor can be sure that his manner of speaking belies his actual words.

To tell singers in tones of petulance or impatience, "Sing happily!" is about as effective as giving them a military com-

1 : October 19, 1968

mand, "You *will* enjoy this music. That is an *order*." The words say one thing; the tone and phrasing convey an opposite meaning. Equally unsettling can be the revelation that his choir's apathetic response, its dreary performance of emotionally intense music, reflects not his instructions, but the droning monotony of his speaking tone.

While to some extent the conductor's speech inflections represent his inner feelings and attitudes, and thus might seem beyond conscious control, much can be done to modify and direct their use. Actors and speakers *learn* the art of swaying audiences through the use of controlled speech inflection. So must the conductor, if this powerful asset is to enhance his effectiveness. Without its help his tone may betray his words by conveying the wrong meanings, moods, and connotations and the music will suffer.

COMMUNICATION BY EXAMPLE : USE OF RECORDINGS

Between verbal and completely non-verbal techniques of communication lies the use of recordings as examples, which partakes of both types. It is non-verbal because it conveys specific sounds directly; it is verbal both because it is aural, and because its maximum effectiveness often depends on verbal explanations and comparisons.

In some circles it is regarded as poor technique, too time-consuming, vaguely unethical, or merely unsporting to use recordings in rehearsal. Yet as a means of teaching tone, notes, language, blend, expression, and a variety of techniques and subtleties it is virtually unparalleled. In this era when recorded sound is a principal means by which the great majority know music at all, it can be presumed that singers will respond to it readily. The availability of great portions of the choral repertoire in professional performances is augmented by some publishers' practice of recording new works they wish to promote. In addition, recordings of vocal production and choral techniques provide live samples of sound which are far more communicative than would be reams of printed instructions on how to produce them.

The objection that playing a recording in a rehearsal stereotypes the choir's future interpretation of the work must be balanced by the realization that for the "average" choir such stereotypes represent an improvement at the outset. Because the professional, recorded performance is so much better than anything they have done with the music it acts to raise the level of their sensitivity and response. If they can only imitate what they hear, the chances are that this alone will make them sound better.

Of more importance is the fact that the recorded sound conveys a non-verbal concept directly. With a minimum of verbal instructions, concepts of tone, rhythm, melody contour, blend and language are clarified by the sound, and communicated far more accurately than is possible by words alone. Progress in developing choral skills results from the individual's conscious attempt to improve present vocal habits. What more graphic concept as to the desired direction of such change can he be shown than a finished performance, either of a complete work, or the production of a specific tone quality? And what more direct route to the desired change than an immediate attempt to imitate that performance? If this imitative attempt can be recorded and played back for side-by-side comparison with the original model, the values of the whole procedure will be confirmed and multiplied.

Indifferent performances sometimes heard in festivals force the conclusion that some singers have never been led to compare the sounds they *do* make with other sounds they *might* make. A festival atmosphere is conducive to such comparisons because singers hear their peers, of approximately similar backgrounds, making different sounds and exploiting different tonal techniques. This is often most beneficial to choirs whose conductors have failed to communicate to them a wide variety of tonal experiences. The conductor who becomes aware that his choir is deficient in its ability to produce a variety of tone might well turn to recordings as a convenient, effective remedy.

The record library

A library of proven recorded examples is of great value to the conductor. This should include as many techniques as possible, skillfully demonstrated and artistically achieved. Among these should be instances of:

a. *Expertly-produced tonal styles* ■ This should include only the very best recordings of rich, vibrant, resonant, rhythmic vital choral tone. Any musical style is acceptable, but for purposes of demonstration there is a certain advantage to examples of simple materials with which singers can relate easily, such as hymns, folk songs, or even familiar popular songs. The point will be lost unless the recording itself is of such quality that the sound will be reproduced each time the record is played.

b. *Specific choral techniques* ■ Any recording which illustrates sustained, expressive phrasing, expert breath control, sensitive dynamic shadings, contrapuntal clarity, uniform vowel quality, rhythmic vitality, clear enunciation and diction, mood, coordination of tone quality with musical meaning, or other choral techniques with which his choir may have to grapple, is a potentially valuable tool for the conductor.

c. *Specific instructional materials* ■ Recordings dealing with tone production, class voice methods, diction, or other techniques in which systematic use of devices has been put into recorded form, should be included.

d. *Professional performances* ■ Most of the classics are available, and the publisher should be asked if a demonstration record is available for the particular new piece being begun. If more than one recorded performance of the same score is available, the contrasts will be most instructive for the choir.

e. *Demonstrating singing styles* ■ To confront a choir with the tonal products and interpretive styles of such widely divergent choirs as the Mormon Tabernacle Choir, the Kings College Chapel Choir, the Robert Shaw Chorale, the Fred Waring Glee Club, the St. Olaf Choir, and a current popular group — to name but a few — automatically casts their own work into a varicolored and brilliant perspective which needs little explanation. The fact that such diversity includes sharp differences of concept tends to remove any possible invidious comparisons with their own singing, and allows them to evaluate it in terms of a variety of criteria which have proven "successful".

Arguments about the use of recordings often say more about the predilections of the disputants than about the question itself. Those who contend that the fastest way to learn a piece is first to hear it as a whole point to the recording as the most convenient, generally available means to that end. Choir members, after all, "learn" pop styles and musical commercials by precisely this means all the time. Why not, then, take advantage of these habits to help them learn choir music? Certainly this seems preferable to the grinding process of leading them into an imposing musical maze whose complexities they can conquer only with great difficulty.

Especially where difficulties are largely notational, the communication of a recording is the fastest means to achieve mastery of a style. For example, it is curious but demonstrable that jazz and pop styles are often very difficult for singers to produce by working from notation alone. Their singing tends to sound square, awkward, and not at all idiomatic, because the notation needed to write down the rhythms of these styles is necessarily complex. But if the conductor provides a recorded performance after they have tried to extract the music from notation, he will note with awe the speed and ease with which problems melt away, as musical meanings which the notation presented with technical imperfection are related in the singers' minds to sounds which are already familiar.

To a lesser degree, the same benefits accrue in choral works with complex contrapuntal lines, thick and unaccustomed harmonic settings, irregular rhythmic patterns, and even simple dynamics. A flexible and imaginative use of recordings not only speeds up rehearsal procedures by communicating concepts in the most efficient forms, but can lead a choir past bogs of tedious frustration to the pleasant meadows of accomplishment.

3 | The Conductor's Communicative Techniques (II) : Non-Verbal

Many of the most important meanings the dynamic conductor conveys to his choir never find their way into words. A communicative flow begins in the moment that singers give attention to their conductor; before he speaks at all, conscious and subconscious meanings are communicated by what he does or fails to do. Throughout the rehearsal or performance these continue to flow, and they may even be strong enough to supersede much of his verbal communication. "What you do speaks so loudly I can't hear what you say!"

The variety of means by which this communication is carried is virtually limitless, and can only be suggested in the following discussion of its more tangible forms. More than merely cataloging techniques, this should re-emphasize to the conductor that, like the showman, he communicates *something* during every moment he is in front of his public. His conscious development of command over these non-verbal communicative techniques will pay continuing dividends in increased effectiveness.

EXPLICIT NON-VERBAL TECHNIQUES

Look them in the eye.

Eye contact is the most forceful non-verbal communication possible. Its presence conveys authority, sincerity, knowledge, and purpose. Its absence reflects uncertainty, weakness, vacillation, and the tensions of embarrassment. It is by far the most direct and immediate means of commanding attention. If the conductor is personally troubled by inner conflicts, fears, and uncertainty, an ability to maintain eye contact may be the most difficult challenge he faces; by the same token it is probably the most crucial. Until he commands sufficient poise to use it freely and naturally in rehearsals and performances, his potential as a conductor will be severely constricted. To use eye contact effectively he must have a thorough knowledge of the music and a secure conducting technique. His gaze must not be glued to the score, either to cover his insecurity about the music or as a means of keeping his conducting abreast of what the choir is singing. If he is to conduct the *singers,* and not just the *score,* the fundamental evidence will be an unflinching, direct eye contact by which he establishes and holds command.

Talk to singers, not at them.

Command starts with habitual eye contact, and extends to the manner in which directions are given: the choice of words, inflection, and general tone or attitude of whatever is said. One speaks differently when talking to fellow human beings than when issuing a dictatorial proclamation to the subservient masses!

Use the hands meaningfully.

Second only to the eyes, hands are principal agents by which non-verbal meaning is conveyed. The right hand is ordinarily concerned with conveying the basic metric pulse through the beat pattern (see below), while the left hand indicates such varied matters as cues and entrances, cut-offs, dynamics, phrasing, mood, and special nuances. Most scores contain moments when these expressive elements are sufficiently urgent to require the effort of both hands, at the momentary expense of the beat pattern. The conductor must train his hands not only to make the right motions for the score's requirements, but *not to make meaningless motions.* Like unneeded words, these only confuse communication. A left hand which only mirrors the right hand pattern or waves limply with no discernible intent should be dropped at the side until it is needed to indicate a specific meaning distinct from that of the right hand for it to indicate.

An essential element of hand use, too often ignored by amateur conductors, is a basic graceful hand position. To some this comes naturally; to others the "natural" position is stiff and ungainly, becoming a real factor in conveying subliminal tension to singers Subtle shadings of tone or expression, as well as rhythmic indications of precise clarity, are the language of hands schooled to be graceful, supple indicators.

That such artistically controlled hand motion is usually reduced in size in no way diminishes the intensity of its meaning. David Willcocks, one of England's leading choral conductors, was observed in rehearsals of the London Bach Choir and the famed King's College Chapel Choir to rely on exactly this kind of control. His hand motions were invariably graceful, and seemed to embody a separate, tangible expressiveness of their own. He repeatedly controlled rhythm, phrasing, and dynamic shadings with motions of the right hand alone in motions no more than two or three inches in amplitude.[1] The sensitive response by his singers was remarkable, the more so when it is recalled that the Bach Choir numbers over 300 members.

1 : October 21-22, 1968

It is virtually impossible to place the hand in an awkward position if the middle two fingers are always held together. This is suggested as a starting point for the conductor seeking a naturally graceful basic hand position. Once such a position has become habit, he will be able to elaborate on the meanings his hands convey by modifying this position in response to his inner impulses about music. Example 3.1 shows representative hand positions, with and without baton, which contrast reasonably graceful positions with others that are tense and awkward, and too often seen in inept conducting.

EXAMPLE 3.1 : BASIC HAND POSITIONS

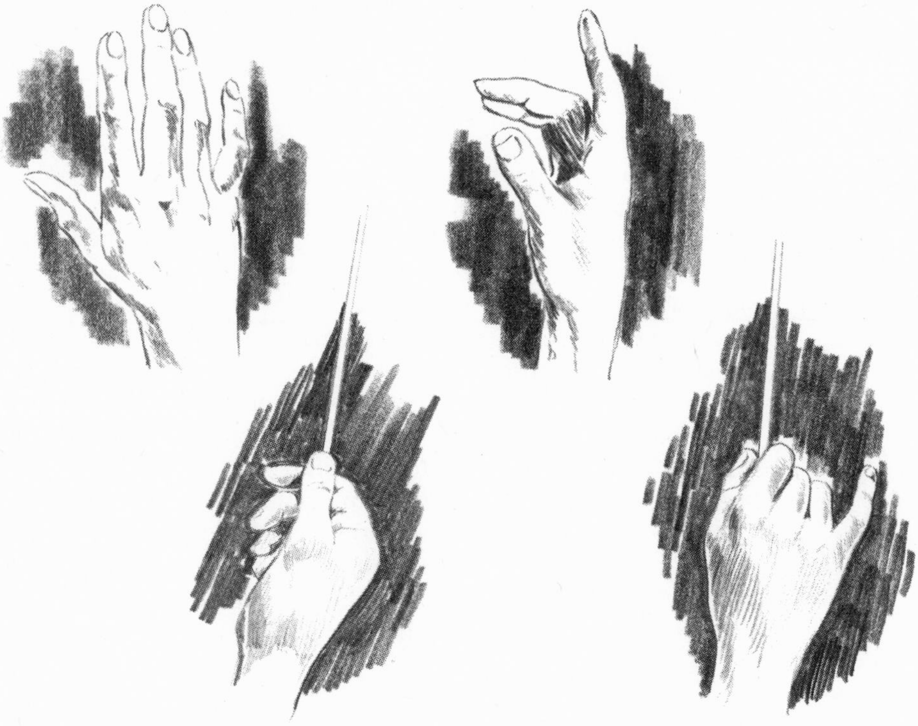

AWKWARD HAND POSITIONS OFTEN SEEN

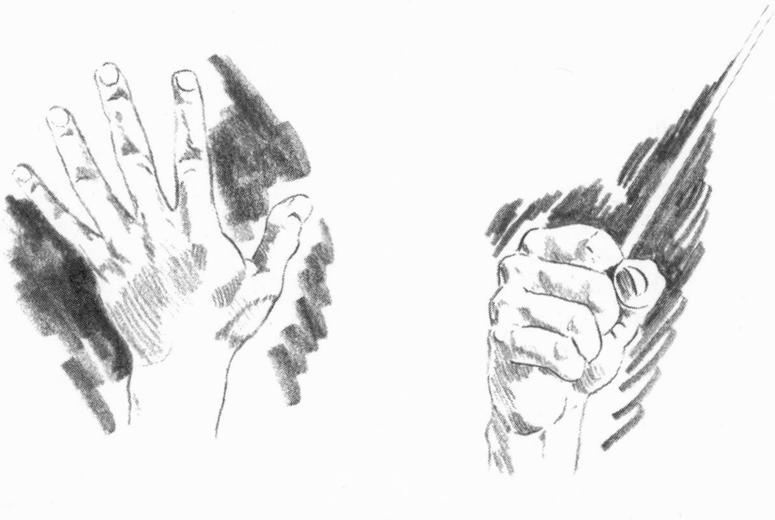

Lift head from score.

This has already been cited in its relation to eye contact, but it involves a separate non-verbal communication which is urgent and potentially devastating. If the conductor must watch the score exclusively, this tells his singers first that he is not assuming an insistent command of their attention (by way of eye contact), second, that he is insecure in the music himself, and third, that it is all right for them to bury their noses in the music because that's what *he* is doing. And all of this is communicated before any aspect of the music itself has been even considered! Any of these attitudes will effectively undercut practically anything the conductor may wish to build in musical performance. While it may not be possible to memorize every score, adequate preparation will allow the conductor to check with the score first, then look at the singers as he conducts.

Develop a posture of command.

Assumption of leadership starts with a stance which emanates readiness to lead and imparts confidence in that leadership. Fidgeting, shuffling, slouching, or presenting a timidly uncertain approach to the group instantly establishes the wrong mood. Any mood consistently conveyed by the stance and physical poise of the conductor can dominate everything that takes place in a rehearsal or performance. Even as he develops a basic hand position, he should establish a basic posture from which all of his conducting motions will emerge. Many have found that the most commanding posture is a position similar to military "Attention", standing tall and straight, heels together. A stance which places the feet too far apart looks awkward when viewed from the audience and imparts a rolling, ape-like quality to most of the motions that emanate from it. The most successful conductors maintain a convincing posture of command throughout the performance.

Acknowledge applause graciously.

Bowing, among amateurs, is too often an embarrassed, stumbling fidget, communicating self-consciousness and lack of poise. A consideration of how to acknowledge applause may seem far-fetched in a discussion of communicative techniques, but the conductor should remember that when he is engaged in such acknowledgement, both the choir and the audience are watching. The style of his response culminates the performance by conveying a mood which may range from dignified pride to fumbling self-awareness. Whatever he does is likely to have a tangible impact upon the sensitivities of all who are watching. A little practice of the following essentials of bowing in front of a full-length mirror will go far toward achieving control of a body movement that is inherently awkward.

a. Keep the heels together and the legs firmly straight for the entire duration of the bow, *and afterward.*

b. Bend from the waist *only:* not the arms, not the shoulders, not the neck. Bend to about a 45° angle.

c. Don't look at the audience during the bow. To do so requires that the neck be bent backward — a very awkward contortion which tends to convey obsequiousness.

d. Move with a slow, deliberate pace; don't jerk down or up.

e. Keep the hands in a graceful position, held still, with both at the sides, or possibly with one in a relaxed position at the waist.

f. Present a countenance which manifests friendliness and genuine pleasure. A grim expression communicates disdain or conceit; a frown, displeasure; a silly grin suggests immaturity or nervousness, or both. A controlled expression reflects the conductor's appreciation for the audience's response, pride in the group's performance, and his dignified satisfaction in the entire event.

Control or eliminate mannerisms.

Unnecessary, nervous motions such as shuffling music, adjusting the music stand, shifting feet, toying with glasses, hair, or clothing all convey uncertainty and lack of poise. Unconscious tics and reflex movements distract the audience's attention from the music. In rehearsal they can so divert the singers' attention that the conductor is able to convey little about the music. Each meaningless motion lessens the impact of motions intended to convey musical meaning. If the choir has to learn to ignore *some* motions, it is only a short step to ignoring *most* motions.

Use facial expressions effectively.

A summation of the mood and meaning of the music should show on the conductor's face. When it does not, singers can be excused for responding with a colorless, unexpressive performance. The dynamic conductor uses his face to draw deep personal response from his singers. By his expression he speaks to them as persons in direct, non-verbal ways, and since this commands their attention, they invariably respond. There are conflicting views as to whether the conductor should sing or mouth the words with his choir, but regardless of any final dictum in the matter, this technique will probably continue to be used, because many conductors find it the fastest way to cue uniform diction. It is a direct outgrowth of facial expression and must be employed with forethought and discrimination. If the conductor sings *all* the time, or makes a fetish of enunciating every word, he probably wastes effort that could be directed to other communicative devices. However, enunciation of attack words, coupled with a facial expression which encourages confidence and emotional intensity, is easily the fastest way of insuring a coordinated attack. It is far to be preferred to the direction of a conductor who shuns all facial expressions except a "dead-pan" stare and gives his singers no visual support whatever.

Demand the unexpected.

Music with a bright mood is sung by some choirs with a sad, listless manner, while solemn music may be given a banal or flippant performance. If the conductor realizes that his choir is singing without thinking, some forceful reminder is called for. To dramatize for the singers that they are not conveying the mood of the music, he may exaggeratedly mimic the inappropriate mood of the choir. The shock effect, for example, of a comically doleful face made suddenly by the conductor during a lethargic rendition of a bright piece has been found to be a most effective way of reminding the singers instantly and wordlessly of the music's requirements. Their response is almost invariably a smile and increased vitality of performance. The audience of course does not see the face-making, but it instantaneously conveys a concentrated group of meanings to the choir. Many similar graphic gestures used on the spur of the moment serve to keep the choir on its mental toes, and reinforce their assurance that the conductor's motions do have meaning. Like the use of "bad tone" discussed in Chapter 4, this device, by dramatically showing what is *not* wanted, underscores the nature of what *is*.

Control self-consciousness.

No conductor is superhuman, and each is subject to all the frustrations, doubts, and introspection that may trouble many of his singers. Being troubled by the impact of massed eyes or wondering whether the ever-present problems in achieving the desired result spring from one's own ineptitude are but facets of a self-conscious sensitivity the conductor must learn to control. It takes resolve, courage, and patient endurance to continue to conduct with equanimity in the face of continuing frustration. Yet the moment that tides of doubt overwhelm a conductor, the fact is communicated to his singers in many non-verbal ways. His manner changes, his directions falter. He may take refuge in temperament, allowing his insecurity to become an acknowledged factor of the rehearsal, and thus commit a serious and lasting mistake of leadership. The dynamic conductor understands the need to control at least the outward manifestations of his self-consciousness and learns, more and more, to give few visible signs of whatever inner turmoil may beset him. Perseverance in this control of his personal problems not only benefits his relationship with his choir but enables him gradually to conquer his self-consciousness.

Use efficient, meaningful beat patterns.

Example 3.2 lists the commonly-accepted beat patterns for the principal meters. These are well-established formulas of common currency, and comprise one of the most basic elements of a conductor's training. Books on techniques of conducting and performance practices deal exhaustively with the mechanics of beat patterns and their meaning as indicators of tempo, rhythm, attack, release, phrasing, and a host of other specifics. The present discussion assumes that such matters have already been explored in depth, and is concerned with beat patterns as important non-verbal communicative techniques.

Some opinions tend to discount the value of precise patterns for choral conductors (as distinct from instrumental conductors) on the grounds that such specific formulas tend to over-mechanize the subtler nuances of expressive choral singing. Such arguments seem weakly founded. It may be true that accomplished choirs who have developed sensitive rapport with their conductor may not always need a continuous precise beat in order to sing expressively. But this clearly is the result of having learned so thoroughly the musical meanings which the beat pattern imparts that the model is no longer mandatory. However, whether implied or specified, these meanings are necessary to an artistic performance, particularly with choirs of lesser skills.

More subtle matters than the specific technical meanings of the beat patterns are conveyed by the conductor's attitude about them and his proficiency in their use. Until the rapport suggested above is a reality, the choir has no choice but to rely on its conductor's ability to convey explicit information and assurance through his conducting motions. If those motions say things they can understand, they are able to respond. If they must sift meaningful motions from a blur of imprecise gesticulations or are constantly confronted with motions which contradict the apparent meaning of the music and perhaps even the facial expressions of the conductor, the choir will tend increasingly to ignore the whole procedure. When this happens, the singer must seek meaningful guidance from some other part of the conductor's activity or from the empathy within the group itself in order to continue to function as a performing entity.

EXAMPLE 3.2

THE STANDARD BEAT PATTERNS OF CONDUCTING

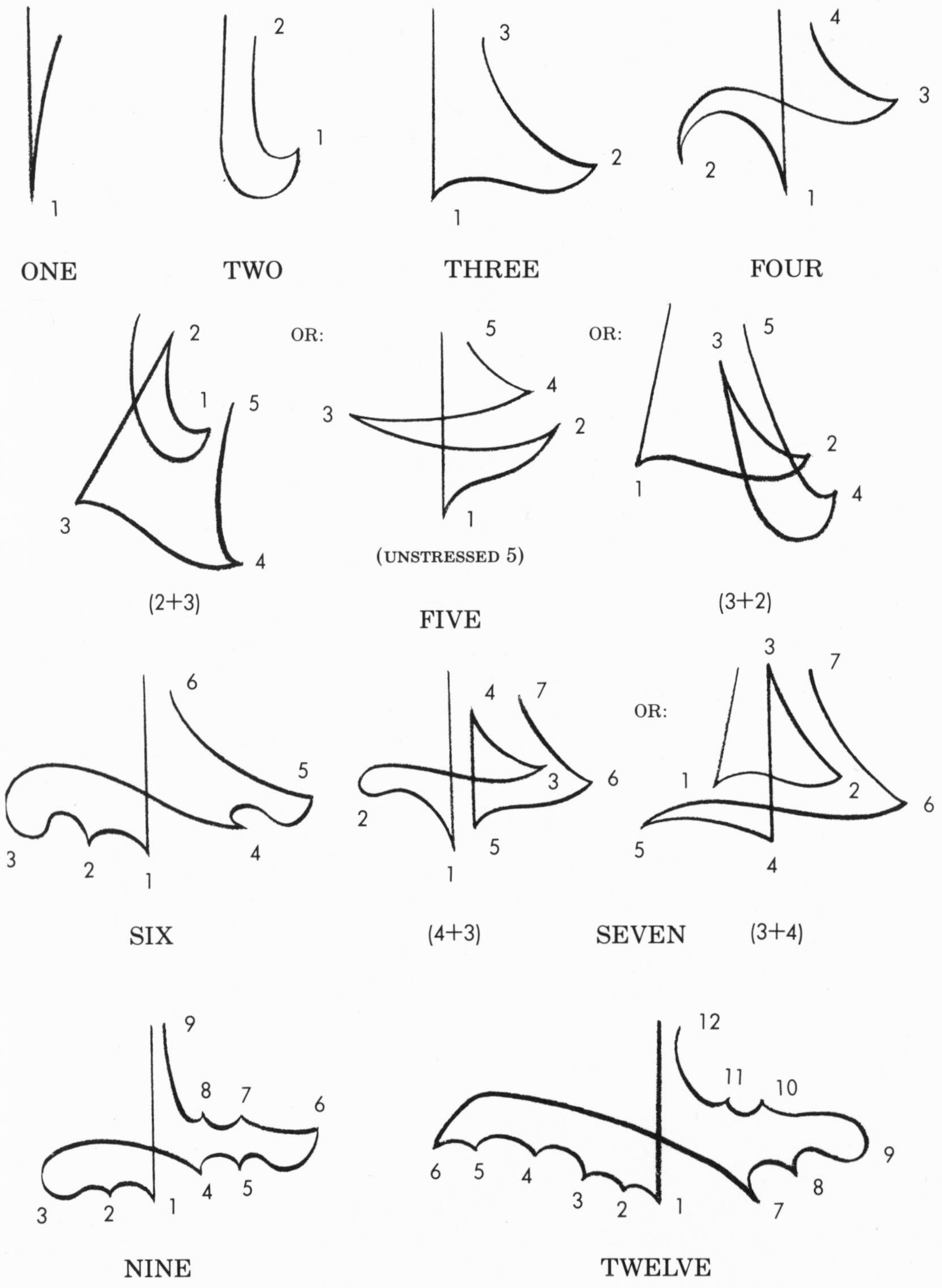

Conductors are invited to test the validity of the following propositions and devices in their own experience.

a. The more economically precise the beat pattern to which the choir can be trained to respond, the greater its expressive power in guiding their performance.

b. Extra, meaningless motions, or flowery elaborations of the beat pattern progressively train singers to ignore beat motions altogether.

c. The more exact the form of the beat pattern which can be integrated into the conductor's expressive demands, the greater will be the singers' confidence in his leadership; precision breeds assurance.

Devices to improve beat patterns.

Control over the efficiency and intensity of beat-pattern use can be measurably improved by the conductor's practicing the following devices:

a. Place the tip of the middle finger of the conducting hand against a wall. Without allowing it to move from its original contact, move the hand and wrist in beat patterns which are as complete and precise as possible. This demands great wrist flexibility, and since the patterns are necessarily restricted in size, extra flourishes are virtually impossible. When the pattern has begun to work with some ease in this position, transfer the concept to live conducting of a choir, imagining the finger to be still against the wall and resisting every inclination to enlarge or elaborate on the pattern. Compress the meaning into the smallest scope available, making clear to the choir that they are expected to respond to this compressed intensity with the same vitality formerly accorded larger patterns. If the pattern is really precise, its beats clear and forcefully indicated, and if a feeling of continuity visibly measures the distance between beats, intense expressive control within a small scope of motions will develop rapidly. This is because the choir must watch the conducting more closely to obtain the conducted information. When their attention is thus more intensely focused, responses are given with greater alacrity.

b. Hold a baton in a normal, graceful hand position. Conduct an intensely rhythmic beat pattern no slower than ♩ = 100, allowing *the tip of the baton* to travel no more than six inches between beats. Practice until the pattern is smooth and intense, without jerky motions. When this is achieved, remove the baton and make precisely the same motions with the hand. The immediately obvious result will be a much smaller motion than previously used when conducting with the hand alone. If the baton has achieved a truly fluid smoothness, *the resulting hand motion will be even smoother.* This commonly imparts intensity to the hand pattern, transforming it into a meaningful measurement of flow rather than a bouncing from point to point. It has been whimsically compared to the motion of "pulling" taffy, since it suggests something of the same feeling of moving against resistance.

c. Engage a choir's help in testing the actual meaning being conveyed by beat patterns. Have them sing a memorized song, asking that they be meticulously accurate in reflecting in sound every hand motion. If the pattern is overly emphatic or bouncy, or contains unmeaningful elaborations, they are to respond with accents, sforzandi, or sliding tones which, although not called for by the score, represent their response to the conductor's signals. He should then try to lead them with only those motions that convey desired meanings. If the choir good-naturedly catches the spirit of the experiment and responds exactly, the conductor may discover points of emphasis he was unaware of making. If a third party serves as impartial referee, judging whether the choir is too gentle or too hard on the conductor, the point will be made with even more force.

ABSTRACT NON-VERBAL COMMUNICATION

In addition to the verbal and non-verbal communication already discussed, the conductor should be aware of other more tenuous ways in which he influences his singers. While these subtle communiques are rarely as tangible or controllable as the means of communication already discussed, they may be of encompassing importance to his over-all success. If the conductor remains completely oblivious of their existence as factors of his leadership, *he may never quite understand what prevents his communicating with his choir as he wants to.* In ways to be delineated in detail in Chapter 9, their cumulative effect shapes the choir's total image of the conductor. Here, these influences are considered in their more immediate communicative aspects, as factors which may open channels through which specific conducting devices can flow, or which may convey undesirable concepts so strongly that any future communication is prejudiced at the outset.

A positive manner

Leadership is effective in proportion to its ability to decide, *and to act upon the decision.* A conductor must quickly discern what is needed in the complex of timed activities which make up his rehearsal or performance. Unless he can also *act* promptly and with assurance in a manner which controls the situation, the force of his leadership is immediately in doubt. Usually, too many things need doing all at once: the tone is wrong, the balance between parts is askew, diction is garbled, and the score's expressive markings are being completely ignored. Which ones shall the conductor do something about?

Some conductors, facing this formidable array, simply keep beating, hoping that somehow before performance time the problems will magically be resolved – perhaps by prayer. Others, in a frenzy of good intentions, attack one particular fault, bringing the rehearsal to a virtual halt while it is worried, probed, scolded, and drilled. Other problems – indeed, whole sections of the music – are hardly rehearsed at all. Of course neither of these extremes overcomes the complex problems. Growth involves the whole organism. A child rarely develops a perfect arm unless the rest of him grows in proportion. So it is with a musical score, which must be developed in its entirety; none of its problems are completely unrelated to the others, and growth in one area may well stimulate progress in another without further comment if the relationship between the two is understood by the conductor. For example, diction problems often spring as much from poor tone production as from faulty articulation; simply improving tone quality may make words more understandable. The conductor's influence should point toward total growth.

Above all, he should never reveal a timid vacillation about how to launch onto the "sea of troubles" which confronts him. Even if he has strong inner doubts as to which of several alternatives might be most productive, it is far better to act, to do something, to show a positive command of the present moment. Even the *wrong* action (which can often be corrected later) is a more dynamic response to a problem in a group situation than to simply let things ride. The fact of positive action itself communicates leadership to the choir and inclines them to grant respect and cooperation, whereas vacillation conveys lack of purpose, and invites disdain.

Action is best impelled from a firm base of knowledge and must be set in motion with skill, purpose, and insight. The conductor who attempts to propel a group very far without these attributes will, sooner or later, be branded as a faker. It still remains true, however, that when the conductor has to make a choice among several courses, an effective rule is: "*If in doubt, do SOMETHING!*"

Pace and continuity

Does the rehearsal move, or drag? Does it start and finish promptly? Does the conductor's total influence impart a sense of momentum, or does it lead the singers to wish he would "get a move on"? Are singers tired at the end of a rehearsal because they have worked hard, accomplished much, and moved continuously, or only because of the tedium or boredom? Does the conductor introduce teaching devices and corrections so that they seem important and interesting challenges, or so that they irritate the singers with what seems to be yet another trivial interruption of their pleasure in singing?

The singers' answers to these questions weave the fabric of fundamental attitudes with which the conductor must work. They precondition the singers' receptivity to more specific techniques in the rehearsal and their responsiveness in performance.

Conductor A starts on time, maintains a fast pace, gives explicit, precise, challenging directions that lead the choir at once to its next objective, maintains an atmosphere of purposeful momentum, and ends on time. He will find that his singers are rarely late to rehearsal, respond with close attention, are interested and cooperatively accept his suggestions, and that their morale is high. They are likely to mention their appreciation of a good rehearsal as they leave.

Conductor B, on the other hand, waits until the majority arrives at rehearsal, which becomes later and later after the announced starting time, gives vague, rambling directions which he repeats several times ("just to be sure everybody gets them!"), talks about all sorts of things, and dissipates the momentum of the rehearsal in halting, poorly-conceived drills which don't correct the faults at which they are ostensibly aimed, and which after several repetitions are finally abandoned without any appreciable result. His rehearsals usually run at least fifteen minutes over the announced limit. He frequently complains that his singers seem bored, pay him little attention, and have to be told the same thing so many times. They talk a lot in rehearsal and tend to ignore most of the conductor's communicative signs. They probably ignore him as they leave the rehearsal.

These two hypothetical extremes are cited to illustrate the pervasive influence of timing and pacing on all the elements of a conducting situation. Conductor A's success grows out of the fact that all of his activities move with the flow of time; for Conductor B no such momentum is ever generated. For the former, "timing" in the sense actors know – sensing the precise instant when the next thing should happen – becomes possible, and sharpens interest. For the latter, things happen, or fail to happen, with little relationship to each other.

Those who maintain that "timing" is strictly an inborn gift should recognize that it is quite possible to correct many of the specific problems of Conductor B's situation by direct action: he *can* start and end on time; he might well plan in advance what he will say during rehearsal and confine himself within those bounds; he can simply not conduct at all while anyone is talking, thus jealously guarding each moment of rehearsal time by projecting the attitude that it is valuable. Each specific fault he corrects will bring him one step closer to a fast-paced, sensitively timed rehearsal environment.

Mood: the emotional environment

Toscanini was known for the towering rages which punctuated his rehearsals. But these were only one facet of the emotional environment which pervaded those rehearsals and the ensuing performances. Samuel Antek gives vivid witness to his legendary impact:

"Such a man was Toscanini. No conductor I ever worked for could create quite this feeling of ecstasy. . . . . .Sitting on the stage in our Studio 8-H at NBC with Toscanini often reminded me of sitting in the sanctuary of a church, or participating in a solemn spiritual rite rather than performing at a concert. Coming from Toscanini, even oaths and curses seemed almost devout."[1]

While few conductors attain such impact, to some extent each creates the climate of mood and response in which he works. This is especially true in choral work, which relies more on overt emotional response than most instrumental performance. It may surprise the choral conductor to realize that what he communicates is directly responsible for the nature and intensity of his choir's emotional responses toward himself, and that he may consciously control many of those responses. They may range from outright, bitter rejection to the most impassioned adulation, with an intervening variety that is virtually limitless. To a remarkable degree the dominant mood of any given moment reflects the conductor's effort or lack of it. Either he has consciously worked to structure that mood, or he has ignored it altogether, *and thus allowed it to be the result of his mistakes.*

1 : Samuel Antek, *This Was Toscanini,* Vanguard Press, New York, 1963, pp. 18, 57

It is probably true that in the "average" amateur choir the prevailing mood at any given moment is pretty well determined by the routines of the choir's function. Concert or service music to prepare, music to pass, roll to take, deadlines to meet, insufficient time – these realities can and do have first call on much of the choir's attention span. It is tacitly – and perhaps ruefully – understood that in the midst of this routine somewhere they are supposed to make some music also.

The conductor's relation to this stream of routine is crucial. He may simply stand by, content to let the tide of events set the mood; this in itself eventually communicates to the choir that his leadership is only nominal, a condition which unfortunately plagues many school and church choirs. Or he may assert a dynamic influence on the flow of routine and by organization and planning turn it into an ally of momentum and progress. This too communicates to the choir, but in terms of challenge and the excitement of forward motion. Two specific ways to exert such dynamic influence are:

a. *Work in a consistent, positive manner* ■ The conductor must be a reliable constant upon whom choir singers know they can rely. Certain things he *will* do; others, he will *not*. This by no means precludes creativity or the unexpected; more probably it intensifies their impact. Nor does this say that the conductor must be a drudge or an automaton, relentlessly doing the same thing over and over. Rather, he is seen as the unfaltering source of progress and accomplishment. Not all emergencies and frustrations can be anticipated, but the conductor's disciplined resolve and positive manner reflect an assurance of command which provides great psychological support to the choir. He is in charge, and they can rely on his leadership. While the projection of this air of authority depends in part on what kind of person he is, how well he is trained, what his ideals are, and how strong his will is, equally important is his conscious choice to assert positive leadership.

b. *Control extreme emotional reactions* ■ Since Toscanini's greatness allowed him the latitude of temperamental outbursts, his relations to his performers was in a sense atypical. A conductor who deals with amateurs or students faces different requirements. Where Toscanini might afford to sacrifice everything and everyone to his phenomenal single-minded devotion to the music, the average conductor cannot ignore the web of personal feelings and relationships which is woven into his environment. Extremes of adverse emotional reaction –

anger, sarcasm, bitter innuendo, arbitrary petulance — tear that web, and in the majority of cases probably do damage that is irreparable.

The conductor who imagines that his position as leader-figure is so secure that he can indulge in such reactions with impunity would do well to check into the *real* feelings of his singers. The tragi-comic figure of the "music teacher" or "choir director" sometimes encountered in fiction: a temperamental, somewhat nutty caricature who imagines himself to be important, but who is actually so divorced from reality as to be generally ignored — emerges as the choir's image of the conductor who too often allows himself the luxury of "temperament".

The truly dynamic conductor develops the showman's sensitivity to what can and what cannot be done within his situation and builds his effectiveness within those bounds. When rapport with his choir is strong, he may be able to use small doses of strong emotion to challenge specific faults, but this is always a chancy procedure. Carelessly shoddy work, too much talking in rehearsal, or some other detrimental breach of procedure may deserve the lash of a skillful conductor's overt scorn or displeasure, so long as they are directed at the behavior rather than the person. When correction is approached in this way the group becomes the conductor's ally, for the misbehaviour wastes their time also. But if they view his actions as a personal attack, resentment and tensions will result which sharply diminish the conductor's effectiveness.

In the long run, a mood of excitement and accomplishment will more effectively control problems than one of repression, retribution, or punitive "discipline". Naturally, discipline is a vital part of musical success, but it must be the inner discipline of common consent if it is to allow the fragile inner feelings of the singers to find expression in music. The conductor who has the poise to maintain a pleasant and creative atmosphere, untroubled by storms of temperament even in the face of the "unusual" pressures which are common to rehearsals and performances, will find it easier to convey musical values to his singers and thus will make better music with them.

Identification with singers

The conductor must be appreciated for his ability to communicate as a human being as well as a leader. A member of the professional Swedish Radio Chorus of Stockholm, describing the group's high regard for their conductor, Eric Ericson, spoke glowingly of their respect for his artistry and skill as a conductor, and concluded ". . . .but he's something special; he's one of *US!*" Such an accolade! Without diminishing their image of him as a leader and trustworthy source of skilled musical guidance, he had succeeded in communicating his warm humanity, with results that were of great benefit to him as a conductor. This benefit was obvious in the choir's accomplishments in the rehearsal, in which, because of the sensitive communication between leader and choir, the group sang a difficult repertory with exceptional meaning and artistry.

Knowledge: the main communication

The importance of the conductor's knowledgeability has been stressed in various ways and will return again in other connections, for it is in the truest sense fundamental. A choir senses immediately whether its conductor *really knows,* is faking, or does not know. If the environment disposes them to accept him anyway, they may not leave. He may even be deluded into thinking he is exerting a dynamic influence on events because they give him surface acceptance; but the chances are small that they will ever make real music together. His charming personality, facility of expression, or the fact that the choir feels a responsibility to prepare a service or maintain an organization may keep it together, but the musical product will always be marred by the fact that the conductor doesn't have the fundamental knowledge or skill to lead them competently. Without exception, great conductors have established firmly that they are masters of what they do. They know the musical score, they are guided by a viable artistic image of how it should sound, and they have a conducting technique that conveys meaning to the singers and obtains the desired result.

Adolescents flock to the leader who not only speaks their language but who has demonstrated that he can move them to do artistically meaningful things, because he *knows.* Children give their love and adulation to a teacher who knows how to make them sing beautifully. Adults give allegiance to the conductor who shows clearly that he knows the music and can challenge their ability to produce it. Singers of all ages respond to the leader who can guide them to real musical achievement which enhances technique with emotional exhilaration. Attainment of such artistry provides its own motivation and contains its own reward.

4|The Conductor and Choral Tone

A choir's tone is its principal product. The conductor's first responsibilities include shaping tone quality and controlling the way it is made. Control of choral tone is achieved only when the choir itself has come to *know* its own sound, and each singer has become personally involved in the process of control.

Conductors who are effective in producing fine choral tone may say that this statement is self-evident; certainly it has been stated often and in a variety of ways. European choirs with long traditions have it so deeply ingrained that they habitually produce a rich tone, no matter what other problems may affect their performance. Better American choirs show a firm grasp of its importance.

Yet it is distressingly true that too many church and school choirs continue to sing as though the word had never reached them. Their tone is harsh, too loud, unbalanced, devoid of resonance and deep support, and just as hard on the singer's voice as it is on the listener's ear. It would seem that if the choir and conductor would only listen to the sounds they make, improvement would be automatic; yet those sounds persist.

Nature of choral tone

Beautiful choral tone results from a process of tonal homogenization. At the outset, individual voices singing together produce diverse, conflicting sounds which must be modified in the direction of one consistent group tone. This modification must derive from each voice its unique characteristics and timbres, produced in a natural way, devoid of strain, and blending with, rather than dominating, other voices. Every choir's tone is thus a unique entity because it is an amalgamation of the unique individuals that comprise it. It must aim at a unity of sound which is neither an absolutely rigid uniformity – virtually impossible in any case – nor the raw cacophony resulting from an unrefined potpourri of independent solo qualities which is a common affliction of bad opera choruses. A beautiful "choral tone" is a sound lovelier than the sum of its individual voices.

A majority of American choirs consist of singers who will never study voice privately and will devote little time to the technical exploration of their vocal apparatus; certainly they have no aspirations to be soloists. This means that many of the normal, detailed disciplines of solo training have little or no relevancy for them, and it is probably idle for the conductor to approach their tonal training by such routes. He needs group techniques which will develop the tonal resources of his choir *as a group*. Certainly it would be nice if every singer would faithfully practice daily exercises in resonance and velocity, but realism says they will not. It remains the conductor's responsibility to develop in his choir at least some of the proficiency such exercises impart during their rehearsal as a group.

Cultural influences

Today the matter of choral tone production is complicated by a new and formidable subconscious influence with which the conductor must reckon. Many "new" concepts of tone quality and singing style are constantly being urged upon the public by current pop and commercial groups or soloists. The long-term value of these concepts is less important than their immediate impact. Many are fleeting, warmed-over versions of ideas long ago discarded as arid. Others are obvious experiments, clearly harmful to normal voice production, and used principally for shock effect. Some, however, only bring up to date folk idioms long established as charming and expressive. If the conductor becomes entangled in value judgments about any of these, he only reaches the dead-end of partisan argument with his singers. The critical fact is that they have heard these singing styles on radio and TV, in stores and motion pictures, *and have made their own subconscious judgments about them.* They may even be attracted to some which the conductor finds objectionable. The "clean slate" of their tonal experience is constantly being written on by other chalk than the conductor's.

Realizing this, the conductor must present his own concepts of tone so skillfully by means that provide such satisfaction to the singers, that they will feel that comparisons are irrelevant. "Pop-commercial tone sounds like *that;* tone for this choral music sounds like *this"* should typify their reactions.

When they sing choral settings of pop-commercial styles as part of their choir's repertoire they will already have the sound of the idiom clearly in mind. It is only when the choir's concept of the various kinds of choral tone appropriate for various styles of music is mixed or vaguely understood that conflicts occur.

Inspired choral performance of any musical style will be frustrated by the lack of a vital, supple group tone quality which uniquely represents a particular choir. The best efforts to master the technical requirements of musical expressiveness – diction, rhythmic acuity, dynamic control, harmonic accuracy, intonation, and purity of style – will be similarly defeated, unless good choral tone is first achieved. Professional singers must demonstrate their grasp of this requirement before they will be hired. When they start to sing, they must immediately contribute and adjust to a rich, malleable group tone. Since amateur singers have not yet acquired this skill, the conductor must inculcate it; he should never be guilty of leaving the matter to chance. If school children are to sing a familiar folk song beautifully, they need to be shown how to make and coordinate the clear, limpid tone of which their voices are uniquely capable. Similarly, professionals need to have the full potential of their already-rich tone exploited by the conductor if they are to sing the Mass in B Minor impellingly. Most choirs fall somewhere between these extremes in capability; it is the conductor's job to discover his particular group's tonal needs and potential and to act accordingly.

Producing vital tone is an experience of great satisfaction to the singer himself. It feels good. This satisfaction helps the conductor in that it spurs singers to greater effort. They quickly become involved in learning how their tone contributes to the group. Some may even be stimulated to explore solo singing. The more vibrant the group's tone, the more firmly "hooked" individuals will become on the basic joy of choral singing. It is regrettable that this type of involvement, so common in capable choirs, so often escapes the understanding of certain conductors, whose choirs never attain even the lowest threshhold of gratification with their own sound and who reflect this lack by listless, joyless singing.

Conductors may dream of rows of carefully selected, perfectly balanced, highly trained voices, but very few ever realize such fantasies. They must work with a random selection of human beings who happen to like singing. Sir Henry Coward stated the situation in a colorful way more than half a century ago, proving that this problem is not new:

"In most choral societies, even in those where the voices are tested, there are a great majority of untrained voices, which may be roughly classified as follows: weak and quavery, worn and tinny, harsh and shrill, strident, metallic, shouty, throaty, cavernous, hooty, scoopy and nondescript. I have been blessed with voices answering to each of the above classes for thirty or forty years and have not wholly got rid of them to the present day – and yet I have survived! . . . . . . Every society is made up of average voices, and my experience is that there is not nearly so much difference as some would have us believe in the average voices such as are to be found through the English-speaking countries. I make this statement with the special object of inspiring conductors with hope, and of assuring them that they have great potentialities at hand in their choirs if they will only make up their minds to expend the requisite labour."[1]

The ensuing discussion of tonal techniques assumes that the conductor faces just such problems. In this situation the first need is to establish a common vocabulary of tonal experiences. Terms used to describe tone must have meaningful non-verbal counterparts in the mutual experience of the group. Many of the techniques to be considered here are concerned primarily with establishing just such a vocabulary. Until this is done, the conductor will lack the means to convey ideas about choral tone to his choir. When the vocabulary pertaining to choral tone is mutually understood, the choir's expressive potential can be achieved quickly and surely.

The tonal continuum concept

A practical, proven means of acquainting a choir with its own tonal resources is found in the use of a tonal continuum concept. This is a dramatic, easily-used introduction to almost any problem whose solution demands that the choir agree upon one specific quality of sound, chosen by common experience from among many possibilities.

The continuum represents graphically the widest extremes of quality possible in the particular aspect of choral sound under consideration. It interprets "extreme" as connoting "bad" or "unusable" and postulates that midway between the extremes lies an "ideal" area of production. Example 4.1 illustrates this for the essential contrast between so-called "bright" and "dark" tone qualities. The aim is to provide a measurement device on which each singer can gauge the group's – and his own – performance. One result of this is to establish in the group's common experience reasonably precise definitions for

1 : Henry Coward : *Choral Technique and Interpretation,* Novello, London, 1914, pp. 19-21

terms that are otherwise vague and loosely used. These definitions are aural: actual sounds produced by the choir are identified as "bright" or "dark", "thin" or "hollow", etc.

Once this method is established in the choir's experience, it becomes a flexible, productive means by which the creative conductor can secure specific shadings of vowels, establish accurate dynamic levels, determine the desirable extent of vibrato in the group tone, and solve many other technical problems. For example, to berate sopranos about singing the word "Seek" with "too bright a tone" may be perfectly justified, but meaningless if the section has never reached agreement on what "bright" means. Exactly *how* bright? What specific vocal adjustments must each individual singer make? The efficient application of a tonal continuum device such as Example 4.1 can quickly resolve these doubts. The subsequent discussions of vowels, dynamics, and vibrato should suggest ways in which the conductor can adapt the concept to his own needs.

In first introducing the tonal continuum concept to a choir, it is best to use terms which are only partly musical but draw on singers' experiences with making all sorts of vocal sound. What terms do they apply to the most distinct qualities of sound they have already made with their voices? Starting in a familiar area, they can be led quickly to separate "singing" sounds from other vocal sounds, and then to begin making increasingly sophisticated shadings of sound within what is understood as "singing".

To begin, reproduce Example 4.1 on a blackboard or chart, and explain to the choir that it represents extremes of sound from "bright" to "dark" which their voices can produce. Point out that many terms are used to describe these qualities, only a few of which are included in the chart. Other terms suggested by individuals should be considered and added to the chart if they contribute to a mutually understood meaning. Since one objective of the continuum's use is to reveal the vague and overlapping nature of commonly-used terms, every shade of meaning understood by the singers should be incorporated in the chart if possible.

Example 4.1 : THE "BRIGHT-DARK" TONAL CONTINUUM

Terms used to indicate extremes of: **"BRIGHT" TONE QUALITY**	**"IDEAL" TONE QUALITY**	Terms used to indicate extremes of: **"DARK" TONE QUALITY**
light ←		→ heavy
white (lacking color) ←		→ dark (murky)
thin (unresonant) ←		→ hollow (overly resonant)
flat (lacking depth) ←		→ round (cavernous)
pinched (tight, strained) ←		→ loose (empty, uncontrolled)
"squeaky" ←		→ "hooty"
shallow ←		→ deep
throaty (or nasal) ←		→ "chesty"
open (blatant) ←		→ covered (obscured)

NOTE ■ Other kinds of contrast not possible to correlate with this "bright-dark" comparison can be the focus of separate continua if the conductor feels they are more meaningful to his choir. Among these might be "sad-happy", "children's choir-opera singer", "whisper-yell", "sweet-angry", and so on. Impossible or unrealistic combinations should be avoided, such as coupling the "sweet-angry" contrast with a request for a contrast between "pinched" and "loose". Refinements will emerge in the singing of experienced choirs, but to ask for them with beginners only causes uncertainty.

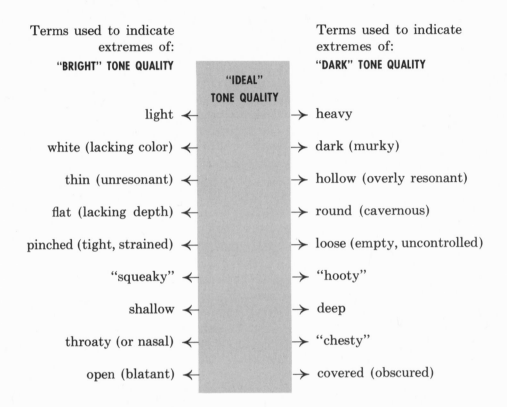

Ask the group to produce sounds (on a uniform pitch and vowel suggested by the conductor) which they feel represent the extremes stated on the chart. It will be immediately apparent that certain vowels lend themselves to each extreme more readily than others. For instance, it is easier to sing EE "brightly" than OO; on the other hand, OO or OH will produce a better "dark" sound. The details of vowel coloring will be examined later, and only the most general agreement about the matter is needed for this first exercise. Since this is frankly an experimentation with the group's tone, it should call for a wide range of possibilities, including forced exaggeration and overtly "bad" tone, and even run the risk of momentary throat strain in securing sounds which are truly extreme.

To point out that these extreme sounds are usually made by physical strain or distortion is valuable. Asking singers to screw up facial muscles, tighten jaw and lips, and strain throat and upper chest to produce the "light-white-thin-flat-pinched" extreme, and to distort the jaw, throat, and shoulder muscles in forcing open the widest yawn position to produce the "heavy-dark-hollow-round-loose" extreme provides them with immediate physical sensation of most of the things the conductor does *not* want them to do when they try for the "ideal" sound. The more automatically singers can be led to improve their posture and muscular poise as the most immediate preparation for singing "ideal" sounds, the more completely the continuum idea has succeeded.

When fairly consistent extremes of sound have been agreed upon, ask the choir to produce what they feel is an "ideal" tone, theoretically about midway between the extremes, *and specifically of a singing quality.* Even though each singer contributes what he considers to be his "best" tone, the group will immediately hear differences among themselves as to what the "ideal" quality actually is. By having sections sing one at a time, each singer has a chance to evaluate a segment of the group tone by deciding where on the continuum the tone of that section falls, in his estimation. Repetition of this process begins to develop a feeling for comparison, measurement, and control in the group. Individual singers can hear how their personal tone production needs to be modified to fit into the group tone more accurately. Use of this device has proven very valuable in solving specific problems encountered in works being prepared for performance.

The most tangible benefits produced by use of the tonal continuum concept are:

Benefits of tonal continuum

a. Each singer is directly involved in controlling the group's tone quality in meaningful, non-verbal ways.

b. A mutually understood vocabulary is established between conductor and singers which can be used to make prompt and sensitive tonal adjustments.

c. Singers become increasingly sensitive to the quality of sound actually produced by their group.

d. The group's concept of their "ideal" tone is clarified and strengthened.

e. Singers develop the habit of comparing and measuring various tonal possibilities as a fruitful and direct method of solving specific problems.

Controlling vowel colors

Most singing is done on vowel sounds. The importance of this obvious fact is not fully understood by many beginners and amateur singers. By clarifying it, the conductor may relate the individual's long experience in speaking vowels to an idea of how he should begin to sing them. The probability that

Accurate Vowel Color = Rich Tone Quality

while hardly an invariably infallible concept, can be used to establish a continuity from which the singer may start, because he already is acquainted with the range of vowel sounds in his speech.

The following devices seek to classify basic vowels by sound alone. In the interest of practicality, this classification will be simpler than that of the International Phonetic Alphabet, although that system is unquestionably the most thorough. However, since it is extremely doubtful that all singers of a beginning or avocational singing group would find the time or motivation to learn the symbols of the International Alphabet, a more easily grasped set of symbols is proposed. Unless all members of a group thoroughly understand whatever system is used, its value as a group device is dissipated. Since the desired understanding of vowel color is aural rather than visual, minimizing technical symbology is the fastest way to the goal.

Various practical systems and simplifications are available, of which the method of "Tone Syllables" evolved by Fred Waring in 1945 is one of the most efficient and successful. A dynamic conductor will to some extent develop his own approach, based on the capabilities of his singers. The following system represents such a construction and argues that if a group can be led to agree on, *and actually control,* ten basic vowel sounds, they will have established usable points of reference from which to make more subtle distinctions. This is a more attainable objective for many choirs than to attempt mastery of as many as fifty distinct shadings of sound identified by some authorities.[1] By analogy, it seems safer in crossing a stream to step on ten large, firm rocks, by-passing forty intermediate smaller stones upon which balance is more doubtful. From the security of the larger boulders one can, of course, always gently touch the smaller stones!

In the following chart these ten vowel sounds are arranged in approximate order from "dark" sounds, controlled generally at the "back" of the vocal apparatus, to "bright" sounds, produced in a "forward" position. The danger of relying on terminology alone to convey these concepts is underscored by even the most cursory examination of the literature explaining such tone productions. Not only do authorities differ; a real terminological chaos exists. Virtually none of the terms has a precise or scientific meaning that is commonly understood or accepted. Dealing with the actual vowel sounds they produce seems the shortest and most effective means to give choral singers a working understanding of the vocal production involved.

TEN BASIC VOWEL SOUNDS

OO as in MOON	AH as in FATHER
OH as in MOAN	ă as in SAD
AW as in LAWN	EH as in RED
UH as in MUD	IH as in DID
o͝o as in SOOT	EE as in NEED

To repeat, it is *crucial* that understanding and agreement be in terms of actual sounds produced by the choir; theory and printed rules – even this list – will not establish the desired pure vowel sounds. Considerable practice must be devoted to establishing in the hearing of the group precisely what shading of sound they must sing together for each specific vowel symbol. Various regional backgrounds precondition singers as to what they consider the "right" sounds of vowel symbols. The restless nature of American culture readily combines in the membership of one choir singers from Georgia, Maine, Kansas, and Texas, with perhaps one or two from England and the European continent thrown in. The resulting divergence of concept as to the "natural" sound of any given vowel can be spectacular.

1 : D. Ralph Appleman : *The Science of Vocal Pedagogy* Indiana, 1967, pp. 175-77

First attempts to establish this common vocabulary involve having the group speak together the word samples given above. In transferring the sounds to sung pitches in various tessituras, differences of vowel color shading will be discernible, both between singers, and between registers of individual voices. Familiar melody lines or troublesome phrases of works in preparation may be used to develop awareness of color shading. For instance, the familiar carol refrain of Example 4.2 will be sung with ease by most choirs.

Example 4.2:

As they are led to focus attention on the sounds they actually make when singing this melody in unison, choir members will observe that the shape of the AW (or OH, see below) vowel changes in practically all voices as they move through the melody's range of a major ninth. The conductor can then concentrate on identifying the points where change or tension exist and should give suggestions as to how the line may be sung with more uniformity of vowel sound. This latter will be helped by incorporating an appropriate register device (see Chapter 5).

This example also underscores the need to agree upon whether the "right" vowel color is OH or AW. Here again, authorities cannot agree. The "authentic, approved" Latin pronunciation is a matter of dispute even among Vatican-approved experts. The conductor should decide by hearing both whether AW or OH sounds richer with his choir and have no compunction about using that sound. The potential displeasure of some branch of expert opinion is far less important than that his choir produce a vital unified tone.

It must be repeatedly stressed to a choir that these ten basic vowels provide only a framework, and that the vowels in some words just won't fit into any one of these. As tonal security grows, the more subtle shadings needed for accurate pronunciation will become easier by reference to these ten sounds. Problems of dynamics, inflection, management of adjacent consonants, registration, and other fine points pertaining to developing an artistic, flexible tone can be handled more readily as the choir develops assurance about vowel sounds. The conductor should certainly be aware of the "stock" solutions to such problems as they are given in books on conducting technique; but final solutions for *his* choir must be hammered out of the raw tonal materials of the moment.

Diphthong precision

Diphthongs (multiple or combination vowels) are a subject of some disagreement as to their number and method of production; once again, the theoretical disagreement is far less important than the beauty and unanimity of the choir's sound. It is not disputed that diphthongs are composed of two successive vowels, and that these have a fixed but unequal time relationship and are uninterrupted by a consonant. Differences of opinion concern exactly which diphthongs qualify as true multiple vowels and which are in fact single sounds.

Four diphthongs are commonly accepted without debate:

OW as in COW	: AH (sustaining vowel)	+	(OO) (vanishing vowel)
IE as in PIE	: AH (sustaining vowel)	+	(EE) (vanishing vowel)
OY as in BOY	: AW (sustaining vowel)	+	(EE) (vanishing vowel)
EW as in FEW	: (EE) (vanishing vowel)	+	OO (sustaining vowel)

Some authorities do claim that the sustaining vowel of the OY sound is a pure OH, and the conductor should determine if the sounds produced by his singers bear this out.

Two other combinations are less clearly defined and offer more room for dispute:

AY as in DAY	: EH (sustaining vowel)	+	(EE) (vanishing vowel)
OH as in BLOW	: OH (sustaining vowel)	+	(OO) (vanishing vowel)

Some contend that under normal circumstances these are pronounced as single sounds; others that they are indisputably diphthongs. The conductor will probably discover differences in sounds among his own singers to bear out both points of view. The important thing is that the group reach a working agreement in terms of sound as to what their practice will be. This may be aided by the following devices:

Example 4.3:

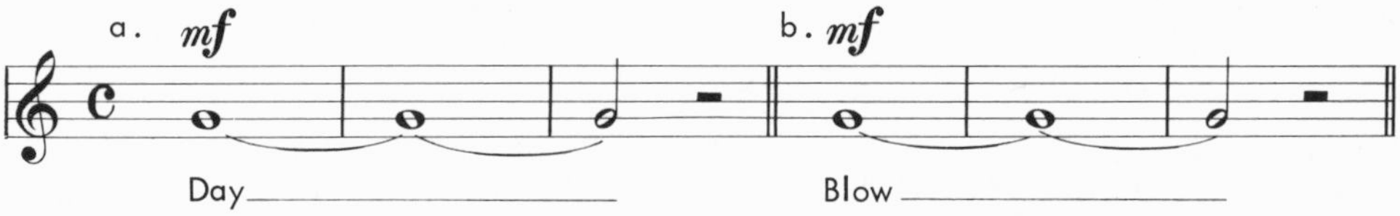

Sing each example twice. During the second time, the conductor stops the tone arbitrarily somewhere in the second measure. The group is asked to judge if, at the moment of stopping, they were singing the whole AY or OH sound, or were in fact singing only the beginning sustaining vowel of the diphthong form. Regardless of which choice predominates, the path to uniform production has been opened, and further practice will develop a secure common habit.

The diction of many choirs suffers from their difficulties in coordinating the elements of a diphthong. The oft-mutilated phrase "Hear our prayer" illustrates why. The word "our" is phonetically composed of

AH (sustaining vowel) + (OO) (vanishing vowel) + R

Singers tend to slight, or eliminate altogether, the (OO) sound, thus producing a sequence that adds up to the word ARE. They must be challenged to enunciate each vowel clearly, and to give each part the proper proportion of the diphthong's total time. This proportion will vary according to tempo, but it will always favor the sustaining vowel by a large ratio. To illustrate the importance of assigning the major amount of time to the sustaining vowel, ask the choir to sing the two vowels with equal duration; the resulting distortion will make the matter obvious.

Example 4.4 :

An even more colorful example of diphthong distortion is often heard in the word "Hail!" Here, either the AY sound must

be carefully executed as a complete single sound, or the component parts of the diphthong rendered fully. If conceived as a diphthong, its parts are:

H + EH (sustaining vowel) + (EE) (vanishing vowel) + L

Omitting or slighting the (EE) sound, as choirs too often do, conveys to the audience an exclamation quite different from the text's intent.

Vowel modification

It has been noted that beginners tend to modify vowel colors as they move between registers of their vocal range. Lack of smooth control over the registers of the voice may produce in singers an almost obsessive fear of high or low tones, usually those lying in the register with which they have had least experience. If the part necessitates singing these tones, the beginner will either fail, or try to sing them using a distorted vowel color on which he has found he can produce tone with reasonable security. This problem can deeply trouble the conscientious beginner, and the conductor must not only be aware that it is a major stumbling block for the singer, but provide him ways to overcome it. The attitude must be strongly conveyed that this difficulty is very much a part of learning to sing, and that no matter how deeply the singer feels his personal problems, they represent no abnormality.

Private voice training usually stresses the development of an "even" scale which smoothes over natural changes of vocal production with firm control. Although the limited individual voice training possible in a chorus will make little difference in voices with acute register-transition problems, there are devices to use in a choral rehearsal that will at least make members aware of the dimensions of the problem. Wise use of these devices may stimulate conscientious singers to strengthen their own weaknesses in the sheltering anonymity of the group. Among such devices are those given in the discussion of registers in Chapter 5. In addition, having the choir sing the simple intervals in Example 4.5 has been found effective.

Where difficulties are intense at the outset, possibly because singers are embarrassed about using tone qualities outside of their "normal" voice, (such as *falsetto* for men and "chest tone" for women), combining these devices with the "bad tone" technique of Chapter 5 leavens the procedure with good humor. In these devices the aim is to make each singer *hear* what happens to his tone and the color of his vowels when he sings in problem areas of his voice. Hearing this helps him evolve his own solutions. Such devices can also identify problem voices that can be helped only by private coaching and, on the other hand, may call attention to voices capable of performing incidental solos or singing with ensembles.

Example 4:5:

Sing in unison:

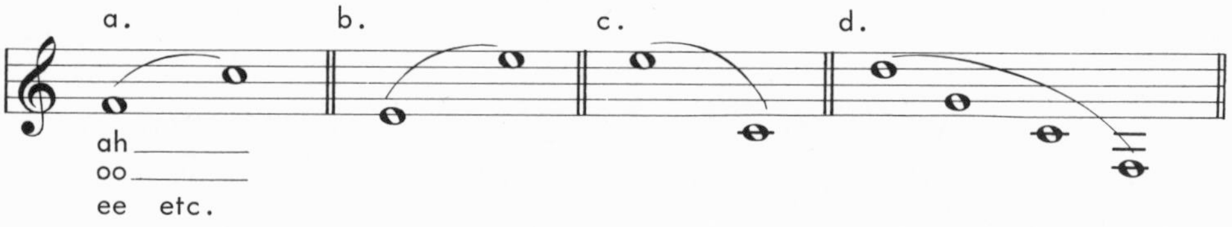

Use the intervals of Example 4.5 with great flexibility, singing them as written, inverted, or filled in with diatonic or chromatic scales. Use a wide variety of vowel sounds, perhaps selecting words or sound combinations which have presented problems in a work being rehearsed. The conductor should bear the following objectives in mind in using these and similar devices:

a. To reveal the location and nature of major changes of vowel color caused by problems of vocal production.

b. To reveal to each singer which vowels are easiest for him and which the most difficult.

c. To demonstrate to the singers as a group that the most resonant, ringing tones they produce also have the most accurate vowel colors.

Vowels to emphasize entrances

In complex contrapuntal passages and thick harmonic textures, where crucial entrances or inner voices tend to be lost in the total complexity, or where an extreme tessitura prevents reinforcing the entrance by added volume alone, slight modifications of vowel color may provide the desired clarity. "Brightening" the tone (see vocabulary established in the Tonal Continuum) even to the point of exaggeration will help to bring out difficult entrances. In example 4.6, alto and tenor lines tend to be lost in the thickness of the total sound and relatively low tessituras.

Example 4.6:

Bach, J.S., *Mass in B Minor, Sanctus* (G. Schirmer)

If the altos are asked to produce a practically pure chest tone, and all tenors and altos modify the vowel in the direction of the next lighter vowel, the parts emerge more clearly. If the first vowel of "gloria" is being sung as AW, it should be shaded toward AH. If it is OH, it becomes AW. Recordings of the Bach Motets by the Thomanerchor Leipzig show that the boys and men of that traditional Bach sanctum-sanctorum use this device — perhaps unconsciously — often and with good effect.

As with the use of "bad" tone discussed later, this raises the question of "using one fault to correct another", which may be regarded by some as a dubious procedure. It is probably true that fully trained professional singers would have little need for such a device, having developed the power and flexibility to sing any pitch on approximately the proper vowel color. Yet it is also demonstrable that most amateurs, including many in highly proficient college and community choral societies, have real trouble in singing certain sounds on certain pitches. With these singers the alternative to modifying vowel color is not an ideal solution based on a perfected vocal technique, but is simply to give up the possibility of making these entrances heard. In addition, singers report that this device not only makes difficult notes audible, but saves vocal strain. If the singers can respond to the conductor's inevitable request in such passages to "Bring out those entrances!" only by singing louder on AW (or OH, which is even harder), it will be virtually impossible for them to comply *without* strain. Seen in this light, modification of the vowel, even though technically a "fault", assumes more justification.

Vowel modification in the other direction is normally practiced by sopranos singing in the range above the treble staff. The notorious entrance in the Beethoven *Missa Solemnis:*

Example 4.7: Beethoven, *Missa Solemnis in D, Credo*

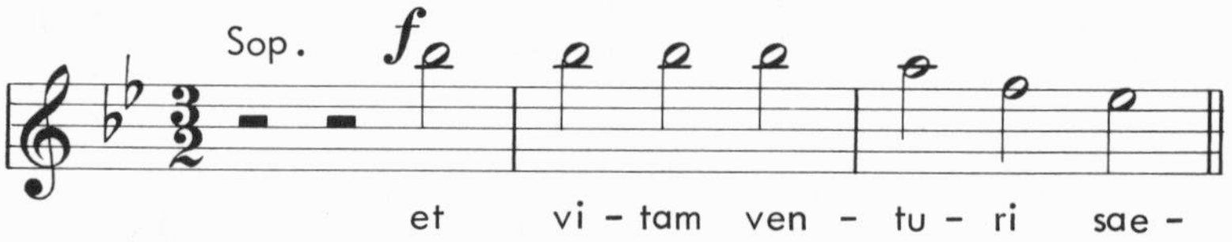

and passages such as that in the Roy Ringwald arrangement of the *Battle Hymn,*

Example 4.8: *Battle Hymn of the Republic,* arr. Ray Ringwald (Shawnee Press)

become shrill cries of wounded agony unless every bright vowel is modified in the direction of darker qualities.

Vowel modification is also useful in achieving special effects. The footnote for example 4.9 gives explicit instructions as to the desired effects. To achieve these, the upper three voices should modify their vowel colors toward brighter sounds and basses should make the "OO" sound still darker.

Example 4.9:

Country Style, Van Huesen-Simeone
(Shawnee Press)

* Imitating a country band:
(1) Girls in three parts on banjo effect— Hard and metallic.
(2) Tenors doing Jews' harp effect— nasal with a ring throughout the 4 bars.
(3) Basses doing a jug bass effect— attack tone low and slide up to proper pitch.

The dynamic conductor will use vowel modification carefully and creatively. The more thorough his score preparation, the better he will be able to anticipate points of vocal difficulty at which use of this device will be constructive.

Articulation of consonants

Consonants shape vowel sounds into words. Unless understood in this context, they tend to become only a collection of clicks, grunts, explosions and muscular contortions of little inherent meaning. The clean articulation of consonants necessary for understanding words results from a sure knowledge of positions of lips, tongue, jaw, and throat required to make each consonant, and the ability to produce these without distorting the on-going flow of tone.

As with vowel symbols, the simplest and most communicative system of signs is most useful to the choral conductor. All the consonants of the English language can be contained in a fairly concise chart, arranged according to the manner of their production. Again it is important that the choir understand that the symbols represent sounds and not alphabetical letters. Some letters have no unique sound, ("Q" is "KW" and "X" is "KS"), or have multiple sounds, ("C" is "K" or "S"), so these are omitted from the chart. Other single sounds which require two letters to spell are added: NG, WH, ZH, and two varieties of TH (voiced and unvoiced).

CHART OF ENGLISH CONSONANTS

EXPLOSIVES:

Voiced *(Pitch accompanies stoppage)*	←*same stoppage*→	**Unvoiced** *(Pitch follows stoppage)*
FULL STOPPAGES:		
B : *Bat*	←→	P : *Pat*
D : *Dog*	←→	T : *Tog*
G : *Got*	←→	K : *Cot*
J : *Jeer*	←→	CH : *Cheer*
PARTIAL STOPPAGES:		
V : *Vile*	←→	F : *File*
Z : *Zeal*	←→	S : *Seal*
TH : *Thy*	←→	TH : *Thigh*
ZH : *Pleasure*	←→	SH : *Shout*

CONSONANTS ON WHICH TONE CAN BE SUSTAINED:

L	:	*Let*	
M	:	*Met*	
N	:	*Net*	
NG	:	*riNG*	(same stoppage as G and K — see above)
UR	:	*pURR*	(Used within or at ends of words, can be sustained)
R	:	*Run*	(Used at beginnings of words, may be rolled, never sustained)

VOWEL-FORMATION CONSONANTS:

(Form to say the vowel, but do not sustain it, passing immediately to the vowel of the word)

W : *Will* = (OO) IH L

Y : *Yet* = (EE) EH T

ASPIRATES

(Made with the expulsion of breath only)

H : *His*

WH : *When*

It will be useful to put such a chart into the hands of choir members, as the information has value only when each singer uses it in his own tone production. Time in rehearsal is too precious to devote to detailed analysis and drill on consonant production, but if each singer has access to the chart, when a consonant problem occurs, the conductor can use the chart to make clear precisely what must be done in articulation and tone in order to correct the fault.

The choir should be shown that failure to make final consonants heard clearly results from one or both of the following causes: imprecise or partial articulation of the consonant by a majority of the voices of the group, or failure of the group to articulate consonants in a precise unison. Do not ask a choir to correct lack of clarity by forcing or exaggerating a consonant sound. Such exaggeration is almost impossible for the group to carry out, and would not completely correct the fault even if the singers could do it. Singers must concentrate instead on articulating precisely, *and together*. A whispered consonant enunciated normally but exactly together by all voices will project with more clarity than even the most forceful attempt at exaggeration. Precision depends on an exact knowledge of the action of the various articulators (lips, tongue, etc.) and "togetherness" comes from intense attention and the accumulation of group experience. It is valuable to train a choir in habits of phonetically analyzing each line of text, as suggested in the previously mentioned *Tone Syllables,* so that the singers become accustomed to thinking of consonants as being placed at precise points within the ongoing flow of tone.[1]

Training devices invented by the conductor should have the following aims:

a. To clarify the rhythmic framework within which consonant articulation takes place. Consonants happen in time, and their fundamental basis is rhythmic.

b. To develop precision and uniform production of consonants; force or exaggeration blur the sound.

c. To relate consonant-making to secure tone-making; since consonants shape tone, the better the quality, intensity and continuity of the tone, the more precisely it can be articulated by accurate consonants. The choir must recognize that consonants do not "chop up" a singing line, but give it shape.

Sometimes the composer has designated in the notation precisely where he expects the consonant to occur in the rhythmic flow, as in Example 4.10:

1: Fred Waring: *Tone Syllables,* Shawnee Press, Inc. 1945 p.5

Example 4.10: Jolley, Florence, *Holy Lord God of Hosts* (Shawnee Press)

In this example the problem is to get all singers to articulate the D consonant cleanly at the specific beat indicated by the notation itself. The phonetic spelling of the words simply reinforces the intent of the eighth note tied to the preceding longer notes. This notation is helpful because it pinpoints exactly where the consonant is to be made. With this matter settled, the choir can more readily maintain a clear, resonant vowel without modification until the exact instant of the consonant.

Unfortunately, few scores indicate the exact location of final consonants with such clarity, and disagreements multiply. Here again, assessment of abolute "right" or "wrong" takes second place to the need for obtaining uniform practice within the group. What will work? What solution will lead partially-skilled amateurs to produce a reasonably precise result? A familiar and typical problem occurs in the fourth chorus of Brahms' *Requiem* when it is sung in English. The word "hosts" occurs frequently in all parts, usually sung on a half note.

Example 4.11: Ibid.

When should the "STS" combination happen? Not only is this one of the most difficult sound combinations of the language, but there is disagreement among experts as to when to attempt it: "on the last part of the second beat" – an imprecise description at best –,"on the third beat"– where it isn't written! –, or even, as the author heard one brave conductor insist, "between the beats"? Some common agreement must be evolved which preserves the integrity of the score, and will work every time in the singing of the choir. One widely successful solution to this problem suggests what might be done in other similar cases. Mentally divide the two-beat duration of the word into two equal parts in strict rhythm and tempo:

Example 4.12: Ibid.

By relating the STS to the preceding vowel tone, and thinking of OṠTS as a separate word to be pronounced within the normal duration of the second beat, technical quibbling is quickly by-passed and the grouping of consonants is clearly understood. Since consonant and vowel are used as integral parts of the same total sound, the close reliance of consonant production on secure vowel tone is stressed.

Precise intonation

It is probably a truism to say that the better the choral tone quality, the rarer will be problems of intonation. A vibrant, rich tone is rarely flat or sharp. But this sweeping assertion corrects few specific faults in the heat of a rehearsal. Indeed, it is probable that no single explanation will account for all the factors that affect intonation, and the choir might not comprehend such an explanation if it were formulated. The conductor should continually explore his choir's intonation problems and try to develop in the singers a *tonal* awareness of what *intonation* means. While calling their attention to specific faults when these can be isolated is helpful, he should also provide devices to enable singers to develop habitual intonation control. The following devices have proven useful:

a. *Relate accuracy of pitch to vowel color* ▪ Instill in singers a habit of thinking as follows: "An accurate and resonant vowel color usually produces an unstrained and resonant tone; if any tone can stay in pitch, such a tone should. When I have intonation problems, I should first check to see if the vowel color I am singing is accurate and resonant". While certainly not an infallible panacea, this thinking focuses the singer's attention on one phase of the problem with which he already has had some experience, and which may serve as the basis of a specific remedy.

b. *Resolutions into perfect unison* ▪ Discrepancies of pitch can be heard most clearly against a perfect unison. To reveal these and to clarify the concept of precise unison, have the choir sing middle C♯, pianissimo, on OH or OO. Men will probably need to use falsetto, and women should lower the head tone out of its usual range, producing it very gently and without strain. As all parts maintain a uniform vowel color and dynamic level, move various sections to other pitches in sequences such as the following:

Men sustain C♯ while women move up to D.

Altos sustain C♯; men move down to C, sopranos up to D.

Tenors sustain C♯; altos move to D, sopranos to D♯, basses to C.

In each sequence, let the dissonance settle into a clear balance, and then instruct the choir to move back to the original C♯ *and decrescendo at the same time.* The result will be a tangible feeling of "relaxing" into the unison. Intonation becomes increasingly precise with repetitions and elaborations of the device, as singers begin to "feel" the center of the pitch and sense its location within their composite tone; the blend and color of vowels will also steadily improve. Manipulation of this device in various ways has proven valuable in clarifying harmonic textures of great complexity, by helping singers of one part to hear their pitch more accurately in the midst of the total fabric.

Increasing dynamic sensitivity

To fulfill the expressive possibilities of choral tone, the conductor must depend upon at least four fundamental conditions in the area of dynamics:

a. The singer must be aware of the dynamic symbols in the score.

b. Those symbols must produce instant and tangible response in the sounds the singer makes.

c. The conductor must be able to exert a moment-by-moment influence upon the flow of the dynamic-expressive musical line.

d. The singers must develop an empathy of performance which integrates the first three conditions above with all the other skills at their command. The better they are technically, the more aware they are of the expressive possibilities at any given instant, and the more coordinated and meaningful will be their responses.

The effect of these conditions is cumulative, and expressive performance displays the full impact of the sequence. Too often, inadequate or uneven preparation of the first two conditions forces the conductor, by attempting a heavy stress on the third, to try to create the entire dynamic-expressive fabric of the music in the moment of performance. This is like trying to put an ornate roof on a house whose foundations are of sand. Weaknesses show through; stress and strain brings on the collapse of the entire structure. It is virtually certain that nothing like the fourth condition will ever be reached.

At the outset, training must equip singers with the terminology of dynamics and make them acutely aware of the presence of dynamic symbols in the score. Beginners tend to overlook these entirely, seeing only that with which they are familiar: the words, and the more obvious elements of notation. The difference between amateurs and professionals in this regard is striking. The conductor of amateurs who has the privilege of working with professional musicians comes away from the experience awed by how alert to dynamic markings these singers were in contrast to his own, who, it seems, must have every separate symbol pointed out. This poignant reminder of the amateur's uneven absorption of dynamic disciplines helps to explain why expressive singing comes so much more slowly to his choir than he wishes. It may also provide cause for introspection about how effective his own training devices in this area have been.

Simple devices should be created by the conductor to make his singers notice dynamic markings in the score and respond to them. An effective means is to require them to start a piece again from the beginning every time they fail to heed a dynamic or expressive marking. Also, it will help to explain the standard dynamic markings at the outset in colloquial terms, such as those below, and follow such explanations with group practice in singing chords at various designated dynamic levels to establish their meaning in sound.

Standard dynamic levels

fff	(fortississimo)	: the very loudest tone the choir can control
ff	(fortissimo)	: very loud, full, forceful, with a sense of power
f	(forte)	: loud and strong, with power held in reserve
mf	(mezzo-forte)	: moderately loud, as in pleasant, animated conversation
mp	(mezzo-piano)	: moderately soft, subduing the same conversation
p	(piano)	: soft, as in intimate conversation
pp	(pianissimo)	: very soft, with the intensity of an eager whisper
ppp	(pianississimo)	: the very softest tone the choir can control

It is important to emphasize to the choir continually that control of dynamic levels profoundly affects their choral tone. They must realize that dynamics are not separate technicalities added on after choral tone is mastered. They must be led to understand that dynamic symbols will have little valid meaning for them as singers until those symbols are converted into integral components of the group's entire choral sound. Devices which have proven effective in training groups to control dynamic levels are:

Comparing dynamic levels

Using such chords as the following on various vowels or words, have the choir sing different dynamic levels which the conductor specifies at random by pointing to a chart on the wall or blackboard.

Example 4.13:

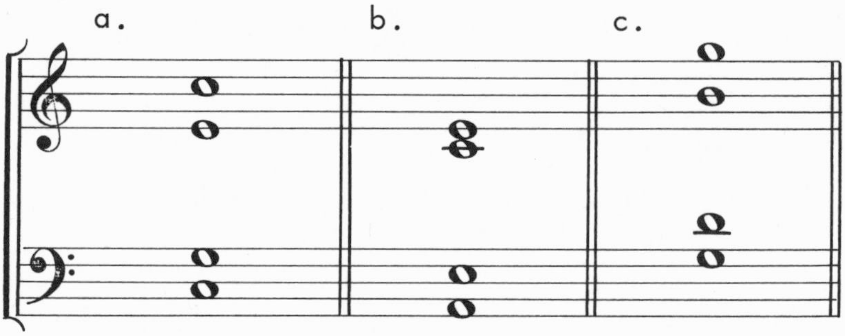

Suggest a pseudo-geometrical relationship between the levels as a means of encouraging each singer to explore the means of controlling the force of his own tone. Starting with the *p* level, establish a fairly consistent sound throughout the choir. Then say, "Now make the pianissimo just half that loud." The resultant softening will be in varying degrees, but should soon settle into a uniform level. Having reiterated that *ppp* means "the very softest tone the choir can control", suggest that it should now be "half as loud as the pianissimo you just sang".

If their full attention has been caught up by the process they will discover that they can control levels of volume which are not only soft and loud, which was the principal aim, but are also touched with evident emotional connotation, about which the conductor had said nothing. The door to real expression has been opened for them. They have also discovered something about the ease and intensity with which a group can vocalize soft tones, and the discovery is beneficial to both their vocal health and their morale.

Extension of the device to all levels, being sure that louder dynamics are produced with deep support and a complete lack of throat strain, will establish a reference for reasonably accurate dynamic shadings throughout the entire range. When this is repeatedly applied to specific compositions in rehearsal, the need for the unnecessarily rigid geometrical concept will gradually fade away, replaced by real expressive control. Continual use tends to make accurate dynamic shadings a matter of habit, like the instrumentalist's fingerings and embouchures.

As frequently stated, a rehearsal device has the greatest value when it springs from a piece the singers expect to perform. Since dynamic markings are often the last aspect of musical notation to receive singer's attention, the conductor must seek passages in the music where dynamic markings can be dramatized. This will occur in passages where the omission or misinterpretation of dynamic symbols may disrupt or completely destroy the musical meaning. Example 4.14 presents a problem of dynamics to the women's voices, since their entrance, while rather high, is marked *pp*. Unless this dynamic level is accurately produced, however, their parts will tend to obscure the principal melody sung by the men, which is continuing at its initial *p* level.

Example 4.14: Schumann, Robert (arr. Churchill) *I Gaze On the Garden* (Shawnee Press)

The inventive conductor will have the choir sing at "wrong" dynamic levels to reveal the logic of the score's markings if any are printed, or the dynamic demands of the music's inherent structure. In the case of Example 4.14 some of these might be:

a. All parts sing the entire passage *ff*.

b. Men sing *p,* as indicated, while the women sing *ff*.

c. Men sing *fff;* women sing *ppp*.

Against any of these distortions the specified dynamic balance will seem to the choir not only "best", but probably "most natural". The process has also accustomed them in a small degree to judge the score in terms of its printed dynamic values. Accumulation of enough such judgments builds habits of dynamic singing.

Changes of dynamic levels, accents

The realm of changing dynamic levels, accents, and special effects is so vast that it is most productive to deal with each problem in its context rather than trying to build an all-inclusive vocabulary in advance. The conductor's prior study of the score will warn him of such problems, and since some of the symbols are almost certain to be new to his singers, he can prepare necessary devices. The list of symbols is long and involved; it is futile to hope that the average choir member will learn more of them than are brought forcefully to his attention by meaningful use. Example 4.15 shows the frequency and importance such symbols can assume in the composer's or arranger's desire to produce an expressive musical texture. The great majority of notes in each voice part carry some specific dynamic symbol, accent, or change of level.

Example 4.15: *Antiphonal Hosanna,* Gregor – Ringwald (Shawnee Press)

Accurate performance of this work requires that singers have control of these dynamic concepts and techniques:

a. A clear working distinction between *mf, f,* and *ff.*

b. Crescendo.

c. The > accent: sudden dynamic reinforcement of a tone.

d. The – stress mark: dynamic reinforcement with added agogic (durational) emphasis; sometimes called a "weight mark".

Work on this example makes it clear that the problems are as much tonal as dynamic. A choral tone which lacks adequate resonance and support, purity of vowel, precise intonation, consonant articulation, or blend of over-all quality will fail to produce even the simplest shadings of dynamics with any accuracy. Instead, the singing will usually be just loud and blatant. The conductor must be able to determine how much of his choir's difficulty with dynamic shading results from fundamental faults of tone which he can correct. This will lead him to deal with the real causes, which are the tonal deficiencies, rather than to belabor only the symptoms: "too loud", "too soft", or "too something else".

Rhythmic vitality in slow tempi

Robert Shaw once observed that the majority of all problems of choral performance are fundamentally rhythmic. Nowhere is this more readily demonstrable than in the production of a continuously vital tone. A principal dimension of tone is its duration, which postulates a precise beginning or attack and an equally precise ending, or release. Between attack and release consider tone as a live, moving entity, whose vitality depends on its sense of motion through time.

Choirs can be shown that their flaccid, unrhythmic, poorly-timed tone quality, beset with problems of intonation, lack of resonance, ragged attack, poor diction, and all the other ills commonly afflicting weak performance, will yield more quickly to rhythmic discipline than to any other solution. For rhythm to be understood at all, it must be *felt.* Its essence can be comprehended only by direct physical involvement.

When a tonal problem resists usual devices, an abrupt, dramatic, and strongly rhythmic change of pace, if possible based on "off-beat" methods, will demand fresh attention and vigor from each singer. Requiring rhythmic involvement of a novel variety casts new light on a work. In Examples 4.16 – 4.18 such techniques are applied to music of contrasting styles:

Example 4.16: Bennet, John, *Weep, O Mine Eyes* (Bourne)

At the outset, choirs will encounter the following problems with the work cited in Example 4.16:

a. A persistent tendency to flat.

b. Scooping, ragged attacks.

c. Failure to resolve suspensions and harmonic progressions together.

d. Dynamic imbalance, based on uneven vowel color and tone as well as simple inattention to dynamic symbols.

Each of these problems is related to rhythmic faults. Since *Adagio ma non troppo* leaves considerable latitude as to the exact tempo, singers feel little security in the half-note unit of beat. This unsettles all attacks and makes a coordinated movement through the harmonic rhythm almost impossible. The resulting subconscious vagueness heightens the tendency to produce wrong vowels, which in turn produces a vapid tone almost certain to fall below pitch. All this mental confusion makes it unlikely that the singers will notice dynamic symbols. Further, the combination of *adagio* with *pp* too often suggests to the amateur moods of "smooth, unrhythmic quiet", with possible overtones of "dreaminess" or "sadness", rather than the simple slow-soft combination intended. This compounds most of the problems cited.

That this music is *very* rhythmic should be immediately obvious to the conductor. The strong metric accent implied by the harmonic rhythm, and the systematic preparation and resolution of suspensions impart a clearly-articulated momentum. If the choir fails to perceive this because of misconceptions about style, some of the following devices may prove helpful. (From the purist's point of view, these do a violence bordering on mayhem to the 16th-century style, but a genuinely durable piece will always survive such treatment. The better its inherent quality, the greater the chance that the "right" interpretation will emerge from an exploration of alternatives.)

To cast this music into a dramatically-altered perspective, ask the choir to sing it in broad swing tempo, 𝅗𝅥 = 120, with a dance-like metric accent, and a tonal style suited to a television commercial. As they sing, have the singers clap the following patterns, using various dynamics and tone qualities:

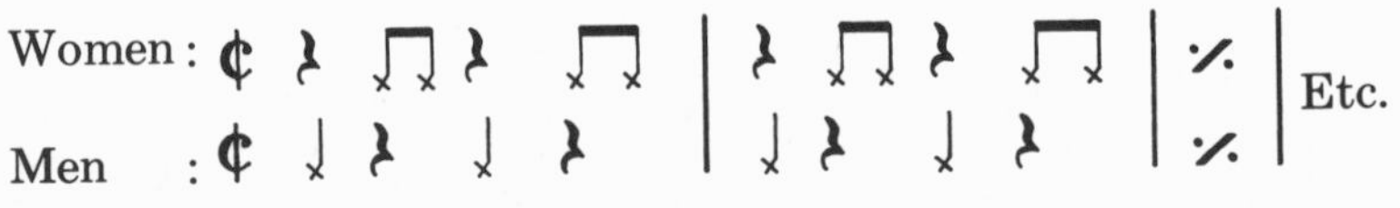

Vary these devices by singing the parts staccato on the syllable "DOOT", stressing a round, dark vowel color, and a short, distinct staccato. The dynamic level should never be allowed to rise above *p*.

The choir must understand that this device is an exercise intended to make them look at the music in a different way, *after which they will return to the directions given in the score.* If this exercise produces the expected vitality of tone, the fact should be called to the choir's attention, and they should be urged to transfer this vitality to the "correct" rendition. Repeated reference to this vitality in future rehearsals should bring noticeable progress toward the score's clear intentions: an intense, quiet, flowing tone, infused with a vibrant vitality, reflecting a strong underlying rhythm. This device has proven to be strong medicine in curing similar ills in *a cappella* works, both sacred and secular.

Rhythmic vitality in fast tempi

Example 4.17: Bach, J.S., *Praise Him*, Paterson

Example 4.18: Stanton, Royal, *Glory in the Highest, glory!*
from *God's Son Is Born*, J. Fischer & Bro.

Examples 4.17 and 4.18 reverse the procedures of 4.16. Each is in a fast tempo, the Bach being marked *Allegro* (₵ meter), and the Stanton *Vivace*, 𝅗𝅥. = 84. While the musical styles are quite different, both illustrate that music of faster tempos, regardless of style, involves tonal problems with which the conductor must help his singers. First rehearsals of these examples will expose the following flaws:

a. Muddiness of harmonic progression; uncertainty as to the exact tonal shape of each chord, resulting from poor intonation and wrong melodic intervals.

b. Blurred dissonances, resulting in the chord sounding simply "wrong" instead of dissonant.

c. A tendency to shrill and blatant tone because of the loud dynamics (all *f* and *ff*), coupled with insecure harmonic progression. This gives free rein to a normal tendency among amateurs to try to compensate for errors in loud passages simply by singing louder.

d. Poor diction: faulty vowels and unarticulated consonants.

As with the problems of Example 4.16, these matters relate directly to rhythmic causes, but instead of concerning deficient rhythmic vitality, they represent uncontrolled rhythmic momentum. The very ebullience of the music's drive can result in poor coordination between parts and an uneven rate of accentuation. Again, "abrupt and dramatic change" may prove helpful.

a. Sing the passages in hymn-like quarter note meters, (♩=60) molto legato, *mp*.

b. Sing each troublesome chord as a three-beat note, followed by a fourth beat of rest in the same tempo.

c. After the slow-tempo drills have achieved accuracy of tone, balance, and rhythm, speed up to ♩ = 100. Demand that the improved accuracy of the slower performance be maintained. It is helpful at this tempo to have singers tap or clap the metric pulse indicated in the score, even though the tempo is slower than the final version will be: for Bach, clap half notes; for Stanton, dotted half notes. Again, it is of the utmost urgency to return to the correct score tempo, carefully maintaining the progress achieved.

The problem of vibrato

Vocal *vibrato* is a normal pulsation of pitch or intensity, about six pulsations to the second, regarded by most authorities as characteristic of a resonant, well- produced individual tone quality. It is often confused with *tremolo,* or *wobble,* which are muscular contortions resulting in a wider range or faster rate of pitch change. Untrained, or bad-habit-ridden singers, unable to hear what they understand to be vibrato in their own tone, consciously add tremolo or wobble in the attempt to make a "rich" tone, and produce a sound with such variations of pitch that it is practically useless as an ingredient of choral tone. Solo singers, accustomed to the freedom of singing without the need for accommodating to other simultaneous vocal sounds, sometimes sing tones that because of their vibrato rate are glaring contrasts to a surrounding choral tone. Where the texture of the music calls for raising a solo line in relief against the choral sound, such tones are valid. Where it does not, they are wrong.

Choirs can be trained to sing with varying degrees of tonal pulsation, as various recordings currently on the market illustrate. The conductor's concept of the tone he wants his choir to produce should include a well-defined position on this matter. If he leaves it to chance, his group's sound is almost certain to be dominated by the voices which are afflicted by varying degrees of tremolo or wobble, resulting in blurred pitch and vowel color, and a general inability to produce a ringing, resonant tone.

Adapting the *Tonal Continuum* device to the matter of vibrato-tremolo is a workable way of clarifying the choir's own concepts. The continuum in this case would range between the extremes of "Absolutely straight tone" and "Wobbly tone", in which the pitch changes are better than a half-step in amplitude. When the singers locate their own production somewhere along the continuum, call their attention to the fact that when individual tones vary widely in pulsation rate, the group tone is inevitably a blur. By smoothing out such pulsations *together* greater clarity is achieved; but if the process is carried to the "completely straight tone extreme", the tone tends to become cold and lifeless. The more firmly such differences are established in the mental ears of the singers as a result of what they have sung, the more their "ideal" tone (as in the Tonal Continuum) will be found to have drawn strength from both extremes: the clarity and precision of "straight" tone, resulting from the elimination of tremolo and wobble, and the richness and intensity of a well-produced vibrato tone.

Father William J. Finn some years ago put the relation of vibrato to choral tone quite concisely:

> "It is true that Caruso, Gigli, Scotti, Frances Alda, Galli-Curci, Jeritza, and many others showed wide vibrato range upon measurement, but it is also true that probably no living choral conductor could develop an artistic chorus from among them and their colleagues . . . . . . .It would be interesting to listen to a chorus of high-powered vibratoists tangling itself into the net of an eight-part motet by Palestrina, or even a simple *a cappella* fugue by Bach."[1]

The American Academy of Teachers of Singing, however, imply a somewhat different view in a Paper issued in 1966; in speaking of the values of choral work to the solo-oriented singer, it says,

> "In . . . groups where 'imitation', the so-called 'straight tone', *or other dubious methods are practiced,* he [the

1 : William J. Finn : *The Art of the Choral Conductor,* C. C. Birchard, 1939, pp. 88-89

singer] has nothing to gain and much to lose."[1] (this author's italics).

From these extremes it is clear that much of the divergence of view about the desirability of vocal vibrato springs from the natural difference between the soloist's attitude and that of the chorus singer. Between these extremes, and considering his own singers' tonal resources, each conductor must stake out a position for himself. His decision, here as elsewhere, is the crucial one as far as the sound of his choir is concerned. Certain demonstrable facts should guide this decision:

a. *Clarity of tone springs from uniformity of vibrato rate* ▪ A section or part must "speak with one voice" when they sing the same vowel on the same pitch. If tone color, pitch, and vowel are to be accurate, they must not be blurred by conflicts in the pulsation rate. Either that rate must correspond exactly in all voices:

Example 4.19 : 

or vibrato must be virtually eliminated in the direction of a "straight" tone. If each tone is allowed complete freedom of vibrato, a slight blur results:

Example 4.20 : 

The condition is severely aggravated by the presence of one or two voices with uncontrolled tremolos or wobbles:

Example 4.21 : 

While it is true that very little conscious control can be exercised over the pulsation rate of *true* vibrato, since it is a subconscious quality of well-produced tone, it is also true that voices singing together with proper production tend to establish a uniform pulsation rate.

b. *Musical style affects the amount of vibrato required* ▪ Father Finn referred to Palestrina, and the implied need for "straight" tone in performing his music. On the other hand, singing Brahms with that same tone can destroy the meaning of the music. The two styles demand different expressive means. Choirs known for singing Renaissance styles with great purity by using the "straight" quality often founder when they move to Romantic repertoire for this very reason: the tone is wrong. This underscores the value of a group's at-

1 : Amer. Acad.: *Choral singing and the responsibility of the Choral Director.*

taining control over their vibrato so that they may sing more than one style of music with validity. Groups which sound the same singing Victoria, Beethoven, and Richard Rodgers should not be applauded for consistency; they are consistently wrong. The conductor's prior study and good taste must determine the choral tone suited to each style.

c. *Ultimate control of vibrato must be a non-verbal group agreement* ■ The sounds produced by the choir will show whether such an agreement has been reached. If those sounds are fuzzy and out of tune, it has not. Theory and verbal statements about the "right method" are virtually without meaning until experience has brought about a non-verbal understanding between singers. This means that the conductor must provide his singers with experiences (such as Tonal Continuum devices) through which they can evolve such agreement in their singing. His efforts will probably achieve greatest success if he starts with tones at the "straight" end of the spectrum; but he must keep in mind that many other qualities are valid, *depending on what the group can actually be led to produce with unanimity.* The "problem of vibrato" is only one phase of the larger aim of building a rich and vibrant choral sound. It is quite possible, indeed, that choirs not afflicted by glaring tremolo or wobble problems will be able to bypass direct reference to vibrato simply by focusing on that more inclusive aim.

5 | The Choral Conductor's Role in Voice Training

To what extent is the choral conductor involved in the voice training of his singers? This question would be answered in a wide variety of ways if asked of all choral conductors presently active in America. At one extreme are choirs in which the singer's continued membership depends on regular private lessons with the conductor himself. In the center is the great majority of choirs in which there is an unspoken agreement to ignore the matter altogether. At the other extreme is the nationally-known conductor who was heard to express to his choir quite derogatory opinions about the value of voice training and voice teachers in general. Against this background of diverse practice and opinion, the purpose here is to consider what seem unavoidable phases of voice training with which the choral conductor must be involved in his attempt to produce an artistic *choral* result.

Choral vs. solo voice training

Since he deals with many more choral singers than soloists, his involvement with voice training is oriented toward the particular needs of the former. His concern with the vocal production of an individual singer is rightly limited to that which affects the tonal product of his choir. Such specific guidance as he gives to choral singers and soloists must be limited to modifications of voice production that benefit the choral tone as a whole. To this extent he is a *group* vocal coach. Since his objective always concerns the sound of the *group,* and only secondarily the techniques or triumphs of any solo voice, he is *not* a private vocal coach. While his understanding of the functioning of the voice and his methods of teaching vocal production must be thorough, comprehensive, and well prepared, all of these must be directed toward the choir and not the individual.

Some private voice teachers forbid their students to sing in choirs on grounds that vocal techniques of choral singing differ from, and in the teacher's opinion are detrimental to, those needed for solo production. While the validity of this position may increase as soloists develop more advanced skills, it remains to be demonstrated that in the beginning and intermediate phases of their training, these singers can appreciate enough about the refinements of vocal production to be aware of the small differences between solo and choral singing to which the teacher objects. On the contrary, until a wide experience in fundamental tone production is acquired, it probably benefits any singer to take advantage of every opportunity to sing in a controlled situation. Among such opportunities, choral training under a competent conductor whose knowledge of the physiology and function of the voice is secure certainly qualifies as constructive.

There is no question that the demands of solo singing *do* differ from those facing the choral singer. Concepts of projection, expression, tone quality, and rhythmic freedom are shaped by the fact that the tone is solitary, and so not constrained to coordinate with other simultaneous vocal sounds. Disciplines involved in equipping the voice to be the only vocal sound in a musical complex are of a different order from those which train it for the precise coordination required when it is to be just one component of a group tone.

This is not to say that these demands are necessarily contradictory. A completely trained voice should be flexible enough to function well in either setting. A comparable case is the concertmaster of a symphony orchestra, who is expected to be the outstanding group player in the violin section, second only to the conductor in his influence on the quality and uniformity of the group tone they produce. He is also called upon to play incidental solo parts in a completely personalized manner, with a tone and style providing individual contrast to the group tone.

Not all violinists are concertmasters, nor all singers soloists. Those singers aspiring to solo achievement should be given every assistance in securing the very best private instruction, and should be expected increasingly to devote their effort to solo singing. It is safe to assume that the majority will never become "completely trained" voices, preferring to remain choral singers of varying degrees of proficiency, for whom the choral conductor will be the sole source of vocal instruction. Comparisons of relative merit between the two styles are meaningless and invidious. While some very skilled choral singers make poor soloists, it is equally true that very proficient soloists can be the most inept of choral singers. The role of vocal training in a choral situation is most clearly defined by the conductor's decision as to whether his choir is a vehicle for training potential soloists or an organization devoted to producing choral sound.

Conductors and voice teachers

Some choral conductors find themselves seemingly in conflict with private voice teachers with whom their choir singers study. Such conflict is often more apparent than real, but it is incumbent upon the choral conductor to dispel it by actively fostering the best professional relations with voice teachers. Even if choir membership is predicated upon personal voice coaching with the conductor, as is the case in some college and church choirs, in choir rehearsal the conductor should make it clear that his suggestions regarding voice techniques are aimed solely at choral tone production. His success in clarifying this focus to his "voice training" activity will guide the conductor around thorny problems which often beset those whose teaching of vocal technique is regarded as an infringement on the territory of the private teacher. If the conductor also wishes to establish himself as a private teacher, he must realize that he invites just such problems by seeking to play a dual role.

Another possible source of misunderstanding is the delicate matter of whether the choral conductor, in his more public position, will recommend certain teachers and ignore others. A conductor in a public school or college is often ethically constrained to make no recommendation at all, on the theory that the representative of a public-supported institution should state no preferences. Yet the conductor cannot avoid observing which private teachers seem to produce beneficial effects in singers, and which ones lead singers to stagnate, lose interest, or actually damage their own voices. When singers ask for advice his impulse in the midst of a busy schedule may be to recommend teachers whose students seem to be making obvious progress, and to say nothing about others. This can lead to ill will and unpleasant relations among members of the musical community, and it places the conductor in a position which is hardly tenable in the event of direct criticism. A possible solution for the problem is for the conductor to maintain and post an open list of voice teachers, on which all of the community's instructors are invited to list their qualifications and the kind of voice students they are interested in working with. No recommendations are intended or stated. Very soon, teachers whose efforts are soundly productive will acquire word-of-mouth reputation fully as forceful as the conductor's recommendation. Further, the conductor will be credited by voice teachers with a fair attitude in giving equal opportunity for all of them to become known to his choir members.

Far from being in conflict, the activities of private voice teachers and choral conductors in a community should be mutually beneficial. The dynamic conductor's influence increases interest in private study, and his performances afford opportunity for public solo work by students of the voice teachers. On the other hand, artistry in cantata and oratorio solo performance is certainly enhanced by individual coaching, and the conductor's presentation will benefit from such skilled private assistance. Bickering and dissension such as that which mars the musical life of some communities only reflect shame on all concerned.

Advantages of group training

For the confirmed non-soloist choral singer there are distinct advantages to vocal training acquired in a group environment:

a. The influence of self-consciousness is minimized.

b. Hearing other voices meeting similar problems provides a chance for comparison not readily available in the private studio.

c. Immediate feedback from peers and conductor about the individual's vocal production helps him learn to control his voice in ways that will benefit the group.

d. Opportunity is provided for comparison and contrast of tonal concepts in non-verbal ways, making these concepts much more meaningful to the singer than can theory or verbalization.

e. A friendly group environment encourages timid singers to explore their vocal resources, which they might be too self-conscious to attempt alone.

DEVICES FOR GROUP VOCAL TRAINING

Problems in teaching laymen to sing usually arise when the instructor's words fail to convey his precise meaning or concept. At that juncture, no matter what "school" or "method" of voice culture framed the concept, words become dreadfully imprecise tools for etching concepts or conveying insights about voice production.

To escape such an impasse the conductor must develop the skills of non-verbal, conceptual communication discussed in

Chapter 3, and foster an attitude of controlled self-help and experimentation on the part of the singer. In the final analysis, each student must re-discover in his own singing the concepts which "the poor power of words" dams up in the instructor's mind.

The conductor must also carry on instruction at the level where the *singer* is, rather than where *he* is. The more "lay-ish" the singer, the more urgent this rule is. The sequence and speed of instruction must be structured in terms of concepts that the student shows he is ready to use. While it is true that the steps and levels of this structure ideally should be built upon a comprehensive, technically correct exposition of voice training, it is also true that if the singer doesn't personally experience each step in sequence, the comprehensive grand design is lost on him, and everything beyond the last point he really understood seems hopelessly technical or pointless.

Thus the non-soloist choral singer who never studies voice privately may find it hard to distinguish between "solo voice training" and "choral voice training". The distinction may be clear and important in the mind of the conductor, but since the singer's horizons are more limited, many of the "choral tone" devices of Chapter 4 qualify fully as "voice training" in the singer's understanding.

Other devices will be suggested below, which, although structured for group use, serve to focus the singer's attention squarely on his own production: precisely how does *his* voice accomplish *this* vocal challenge? In using these devices, the conductor should never permit his attention to be drawn too far away from group objectives by glaring tonal faults in individual voices which are suddenly given unwelcome prominence by some teaching device. Though such faults obviously cannot be ignored, efforts to modify them must relate more to the group tone than the individual's.

Unison solos

When an entire section or choir sings a solo melody in unison in rehearsal or performance, interest is heightened and attention is focused closely on the sounds being produced. Singers hear both the musical values of the work and the manner in which voices relate to those values. Blatantly deviating tones stand out sharply and the contrast to surrounding tone qualities is likely to impress the singer and cause him to make a desirable modification in his singing.

Unison solos distribute responsibility for tone quality equally among singers. Since the desired blend will be accomplished *only* through conscious, inner-motivated cooperation, each singer must feel responsibility for his contribution. Example 5.1 cites a group-solo melody which demands the utmost in tonal and dynamic control. It is useful not only for the alto section for whom the composer wrote it, but for all other sections or even the entire choir.

Ex. 5.1: Williams, Ralph Vaughan *Mass in G Minor Kyrie*
G. Schirmer, Inc.

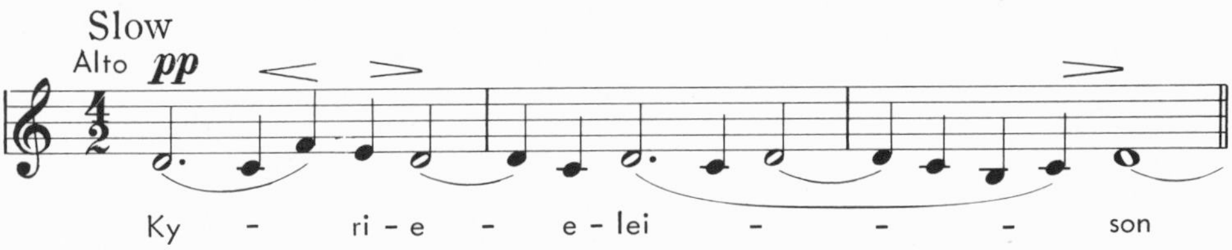

Such melodies call for scrupulous observance of every dynamic and rhythmic indication; these alone contribute measurably to the beauty of tone. By achieving them and hearing the melody as the unified production of many voices *including his own,* the singer can acquire a remarkable degree of non-verbal control over his voice. He helped produce that sound, and although he couldn't relate in technical terms how he did it, he could probably reproduce it — and *that* is what the conductor wants.

The usefulness of the unison solo device can be expanded by altering the manner of performance for purposes of comparison. Changes of tempo, dynamics, or vowel color should be called for; altered tone quality may be evoked by suggesting different moods, requiring a change in vocal production. For example, a tangibly different quality would result from the melody's original mood of intense, quiet joy, if it were then sung as a song of mourning. Both might be *pianissimo,* flowing in rhythm, and rich in tone; but most singers would produce an appreciably different quality consistent with the differing moods. Carrying the idea of mood changes to extremes not suited to the music being rehearsed (as for instance singing Example 5.1 as a military march) can provide a useful contrast of perspective, through which the validity of the original musical concept emerges clearly, and which illustrates to the singer the many moods which his voice can achieve.

Unison solos need not be considered only as rehearsal devices nor limited to melodies originally written for group performance. Several of the arias from Handel's *Messiah* lend themselves excellently to use as group solos. Musical repertoire abounds in passages which call for the unique, expressive sound of carefully-honed unison singing, ranging from the glories of Gregorian Chant to the invigorating impact of a well-turned popular melody. While this device can be therapeutic for certain vocal ills, it is also a performance resource of real beauty, too often neglected.

Tone matching

When tonal problems persist, rehearsal time can profitably be devoted to tone-matching between individual singers or small groups. To isolate and modify mis-matches of tone, pitch, or vowel sound, have a section or the entire choir attempt a unison sound. If it is apparent that no unanimity of quality or pitch exists, ask one individual to sing the desired pitch, which is then to be matched by each singer in turn. This will make each person aware of differences in pitch or vowel color, so that he may attempt to modify his tone. This procedure also shows the conductor which singers produce the most dependable tone, and he may wish to re-arrange seating to place them in positions of sectional leadership.

Tonal mis-matching and lack of blend spring from one or more of the following causes: 1) Inaccurate vowel colors, 2) faulty resonance, 3) inability to sustain proper intonation, or 4) breathy-throaty, unsupported production. Example 5.2 shows a device which allows the singer to identify his particular problem in a simple context. Use of such contrasting pairs of vowel colors has proven of real value in helping individuals and sections identify their vocal differences and attain more uniform production. In using this device it should be clear that the conductor must call for consistently perfect intonation, and a deeply-supported, resonant tone. Whenever possible, the conductor should relate this device to a problem which is impairing the sound of a work in preparation. Such timeliness has the double advantage of increasing the effectiveness of the device, because singers can immediately see its application, and lessening the chance of embarrassment to individual singers who may feel they are being singled out for their vocal faults if this device (or any other) is not directly related to the job at hand.

Example 5.2:

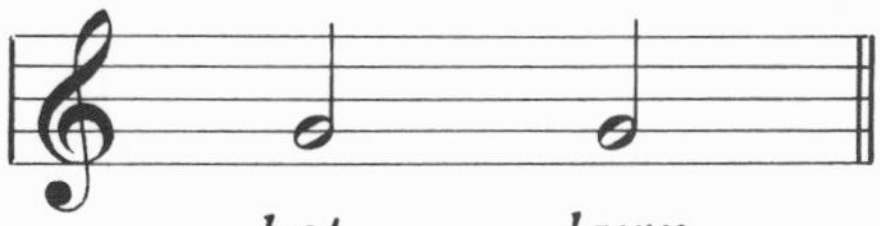

hot	*lawn*
sad	*ed*
see	*sid*
gone	*home*

Use of "bad" tone

A choir needs a common stock of tonal experiences, identified by mutually-understood terms, if it is to develop precise concepts of tone control. If the conductor applies only the broad terms "good" and "bad" in trying to help his choir control tone quality, he will be understood in as many ways as there are singers. Since the possible shadings of those terms are virtually limitless, they must be more carefully defined, and attached to specific qualities of sound within the common experience of the choir if they are to have any precise meaning. If common agreement leads singers and conductor to settle on a certain tone quality as "good", the word then becomes a symbol for a mutual non-verbal experience which is more precisely understood than the word can ever be. The most direct way to develop such associations between sounds and words is to have the choir produce a wide variety of tone qualities, beginning with the general terms "bad" and "good", and working toward finer discriminations between more subtle qualities. As each new shading of tone is identified it should be associated with a descriptive term which all agree upon. Techniques of the Tonal Continuum (Chapter 4) are most useful in having the entire choir engage in such tone production, but on occasion the conductor's voice may serve as a model.

By asking a section or choir to sing a melody with what they consider not merely "bad" tone, but more specifically, "bad, *harsh* tone", or "bad, *breathy* tone", the conductor confronts singers with differences in their own concepts as revealed in their performance. This immediately casts the probable nature of contrasting "good" tones into relief. For beginning groups the most important thing which this may reveal is simply that their "good" tones are *different* from their "bad". As already suggested, some choirs sing as though they had never encountered this fundamental concept. By isolating various shadings of "bad" through conscious attention and the use of good-humored exaggeration, the way is opened for the conductor to identify specific qualities of "good" tone production, giving each a graphic word-designation ("clear" or "focused" as opposed to "breathy"; "smooth" or "velvety" for "harsh", and so on) which will identify the newly-understood quality in the minds of the choir members as they attempt to reproduce and control it.

For a majority of singers in the choir the cacophony created by the "bad tone" device will be in such sharp contrast to their concepts of "good tone" that understanding of the differences between the two will be automatic. For some, however, it may come as a revelation (relatively unencumbered by embarrassment or self-consciousness) that what their peers consider "bad tone" is uncomfortably close to their own normal or even "good" tone. Few conscientious singers can remain unmoved by such a discovery.

This device must obviously be used with care, gentle good humor, and a keen sensitivity to personal feelings. As a means of ridicule, apparently directed at one individual, it can be devastating; yet perceptive application of its cutting edge to a choir's tangled sound can quickly remove many undesirable tone qualities.

Problems of vocal registers

For four hundred years, teachers in the broad stream of voice culture usually identified by the label *bel canto* have insisted that the human voice, male and female, functions essentially the same way, women using principally the upper register, and men the lower. The road to the development of a beautiful voice, it is maintained, begins with the separation and strengthening of these two principal registers in every voice and leads eventually to their becoming balanced and coordinated.[1] In the literature of voice training the terminology by which this process is described comprises a catalogue of contradictions. Private voice culture is an active battleground, on which various "schools" and "methods" have long contended. Recurring skirmishes are fought over the exact number and training of "normal" registers of the voice, with all contenders being able to array apparently imposing authorities and "scientific evidence" to support their respective points of view.

Register devices

The choral conductor may unwittingly be caught in the crossfire of this battle unless he clings single-mindedly to one concern: producing beautiful choral tone. Actually there is no *need* for the choral conductor to become involved in these disputes, which concern solo tone production almost exclusively. As far as voice registers are concerned, his job is to make choral singers aware of what they can and cannot do with their voices. Every man who sings is aware of his falsetto, which he may regard with attitudes of assurance, puzzlement, or embarrassment. Similarly, most women are familiar with their various shifts of vocal register if only because they "can't sing certain notes very well!"

In his quest to produce a valid choral tone, the conductor must confront individual problems of transition between voice registers and provide possible solutions through devices designed for the whole group. Successful involvement in such group devices is usually of direct benefit to the individual singer's tone production. Used in moderation, without strain, and with full recognition of the limitations of growing voices,

1 : Cornelius L. Reid: *Bel Canto, Priniciples and Practices,* Coleman-Ross, passim. (New York, 1950)

the following devices have been found valuable as means to help high school singers explore their vocal potential. Their principal effectiveness, however, is with adult choirs, where they will serve effectively to improve clarity and uniformity of group tone.

Unifying women's chest tones ■ Stressing ease of production, uniform vocal color, and accuracy of pitch, ask all the *men* to sing in unison:

Example 5.3:

When a unified sound has been achieved by the men, say to the women, "Please sing the same sound." It is not enough to say "the same pitch", since it is the *quality* of the "chest register" which must be imitated. Some women will find this difficult. For them, repeating the comparison with men's voice quality a few times will be encouragement to explore their ability to make the "same sound" and thus learn what the term "chest register" means in their own voices. A comparison between altos and sopranos frequently reveals that individual sopranos sing an easier, more secure "chest" tone than many altos. This should help dispel the misconception that such tones are inherently "alto" in nature. Once the concept is established, the conductor should call for this "chest" quality in choral works in preparation, particularly when voice parts lie in the range:

Example 5.4:

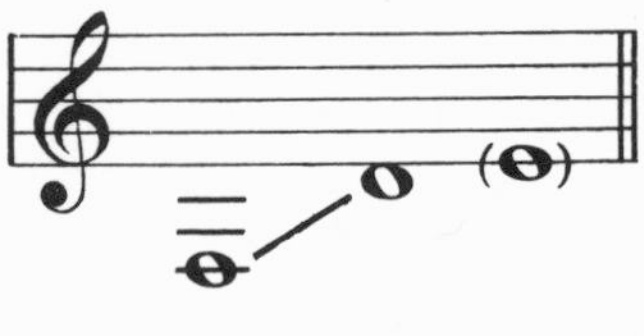

Encouraging men's falsetto ■ Reversing the above procedure, ask the *women* to sing:

Example 5.5:

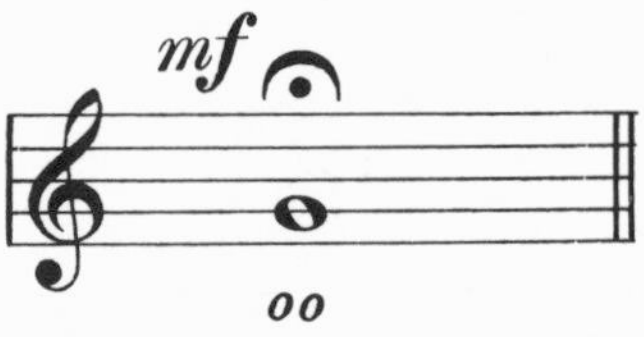

followed by the men, again on "the same sound". Good-humored encouragement may be needed to bolster their resolve to try the sound at all, but gentle persistence will reveal to the men tonal resources they may not have realized they possessed. Graphic instructions such as, "Make a hooty tone", or "Make a sound like blowing across a pop-bottle", while flagrantly unmusical, may ease tensions enough to persuade men to experiment in this valuable area of their voices. As their confidence grows, the conductor must point out to them that the greatest clarity, power, and flexibility of falsetto tone results from the most relaxed production, so that in their individual experimentation the first aim must always be ease. As the group's ability to use falsetto improves, it can often be shown that in terms of clarity and power, within the limited range in which the falsetto functions most readily (as shown in Ex. 5.6), men can out-sing women. The confidence imparted to the men by this discovery leads men to use falsetto more freely, tending to ease the reluctance of both tenors and basses to attempt "high" tones.

Example 5.6:

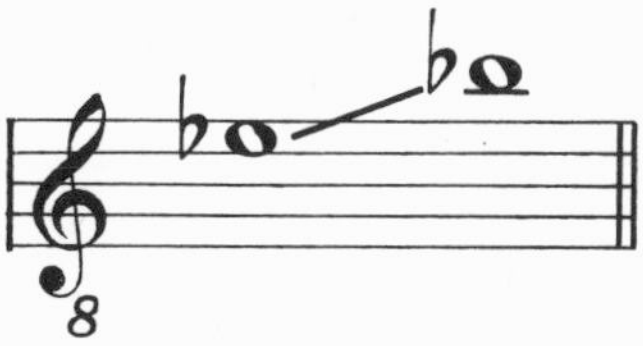

Conductors who hesitate to ask for falsetto singing from male voices should remember that much of the greatest music of the choral repertoire was written in this range to be sung by men and boys. In cathedral choirs which consist of male voices only, falsetto singing is commonplace. The author noted with interest that David Willcocks, working with the Kings College Chapel Choir of Cambridge, almost subconsciously used his falsetto voice to give examples. In a service sung by the Canterbury Cathedral Choristers, four of the five parts of a William Byrd motet were sung by the men, the boys uniting on the single treble part. "Alto" parts were sung by men in their original connotation of "high" parts to be sung in falsetto, or more exactly, counter-tenor range.

American prejudices about "singing like a man" have cast a shadow over the use of falsetto in the minds of many men. Historically and physiologically, however, falsetto rests on the firmest foundations, and the dynamic conductor will do well to encourage and foster its use by his male singers. Wise use of falsetto will reward the singers with added vocal color and flexibility, and a new ease in singing high tones, which they will soon learn to appreciate.

Matching and balancing vocal registers ▪ When a choir can consistently sing tones which clearly separate head and chest registers, they must be led to move from one register to another with smooth control in the range within about a fourth above or below middle C. In this range, both men and women can sing in either head register or chest register, and it is important that they sing these tones in unison at the outset, even though it cannot be expected that men's falsetto or women's chest tones will ever acquire the power and flexibility of their normal voices. For both men and women, the presence of the other gender's "natural" tone serves as a valid model, and the constant comparison thus made possible furthers the most basic objective of these devices: to build homogeneity into the group's tone.

Downward scales are advised because for most singers they involve an automatic lessening of tension. Use of upward scales in this context too often only strengthens habits of tightening and throat strain which may be present in beginning vocalists. Singing these devices should always be done while looking at written or printed notation, so that specific insights called for become firmly associated with visual symbols.

To begin, have the entire choir sing a downward scale, *mezzo piano,* on a dark vowel, from G above middle C to the G below, *entirely in head tone.* For the men the beginning of the scale will be sung in falsetto, and they should be told to continue using that quality downward as far as physically possible, even though they lose power and quality. Similarly, women should be cautioned to resist the inclination to change to chest voice as they descend, even though they too lose power. During repetitions of this exercise in head tone, suggest that each singer make mental notes of the following:

a. On what pitches the voice feels inclined to "break".

b. On what pitches is the most pronounced loss of power observed.

c. Which pitches, if any, can be produced only by straining.

Next, lower the octave to F# – F#, or even F – F, and instruct the choir to sing downward using *only chest register.* It will be immediately obvious to most men that they can meet this requirement only by shouting the upper tones, while most women will find that their production of the same tones involves coarseness or even strain, if they are singing pure chest quality. It should be every singer's experience in using chest tone that moving down the scale brings them into an easier, more controllable production. By contrasting this experience with the greater ease with which they sang the same notes using head tone, singers can gain insight into the workings of their voices, and begin to understand the importance of balancing and coordinating both of their principal registers. Since this device runs some risk of strain for beginning voices, it should be used in moderation and with careful discrimination.

Questions to be asked about the chest tone scales are:

a. What problems do you personally experience in singing the upper tones?

b. On what pitches does singing become easier for you? How do these compare with the pitches in the head-tone scale on which you felt an urge to "break"?

c. On the middle tones of the scale, can you sing with either head tone or chest tone and produce approximately the same sound and power?

Perceptive use of register devices discussed above will improve the power and uniformity of a choir's tone because it tends to:

a. Develop habits of easier voice production in the less-frequently-used register of each singer's voice.

b. Allow the production of natural tone qualities in each register with diminishing strain.

c. Reduce psychological resistance to "high" and "low" tones.

d. Demonstrate to men that upper tones need not be strained for, but that with the use of adequately-supported falsetto, this range becomes increasingly easy to sing without shouting.

e. Develop women's confidence in singing lower tones, upon which much of their eventual power and projection must be based. For adolescents this may be a completely new revelation, as the capacities of their growing voices are shown to include chest qualities they had not realized they possessed. It is also true that many adult sopranos have never satisfactorily resolved problems of vocal production in the range a fifth down from middle D, and these devices guide them in seeking answers, by providing a controlled situation in which they can compare their vocal production with that of other similar voices.

Preparation for choir training

Although he may never become directly involved with solo voice training as such, the choral conductor must be thoroughly trained in voice culture and fully prepared to apply his knowledge to building choral tone. He needs:

A thorough knowledge of how the human voice functions ■ This includes the physiology, psychology, and conceptual basis of the act of singing. It should be based on study *and* practice, meaning that he should have studied about singing, have sung chorally and in solo, and have had private voice instruction, so that he has had occasion to judge the effectiveness of training on his own voice and musical experience. It is a commonplace that an orchestral conductor must have played several and preferably all instruments; the same requirement applies to the choral conductor: He must have sung extensively.

A clear concept of the tone quality he wants his choir to produce ■ This may change and grow, being modified by particular situations. It will be a composite of his personal experience with singing, the choral tone he has heard in listening to other choirs, his experience with producing choral tone with his own choirs, and his personal conception of what an ideal tone should be.

Familiarity with the principal "methods" of voice training ■ He must be aware of the bias and thrust of conflicting ideas about the "right method" of singing, and be familiar with various techniques of class voice instruction. His own concepts of what "teaching voice" entails will be derived from his insight into all methods currently in use. A comprehensive grasp of such methods will equip him tactfully to reconcile divergent points of view present among chorus singers taking individual private instruction from different teachers.

Knowledge of the general history of solo and choral singing ■ His repertoire for choir, including works which involve a solo voice alone or with choral background, will be drawn for the most part from music of the last 400 years. His knowledge of the vocal-choral demands of that repertoire and of the evolving techniques of vocalization which led the composers to write in particular ways will permit him to judge the suitability of specific pieces for his choir, and not blunder into using a work for which his singers have neither the vocal skills nor adequate musical understanding.

Familiarity with an extensive repertoire for the voice, solo and choral ▪ In addition to knowing stylistic characteristics and technical demands, the conductor should have a detailed acquaintance with specific pieces of music, both choral and solo, from having studied or performed them. While his most detailed knowledge will be in the choral field, he should also be thoroughly conversant with leading examples of art song, operatic aria, sacred solo, and folksong setting. The more his knowledge of the problems and demands of such styles stems from direct personal contact, the more effective it will be in preparing him to guide his singers through a wide spectrum of vocal problems.

Ability to anticipate vocal problems in new works ▪ His cumulative experience and study should prepare the conductor to see in advance the exact nature of the vocal problems posed by a new work. The most crucial of these will be its choral problems, but his insights must include just how a work challenges the capacity of the individual to make and control his own tone.

An empathy for the personal psychological ramifications of singing ▪ The vital importance of creating an amiable, empathetic climate for choral singing is cited in other connections in this book. The importance of such an atmosphere as the conductor attempts vocal guidance of his singers springs from the intensely personal nature of singing itself. A person's singing or speaking tone can reflect the subtlest meanings of his innermost thought or mirror in indefinable ways the kind of person he is. The conductor must have the capacity, through the exercise of human understanding, to blend these diverse subtleties into a beautiful composite. Without this sensitivity to human values, the choral music he produces will be cold and detached.

6|The Conductor and Group Musicianship

To say that musicianship is needed by choral singers is like Being In Favor Of Virtue — unimpeachable, but vaguely ambiguous. Terms must be defined. What, exactly, is the "musicianship" they need? What degree of individual musical skill and knowledge of music theory and history must a singer display to be recognized as one who has it? What technical accomplishments can the conductor expect or require of the group? Are these requirements the same as for instrumental groups, or individual instrumentalists? What is the conductor's responsibility for training his singers in developing such skills and knowledge?

Derogatory comments sometimes heard from instrumentalists and orchestral conductors about "what bad musicians chorus singers are" often reflect pique at shortcomings which have slowed up a particular rehearsal or flawed a combined performance. They also epitomize the difference of viewpoint which separates many instrumentalists from many choralists.

Choral singers' musicianship

In its broadest meaning, "musicianship" connotes the possession and exercise of broad musical skills which result from acquired knowledge, persistent practice, discerning taste, and continuous application. This meaning implies the need for a knowledge of style and historical perspective, a grasp of the organizational principles of music such as form, harmony, counterpoint, and instrumentation, as well as skill in performance. In common parlance, however, or when the term is used as part of a derogatory comment, its meaning is usually limited to one specific area. The "poor musician" is seen as one who can't — or doesn't — read music notation. Since this meaning is also the one which most concerns the conductor in the choral rehearsal, this chapter will focus upon it to the virtual exclusion of the more comprehensive realms of "musicianship". Those realms must never be ignored by the conductor, but in the rehearsal his opportunities to impart such knowledge are very limited.

There is little doubt that choral singers, by and large, are less proficient in many of the purely technical disciplines which the instrumentalist defines as "musicianship". The nature of choral training too often allows the singer to by-pass such disciplines, and the omission places him at a continuing disadvantage. To play an instrument, one must learn fingerings, embouchures, or bowings. The fastest way to coordinate all such technical demands into a musical result is to do what it says on the printed page; he thus learns notation at the outset, as the best means to an end. Singing, on the other hand, can spring from the singer virtually complete. Good or bad, the sounds emerge whole. The fact that singing is largely impelled by a mental concept makes it literally *too* easy to produce a pseudo-musical sound simply by imitating what one has heard. "Just play it over once on the piano. . . ." is a temptation which the conductor must resist if his singers are to develop musicianship. To achieve this, they must be moved by a clear insight into what "musicianly" means *as far as their performance as a choral group is concerned.*

Many choirs do accomplish musicianly performance of a high order. It is usually attained by professional groups and is often heard in the work of better school and church choirs. Paradoxically, it would be quite possible to show that individual members of many such groups suffer personal shortcomings in skills of musicianship, but that somehow these faults do not impair the group's final product. The sustaining power of group momentum, when initiated and guided by dynamic conducting, can carry weaker members along to heights of musical accomplishment they could not achieve alone.

This "group musicianship" should be the choral conductor's first concern in developing technical skills. He will certainly be "In Favor Of" his individual singers having the greatest personal skills possible, joyously welcoming any who have them, and urging others to attain them. He realizes, however, that his best efforts in a group-rehearsal setting can at best improve such skills only slightly, and largely by indirection. He knows also that if he waits to attempt musicianly performance until all his singers have developed extensive personal skills and knowledge, he will never build a choir. His influence must show the group as a whole what "musicianship" means to their united effort, and he must supply them with specific things to *do as a group* to achieve their musicianly goals.

A non-technical definition with which to start toward this objective is: *Musicianship is the ability to use musical materials accurately and skillfully and sensitively.* "Musical materials" can be understood as rhythm, melody, harmony, notation, dynamics, style, and (for the singer) vocal technique. This definition puts the concept of musicianship in terms a layman can use, removing some of the aura of the esoteric which musicians sometimes like to cast about it. It also suggests specific things which the group — and, of course, individuals also — may actually *do;* in short, places to start. This can help the conductor in moments of stress. While it may give him great emotional release to berate his choir about what "terrible musicians" they are, it is more constructive to single out the particular deficiency in their use of musical materials which is slowing them down, and provide specific remedies: show them exactly how to count, hear the interval, or use the particular notational device which will overcome the difficulty.

When we all get to heaven, singers will read music fluently and come to the angelic choirs (which by that time we will have qualified ourselves to conduct) totally prepared to meet the demands of the Music To Be Sung Around The Throne. Until that happy day, however, the conductor of amateurs can be sure that most choir singers will not "read", will be ignorant of music theory and history (which provides the knowledge permitting correct choices of singing style) and, in short, will have to be taught most of the "musicianship" he wants their performance to exhibit. The picture, however, is not entirely hopeless, nor as bleak as the angry instrumentalist might sometimes color it. The truly dynamic conductor knows from experience that Henry Coward's optimism in the face of less-than-perfect voices can be transferred to the matter of musicianly performance: Much *can* be accomplished by conductors who "will only make up their minds to expend the requisite labour".

Inventing teaching devices

This accomplishment depends on his ability to invent, adapt, and use workable devices with his choir which stimulate musicianly activity. The ensuing devices have been found to work with just such less-than-perfect choirs, and are predicated upon certain basic assumptions. These are:

1. The immediate value of a "musicianship" device is its capacity to increase a group's skill in accurately using musical materials *together.*

2. Its impact in teaching depends on how explicit it is. The more directly it deals with *one* problem, in *one* context, the more efficient it is.

3. Its long-term value lies in laying a firm foundation for artistic, expressive performance. It is crucial that the choir understand this, for unless they do, "musicianship", "technique", and "skill" tend to become dirty words which connote only the drudgery of dreary necessity. Singers eagerly look forward to performing in an emotionally expressive way; thus the conductor must firmly establish in their minds that the fastest – indeed, the *only* – means to that goal is through the knowledgeable, accurate, skilled manipulation of the technical materials out of which musical expression can be wrought. Every conductor of amateur singers in our culture knows how quickly impatience and frustration mount when expressive singing doesn't come easily to a group conditioned by its society to the facile, "six-easy-lessons" approach to skills. He should also be aware that the conductor is the only one in a position to lead them through that frustration.

4. Finally, use of "musicianship" devices is best governed by the "philosophy of rehearsal devices" stated in Chapter 2. When such devices solidify into a "method" or rigid "technique", their value is diminished.

NOTATIONAL DEVICES

The hardest thing to get many choir singers to do is just to look at the notes – closely. Instrumentalists learn music starting with the written notes; singers with solfege training learn through similar disciplines. But the "average" choir singer, at least at the outset, expects to learn his music "by ear".

Unfortunately, "getting it by ear" *is* possible, at least up to a point, providing enough time and patience are expended. But in the long run this is doing it the hard way, and the conductor would be better advised to persuade singers to learn to read music. He should start by showing them dramatically that reading notation is the fastest means of achieving satisfaction – a proposition not all beginners are prepared to accept. It must be advanced with good humor, perhaps pointing out that until they learn to read notes, they will be like children who must have the comics read to them, since they cannot read for themselves.

Intelligent adult laymen may readily agree that it is important for them to be able to read music, but gaining this skill after years of dependence on rote teaching will seem forbiddingly difficult to them. Therefore the conductor must supply simple, workable means of understanding notation, through which they can capture satisfactory results *promptly*. To some extent this is true at any level of choir work, with the possible exception of the professional. Most choirs fail to heed notational symbols, only because the meaning of the notation has never been learned. If the conductor by-passes the notation and conveys its meaning by demonstration, the meaning of the notational symbol will remain a mystery to the singers the next time it is encountered. If the conductor can show the group that their performance will be immediately improved simply by doing what the notation indicates and explaining what that is, even advanced choirs will experience the satisfaction of improving their own sound through the simple expedient of "looking at the notes".

The danger, of course, is that because the number of technical things to learn is so vast, the unwary conductor will convert his rehearsal into a music theory class, which is a mistake of the first order. The only sure way to make every individual choir singer a technically skilled musician would be to insist that he pass through separate courses in sight-reading, music theory, and music history – which of course is unrealistic. Besides being impractical, such a requirement of choir members loses sight of the fact that the purposes of a choir rehearsal are many, and only *one* of these is instruction in musicianship.

Such instruction in the choral rehearsal must be devoted to whatever is needed in *this* instant to overcome *this* problem which is preventing *this* choir from faithfully reproducing *this* piece of music. If individual skills are improved in the process, as will undoubtedly happen, this is a bonus derived from the conductor's skill as a teacher. With this viewpoint in mind, the conductor will find the following useful:

Proper terminology

The techniques of communication via musical terminology discussed in Chapter 2 are of prime urgency in regard to notation. Notes and other printed markings comprise a language which can and does communicate, even though it is complex and not always precise. Wherever possible, the conductor should use this language and not resort to folksy idioms that "mean almost the same thing." Such idioms only give the singer an excuse for following his inclination to ignore notation altogether. If the conductor talks to his choir in notational terms, they have no alternative but to find out what those terms mean in order to understand him.

This is a simple but frequently slighted discipline. If the conductor describes a rhythmic error by saying, "You held the word 'Lord' too long", singers tend to look at that word for understanding. If, on the other hand, he says, "The dotted half-note at the word 'Lord' was held for four beats instead of three", their attention is directed to the notational values which specify what should have been done. How often conductors want their groups to "start on page so-and-so at the word. . . . . ."! Pages and words are only tangential to notation; "*bar* so-and-so, on the fourth beat" involves it directly, and takes full account of page and word values!

Such examples are easily multiplied, and the conductor will do well to analyze his own usage and list any such evasions he finds in his own work. Whenever his instruction forces singers to use notation, he helps them increase their musicianship; any other terminology delays its acquisition.

Insist on reading.

Much that passes for "reading" in many choirs is only "friendly following". The piano plays along, or the conductor leads with his own voice. This is not necessarily bad as a means of learning repertoire quickly, but it doesn't do much to force singers to rely on notation for themselves. Choir festivals that include reading competition as part of a rating on occasion do require unassisted sight-reading by the group – to their ultimate benefit, if not immediate pleasure. Real "reading" means looking at the notes and producing the music. To suggest to beginners and amateurs that they do this will provoke a "You've-got-to-be-kidding?" response.

Such resistance can be overcome by having each section, as an introduction to learning a new piece, try reading a few lines of its part at sight, *with absolutely no help whatsoever.* Give them *no* preparation, not even the starting pitch or key. Choose lines from different pages of a work so that one part can't prepare while another is singing, or even ask one part to read another part's line. Add an element of competition by having one part rate the accuracy of another.

First attempts may well sound like disasters, but patient persistence will begin to make progress. This device forces singers to look at notation as the only means available to them to meet a challenge, and their efforts are spurred by the fact that they are being observed by their peers. It literally demands that they become involved with interval size, staff position, tonal center, rhythmic values, and all other relevant signs.

The device is of value at practically any level of choir training. Beginners will fumble and strain to produce a simple chord-like folk tune, once they have agreed on a pitch by hit-or-miss methods. The director must insist that they read as much of it as they can with the skills they have, and that they explore *whatever additional information the notation may suggest to them.* Advanced groups should be asked for more complex achievement, but the problem is much the same: to achieve the unknown or not-yet-accomplished exclusively by use of the directions at hand, namely, musical notation.

Obviously, the conductor must provide encouragement and information to sustain faltering efforts and fill complete voids. But these should be kept to a minimum, for the strength of the device is that it forces the group and its individual members to rely on their own faltering but growing ability. This will not happen if "reading" becomes the all-too-usual practice of looking at the score while the pianist plays the parts. That is, after all, only "getting it by ear".

Rather than make the sweeping assertion that "choral singers don't read music", it is more accurate to say that most do not yet use certain notational symbols with the same facility that many of their instrumental brethren do. This is probably because their training has not forced them to be aware of or use these symbols. Most seven-year-olds are unable to read and understand a medical textbook, but does this mean they "don't read"? Better to say they are "learning to read" through the accumulation of meaningful experiences with words. Even adult laymen would have trouble with the medical book, which only the professional specialist has the technical knowledge to read with comprehension. Since musical notation is a complex technical language, which must not only be read but simultaneously performed, a choir of musical laymen will likely remain in the "learning to read" category, but will steadily improve as they are led by their conductor to accumulate meaningful experiences with notation.

MELODIC-TONAL DEVICES

Interval identification

A secure group feeling for interval size may be developed by the use of devices which require singers, briefly but repeatedly, to identify specific intervals by singing them separately or in musical contexts. Such devices give a preliminary "warm-up" period far more relevance than it will have if used merely for vocal calisthenics. Sung with proper attention to tonal production as discussed in Chapters 4 and 5, such devices can serve to "give the singers the feel of the vocal sound"[1] and train them in musicianly habits. Interval exercises should never be memorized patterns, repeated day after day, for their value lies in forcing new identification of interval size with each experience. Nor should they be used for too long in any one rehearsal; five minutes a day for five days, when done in a fast pace with an air of excitement, will do far more good than 25 minutes in one day.

1 : Joseph Klein : "*Singing Technique*", Princeton, 1967 p. 124

1. Specify the pitch, vowel, and dynamic level to be sung: "Sing G in unison on the vowel OH, *piano.*"

2. While the singers sustain the original pitch, name an interval to be sung up or down from it and ask them to try to think the second tone; then, on signal, have them try to sing it. At the beginning use octaves, fifths, fourths, thirds, and seconds. Use major or minor seconds and thirds, as they happen to fall in the key being used, but do not try to have the singers try to distinguish between them. If first attempts produce only sliding sounds, repeat the exercise until a clear interval emerges.

3. Once the second tone of the interval is established, specify yet another interval to be measured from that tone, usually in the opposite direction. The choir thinks it, then sings.

4. Continue the process, using several intervals but staying within one tonality to begin developing a tonal awareness. To confirm the tonal feeling, have the final interval in a series return to the key tone.

5. As their acuity increases, instruct the choir to sing the letter name of the pitches so that the audible form of the interval is related to the notational form by which it must ultimately be understood.

Scale pattern devices

Most music a choir sings is tonal and singers bring with them considerable cultural conditioning in tonal styles. Scale patterns which rely on a feeling for tonal center are thus relevant means of clarifying harmonic concepts and relating interval sizes. Since this "feeling" for tonal center is completely non-verbal, its most important relationships must be understood outside of technical terminology.

1. Have the choir sing in unison, and identify by name, simple scales in major and minor. Use single vowel sounds at first, but syllables, letter names, or numbers should be added as soon as a minimal security of tone is established. Sing slowly, and repeat until each scale is accurately sung.

2. Reinforce the feeling for tonality and scale position by having the choir sing in random order these so-called "tonal magnetism" patterns of the diatonic scale:

Example 6.1:

These should be sung first without accompaniment, pointing out the sense of "natural" direction implied by each initial tone. When the harmonic patterns of Example 6.2 are added in an accompaniment, they will be heard to confirm strongly that sense of direction. This understanding is a valuable step toward some of the harmonic tonality devices to be discussed below.

Example 6.2:

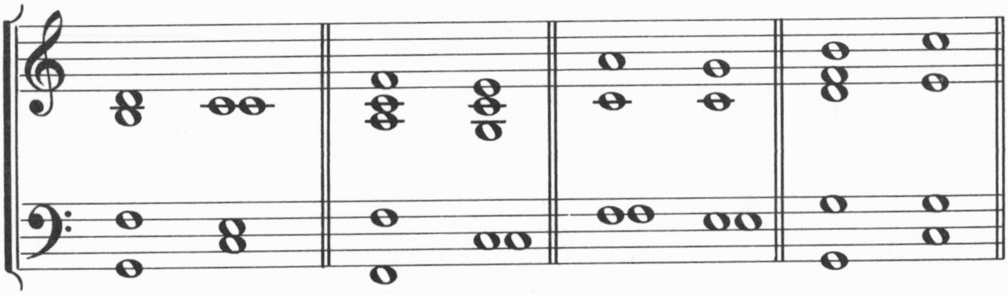

3. Have the choir sing tones and intervals within a major or minor scale pattern, indicated at random by the conductor's pointing to syllable, number or tone names on a chart, such as:

DO	8	C
TI	7	B
LA	6	A
SO	5	G
FA	4	F
MI	3	E
RE	2	D
DO	1	C

Start with the key tone to establish the tonal center. Then move over all of the diatonic tones, with increasing use of more difficult intervals such as sixths, sevenths, and the one diminished fifth found in the diatonic scale. (FA down to TI) When these intervals can be performed with confidence using syllables, letters, or numbers, have the choir try them using notation which contains no helps, as in Ex. 6.3.

Example 6.3:

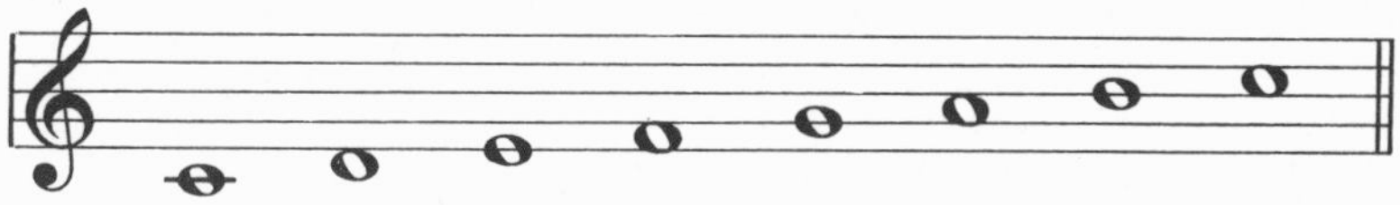

4. Practice intervals not in the diatonic scale. A good place to start is to compare the relative sizes of the major and minor second in terms of sound. Have the choir sing the tones C - D; when these pitches are clearly established, instruct them to "sing the pitch in between", without assistance. The value lies in the brief instant when they actually evolve the sound C♯ by mental effort alone. The next step is to compare the C - D interval, which is part of the diatonic scale in C major, with the E - F and B - C intervals of the same scale, leading them to discover for themselves that there are *no* "tones between". In this aural comparison, the nature of the major and the minor seconds can be established. When this distinction is clear it may be used to approach more difficult intervals. All major intervals in the diatonic scale (thirds, sixths, sevenths) are easily compared with their minor forms, which involve non-diatonic tones. Through clarifying these intervals singers can be challenged to produce any given interval, up or down, from a specified tone, without reference to a tonal center.

RHYTHMIC DEVICES

Meter, rhythm, and tempo

Opaque, confused terminology in this area troubles many accomplished musicians, so it is little wonder that beginners and laymen are often vague about it. The conductor should provide simple, specific working definitions and make singers understand these through physical motions they can feel. The following have been found effective:

THE DEFINITION:	*WHAT THE CHOIR DOES:*
Meter: A basic, unchanging pattern of accents, underlying all other rhythmic elements.	*Tap their heels.* Use simple patterns (1-2-3, 1-2-3-4). Once started, the beat must not change. No speeding up, slowing, changing accents.
Rhythm: Patterns of varying note values superimposed on the meter.	*Clap rhythmic patterns.* Metric heel-tapping must continue unchanged during the rhythmic handclapping.

Example 6.4:

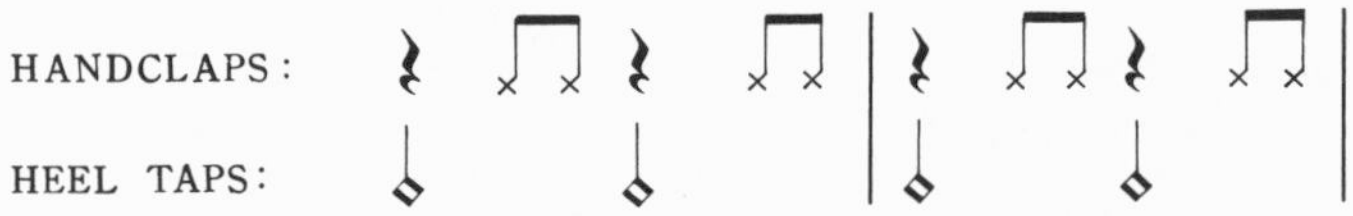

This is best done by simple imitation. Firmly establish the heel tapping of the meter, stressing that it must continue steadily. The conductor then claps short rhythmic patterns over the meter, which the choir immediately imitates. Start simply with divided beats, and work up to more complex patterns, showing that there is no limit to the possibilities of rhythmic variety. Stress separation of hand and foot functions. It may surprise the conductor to find how many rather advanced choir singers have trouble with this separation. If the difficulty is acute, suggest that they exaggerate the clap which corresponds with the metric beat, putting "a separate very light clap between these strong heel tap beats".

Tempo: The speed with which metric pulses occur.

Clap and tap a simple song at various speeds. See Example 6.5.

Example 6.5:

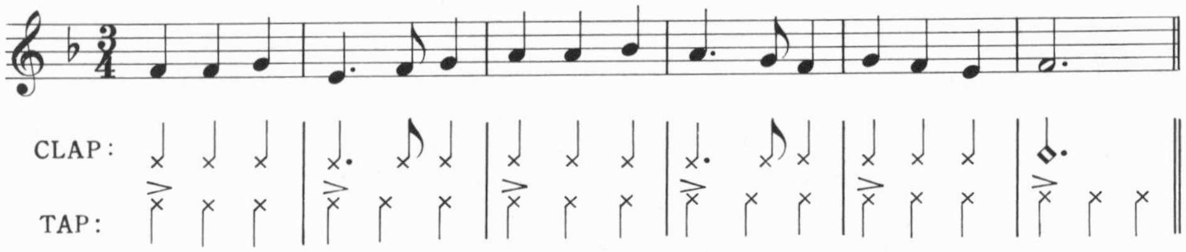

Establish the meter of the song in heel tapping, then superimpose the clapped rhythms. After perfecting this at a moderate tempo (♩ = 72), follow the same procedures at ♩ = 48 and ♩ = 120. In each instance make it clear that the relationship between the meter and the rhythm has remained the same; only the speed has changed. This shows clearly that tempo is separate from meter and rhythm.

The more meaningful these distinctions become in the thinking of the choir, the greater the conductor's responsibility to use precise terminology himself. He should, for example, avoid using the word "time" to refer to any form of meter, rhythm, or tempo. It means nothing, because it is used to mean everything. Conductors say, "You sang the time wrong in that phrase!" This could be accusing the singers of beating two metric pulses instead of three, or omitting a dot on a quarter note, or simply singing too slowly – three distinct, conflicting meanings. While context may sometimes rescue the conductor from this quagmire, it will be much more reassuring to the choir if he uses precise terms.

Building "rhythmic sense"

It has been observed that rhythm must be physically felt to be fully understood. This feeling must become so deeply ingrained that it no longer needs conscious thought. The conductor must reinforce this rhythmic sense through every means, inventing devices which lead the choir to experience it as often as possible. To begin with, he himself must be vitally rhythmic in his communication with the choir. Rhythmic vigor must emanate from his conducting. To encourage the choir to respond with similar rhythmic intensity, the following devices have been found effective:

1. *Silent counting* ▪ Have the choir close their eyes and make no sound whatsoever with voice or movement. The conductor begins an audible metric count ("1-2-3---"), stopping after beat three while the choir mentally carries on the count, clapping sharply when they reach count nine. On the first try this clap may sound like scattered applause, but repetition of the device quickly brings uniformity to the pace of the singers' mental clocks. Extend the problem to longer counts, and even ask them to clap on "beat nine and a half", having set up an initial divided beat pattern audibly. The skills at which this device aims can only be attained when each individual truly feels the duration of time between beats.

2. *Stressing afterbeats* ▪ Inability to accomplish complicated rhythmic patterns, or a tendency to rush tempos, can often be corrected by stressing the afterbeats of the metric pulse. Have the choir foot-tap the meter and hand-clap the afterbeats *as they sing the troublesome passage.* If this combination fails to remedy the fault, remove the stamp-clap and have them sing only tones falling on afterbeats, remaining silent on the metric beats. The silent counting device can be combined with this by asking the group to re-

main silent until a specified afterbeat well into the phrase, at which time they are to sing the note in accurate rhythm and tone.

A very efficient means of clarifying muddy contrapuntal parts is to clap the afterbeats of the underlying meter. This technique, which is such an integral part of jazz and pop styles, can be used in "serious" music to prevent the choir's wallowing along, destroying the clarity of a perfectly singable run because afterbeats are not felt with sufficient force and clarity. The familiar vocal challenge in Handel's *For unto us a Child is born,* which is annually garbled by thousands of singers, can be greatly clarified if the conductor, or even the whole choir, will make sharp claps at the spots indicated in Example 6.6 during a few final rehearsals before the performance.

Example 6.6: *For Unto Us a Child Is Born* (from *Messiah*) G. F. Handel

Such an example may horrify the purist. He may feel that, at least in America, such a rhythmic stress will remind singers of current popular styles. Yet this is probably its principal strength! These styles are vitally, rhythmically alive. If Handel's music can't also be characterized that way, it will be a pompous bore, as performances by some choirs seem each year to be trying to prove with studious determination. It is well to remember that not too many years have passed since the Swingle Singers first made fame and fortune – and a lot of very vital music – simply by singing Bach's and Handel's notes with a little swinging underscoring of the basic metric and rhythmic patterns. This revealed the music's fundamental vitality in a new light, and the public responded with enthusiasm. The most cursory examination of the Swingle's method and similar creative attempts during the last half-century shows that much of the impact comes directly from the clarification and intensification of the afterbeats, and that this alone gives an electric pulse to the style. Every choral style with any relevancy to modern choral practice will profit from such an inner pulse of rhythmic urgency.

HARMONIC DEVICES

Most of the complexities of harmonic theory go well beyond what can be taught effectively in a rehearsal; yet the choir needs every harmonic concept it can absorb if it is to sing with an expressive performance vocabulary. There is, however, one real advantage to learning harmonic ideas in a group situation: whole chords can be demonstrated, so that problems and solutions can be illustrated without reliance on verbal explanations alone.

Fortify tonality sense.

Since tonality is both a melodic and harmonic concept, some devices of a purely harmonic nature are valuable in supplementing those discussed in connection with scale patterns.

1. Recognition of cadential patterns ■ A great deal of music is built essentially on the chord progressions of the authentic cadence. This is particularly true in folk and popular music, much of which is founded almost exclusively on the I, IV, and V chords. The "blues" follows a fairly strict patterning of these chords. Familiarity with this music has accustomed the singer's ear to these progressions, so he will have no difficulty with devices which embody their most specific form: cadences. A vocabulary of sound-meanings for authentic, plagal, half, and deceptive cadences is particularly valuable in helping the choir understand the structure of the music they sing. A "gimmick" effective in establishing the importance of such patterns is familiar to many conductors. As singers come into a rehearsal, the piano is playing simple harmonic progressions, in an apparently idle way, and staying in one key. When it is time to start the rehearsal, the playing stops abruptly, just *before* the final chord of an authentic cadence, leaving it hanging unresolved.

Example 6.7:

The subconscious reaction of most singers will be "Play that last chord!" When this psychological need has been established in the perspective of such an incident, it can be used to confirm the existence of a strong feeling for tonal center. From this, discussion of the function of the cadence and its various forms follows easily.

2. Experiment with non-diatonic chords ■ When chords within the diatonic structure can be read with some facility, chords outside that framework may be attempted. Ideally, a work in rehearsal will provide the kinds of harmonies needed to establish in the mental ear of each singer a clear and accurate concept of chord sounds which are quite unrelated to any tonal center. Example 6.8 suggests some possibilities, and the conductor will want to create others for himself. These chords should be sung quietly, with the best tone quality possible, stressing precision and balance.

The thorough conditioning of singers and audiences to tonal music has unfortunately left persistent subconscious equations of "dissonance equals bad" and "consonance equals good" in the minds of many. Accurate performance of such chords reveals that the truth is more likely that "wrong performance which sounds non-consonant equals bad", and that the wrong performance stems from the singers vague concepts of intonation and chord structure, "dissonance" and "consonance" never really entering the picture, because neither variety of harmony is performed accurately.

Choirs who attempt more advanced contemporary works — either "serious" or "popular" — must overcome this obstacle. While styles of Mozartean purity suffer woefully from faulty intonation and triadic imbalance, it is a curious fact that complex, "close" harmonic styles are even more fully destroyed. They disintegrate into mere cacophony, which obliterates the carefully-conceived texture the composer had in mind. A bad performance of Mozart at least reminds the listener of familiar tonal concepts, but a distortion of more complex styles loses him in an arid desert of strangeness.

Example 6.8:

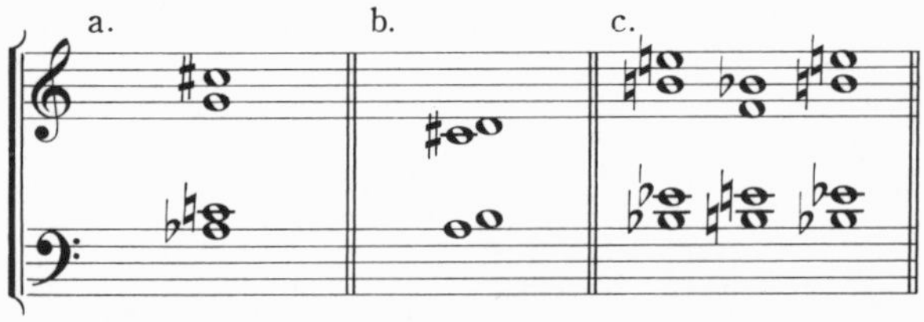

"Feeling" triads and inversions

A singer's ability to sing accurately within a harmonic texture depends on his aural understanding of the relationship between the tone he is singing and other tones being sounded at the same time. One of the most basic harmonic relationships is that within the triad. For many learners, such "reading" as they do depends on their ability to hear and see — more exactly, to *feel* — the rest of the triad of which their tone is a part. This "feeling" for the triad and its inversions is of fundamental importance for every singer, and to help establish it the following devices are suggested.

1. Have the basses sustain the key tone on the vowel OH, assigning other voices to the remaining tones of the triad at random, but always using explicit terminology: "Tenors sing the fifth; altos the major third; sopranos the doubled octave." Move quickly, and demand immediate response. In the instant that a triad is fully established, move the upper voices to other tones. The force of the device lies in making each singer re-think the triad relationship quickly. Use the device in various keys.

2. Assign the root to another voice section, and build inversions by redistributing the chord tones. Use specific instructions, and identify the variety of inversion when it is established.

3. When complete familiarity with the triad and its inversions is achieved, begin adding tones of the seventh and ninth to the texture.

4. Extend the whole exercise to minor triads.

5. Build harmonic progressions by altering single tones in an established chord, as in Example 6.9.

Example 6.9:

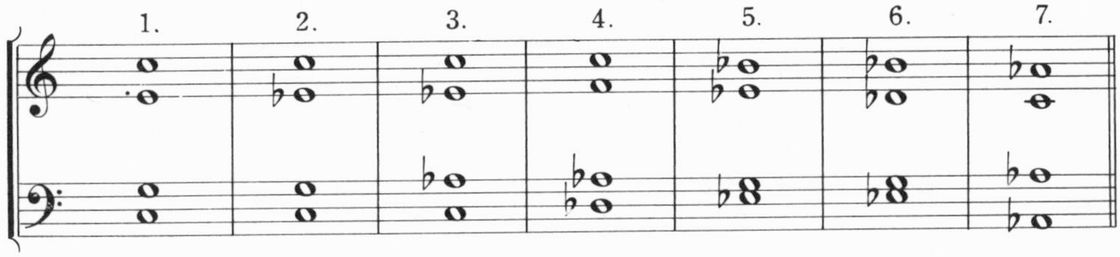

Every part is sustained until specifically told to change pitch.

From chord #1 - #2 : Altos move down a minor second.

From chord #2 - #3 : Tenors move up a minor second.

From chord #3 - #4 : Basses move up a minor second; altos move up a major second.

From chord #4 - #5 : Sopranos move down a whole step (major second); altos move down a major second; tenors move down a minor second; basses move up a major second.

From chord #5 - #6 : Altos move down a major second.

From chord #6 - #7 : Sopranos move down a major second; altos move down a minor second; tenors move up a minor second; basses move down a perfect fifth.

In this example all intervals are seconds except the last bass fifth. Others should be built involving more complex intervals. The choir should be directed to listen for the new triad form which emerges after each move. The device is more effective when it is done entirely by ear, with no chart or printed music involved.

Sensing major and minor

It might surprise some conductors to find just how many of their singers have a shaky sense of the difference between major and minor. In his attempt to correct the situation, the conductor's impulse may be to "explain" the modes in terminology which, while technically precise, is beyond the grasp of his singers. Especially with beginning and intermediate groups, understanding *must* proceed from sound to terminology. Their understanding of the symbols below will develop only after they are sure of the *difference in sound.* Until that happens, they will either ignore the symbols or view them with embarrassed uncertainty.

Example 6.10:

Diminished and augmented chords

If this is true of the relatively simple concepts of major and minor, it applies with even greater force to altered triads such as augmented and diminished chords. Singers can be trained to remarkable acuity in recognition and identification of such chords, if they learn their *characteristic sound* first before they are given theoretical instruction, which should be as untechnical as possible.

Devices dealing with modes or complex chords must be limited to specific music in rehearsal, with no attempt to lead the choir into the thicket of technical explanations which surrounds them. The best that can be expected from the rehearsal situation is to give singers an accurate concept of the sounds of major, minor, augmented, and diminished harmonies, and teach them to identify each by name.

Summary

Those who object that no viable learning results from such casual tasting of these harmonies should consider the case of the small boy who is doubtful whether he will eat the asparagus his mother has cooked for dinner. Never having eaten any, he nags her to tell him "what it tastes like". She struggles with words, but gets nowhere in trying to convey what the boy wants to know. Finally, in desperation, she thrusts a spoonful of asparagus into his mouth, and thereby answers all his questions at once. Similarly, choirs must have their spoonful of major, minor, and altered chords to savor without words before they will be ready for any explanations.

The length and detail of these devices may seem to imply that in spite of statements to the contrary, the choral rehearsal must be turned into a training period in music theory. How, it may be argued, is the conductor supposed to give all these devices to his choir, or build all these concepts into their performance, and still have any time left for learning notes, correcting tone, teaching style, and accounting for all the other necessities which crowd a rehearsal?

Obviously he cannot. This contradiction alone serves to underscore the basic contention of this book: that it is the dynamic, inventive leadership of the conductor which virtually alone accounts for what a choir is able to do. A conductor with such prowess views his mandate to teach musicianly habits with the same equanimity that he accords the obvious fact that it can't be done adequately in rehearsal. He will proceed to mold the occasion to meet the need anyway. His command of these devices will be exceeded only by his dexterity in inventing others. He will fit them into the ongoing pace of events so that they help accomplish what a choral rehearsal must: impart learnings, provide insights, develop skills, and stimulate personal growth so that the choir is prepared to weave the complex fabric of artistic performance. His personal preparation, musicianship, and comprehension of his task will make it possible for him to thread musicianship into that fabric as one of its strongest strands.

7|The Conductor's Many Jobs

The modern Renaissance man

The idea of Renaissance man as it evolved during the 15th and 16th centuries is relevant in many ways to the ideal image of today's dynamic conductor. The Renaissance man was seen as the epitome of the intellectual, social, economic, and cultural ferment of the times, described by Will Durant as

> "a sport of the species and the time, the kind of man we think of when we recall the Renaissance, a type unique in history. . . . . .a mind sharp, alert, versatile, open to every impression and idea, sensitive to beauty, eager for fame. It was a recklessly individualistic spirit, set on developing all its potential capacities; . . . . . in art he was no longer an artisan working anonymously with others on a collective enterprise, as in the Middle Ages; he was a 'single and separate person' who stamped his character upon his works; . . . . .Whatever his achievements, this 'Renaissance Man' was always in motion and discontent, fretting at limits, longing to be a 'universal man' — bold in conception, decisive in deed, eloquent in speech, skilled in art, acquainted with literature and philosophy, at home with women in the palace and with soldiers in the camp."[1]

Leonardo da Vinci was such a man; so were Cellini, Gesualdo, Michelangelo, and many others with whose achievements the age glowed. While each had limitations and shortcomings, his faults sprang from excessive vitality, not timid inertia.

If the choral art is to prevail in our own turbulent age, there is a need for conductors of this stamp. Vital choral music is a "now" thing, a jewel of the instant. It must be polished and placed in its setting by experts who know not only its value but its relationship to all that surrounds it. Otherwise, like the unpolished or misused diamond, its lustre is lost to the world.

1 : Will Durant : *The Story of Civilization,* New York, 1953 V, p.580

The dynamic conductor does many things well. Much of his impact is predicated upon this diversity, which shows his musicianly achievements to be directly pertinent to the life of his times. People think, "Here's a musician who knows his stuff, but can talk my language. He's not some sort of nut, and certainly not a hermit, for he knows a few things besides music. He is interesting to follow and work with."

This is by no means intended to depict his image as that of the hail-fellow-well-met, "public relations", false-front playboy, which is also a recognizable type in our commercialized culture. His diversity must be the product of *achievement*: solid, consistent performance. It starts with musicianly prowess, for if his status as an achieving musician is insecure, most of the rest of what he does will be seen as camouflage or mere fakery. But then it must also involve the matters of communication, technique, and personal empathy considered in earlier chapters, for all are distinct functions of his position. His handling of these multiform aspects of his job may well measure his total impact. Since many of them are tangential to his primary role as "music director", they bear careful examination by every conductor whose situation forces him to be "of this world" as well as in it.

Conductor as musician

As suggested above, a conductor is a musician, or he is nothing. This truism needs constant re-statement, for the pressures of multiple jobs, insufficient time, and limited energy make it all too easy either to lose sight of its dimensions or insulate one's self from its mandates. "Being a musician" in this context ideally implies at least the following:

. . . . . that early in life he found that the non-verbal ideas, emotional values, and technical accomplishments of music spoke directly to his innermost understanding.

. . . . . that he soon developed facility in reproducing or responding to those musical materials in meaningfully communicative ways.

. . . . . that he had systematic training in performance and use of musical materials, developing artistry in some, skill in others, and proficiency in most, and that the total result of such training is that he is competent and knowledgeable in music.

. . . . . that his growth to musicianly stature has been paralleled by development as an intelligent and sensitive human being, with diverse interests and capabilities.

. . . . . that out of his experience with music have emerged clear ideals of musical integrity which obviously motivate what he does with music.

. . . . . that he has become a skilled artisan in conveying musical values to others, by performance, conducting, or teaching, and that he is widely recognized in this capacity.

The high school conductor whose duties include one choir and four classes of mathematics or social studies may feel that his job as a musician is automatically condemned to marginal importance. So may the church musician who must teach a Sunday School class and put out the church paper. Yet the fact that these other duties press heavily on time, energy, and motivation does not alter the mandate that during the moments when he is involved with the choir, *he must be a musician.* The alternative is simple, and regrettably prevalent: he will produce little or no music. That such a musician's position is intolerable cannot be argued. Its widespread existence is further evidence of the urgent need for dynamic Renaissance man conductors whose influence will start to reverse the shameful, lamentable trend in schools and churches which increasingly consigns choral music to insufferable, afterthought situations. Little progress has resulted from tears and lamentation about these conditions; perhaps dynamic leadership, like the grain of mustard seed, can provide the will to move the mountain of indifference.

Conductor as leader

Although broad participation in choral singing might be viewed as the most democratic area of musical endeavor, the act of choral performance itself is essentially autocratic. Expressive group singing rarely results from a majority vote. This means that one person must fill the role of leader, supplying certain essentials of group performance which can *only* be derived from one single source. To do his "job" as leader, the conductor must be:

. . . . . *the focal point* through which all group effort is coordinated. The choir must be strongly enough impressed with the conductor's impact and image, as summarized in Chapter 9, that they automatically direct their efforts to carry out his instructions.

. . . . . *the impetus for group action.* He must lead, and have the inner strength to act. He must be proficient in dynamics of leadership such as vitality, decisiveness, confidence, knowledge, and self-possession. He must be a practicioner of the intensely personal, individualistic use of character traits as devices for communication and motivation. To some extent this spells "personality" in the glib, popular sense, but the difference is that his impetus comes from the depth and substance behind the facade which the popular definition points to. Now, this is not an easy requirement! It is often very, very hard to command a group fully, and even harder to *sustain* that command. How much easier it can be to follow *their* lead, making fine gestures which roughly correspond to what they will do anyway! Or simply to watch the score and wave, "filling" a role which nobody pays any attention to. If the impetus is to start — and stay — with the conductor, he must be guided by the sentiments of the old hymn: "Be strong! We are not here to play, to dream, to drift! We have hard work to do, and loads to lift!" This resolve, of course, must be implemented by devices of knowledge, communication, and the skilled self-control of leadership if he is to accomplish his goals.

. . . . . *a reliable constant.* His singers must know that they can depend on him. They will watch him because they have found that it is worth while to do so. He builds their assurance by leading them into habits of performance that work — every time. He conveys the feeling that whatever else may go wrong, he will carry them through — and he usually does. This assurance involves musical matters first, but is greatly strengthened by parallel security in their respect for his organization and mature knowledge. Such temperamental idiosyncrasies as he permits himself are accepted because they in no way impede the flow of positive qualities they know he will consistently bring them. And this is a delicate balance! Just one tantrum too many erodes his reliability, constancy, and leadership; boredom, slowness of pace, and tedium of technique dissipate motivation.

His greatest assets in establishing a feeling of reliability are orderly, vital rehearsal habits, as suggested in the Five Levels of Conducting in Chapter 3. The greatest assurance, after all, comes from having found for one's self that something works. If the conductor structures his rehearsals to meet the progressively-felt needs of his singers, they will have just such assuring experiences. As they will inevitably be aware that the conductor is the creator of this structuring, confidence in his leadership is automatic.

Conductor as teacher

In the final analysis, the conductor may be a teacher before and beyond anything else he does or becomes. This is a truism in school and church positions, where the substance of what he does is to impart to laymen who do *not* know, that which he, a professional, *does* know. Even in conducting choirs of professional singers a strong element of teaching is present; they are asked to "interpret" the music, which means to perform it as the conductor conceives it. This means he must *teach* them what his way is and how they can achieve it. Since the requirement that the conductor must teach is so obvious, it, like musicianly requirements, may tend to get lost in the pressures of the moment. When the importance of his responsibility in this regard is momentarily obscured, the conductor may lash out in a tempermental blast at the singers' slow learning or apparently bovine inertia. Certainly, teachers *do* get angry. But the best ones rarely yield fully to it, and good ones manage to control it most of the time. It is only poor and insecure teachers who use temperament as a regular refuge.

To do his "job" as teacher, the conductor ideally should have the following qualities:

. . . . . *He knows:* There can be simply no question about this. His knowledge is both extensive and intensive. If a situation reveals to him and his singers that in some particular he does *not* know, he must admit it openly and at once, and then proceed to find out — because, after all, he *should* know where the information can be found. No matter how successfully he may be able to "fake it" for short periods, he is sure to be unmasked eventually, with consequent damage to the trust and esteem with which his right to teach is regarded.

. . . . . *He knows how:* Here he is the skilled artisan at work. His kit of devices and techniques is formidable and effective. Curiously enough, his effectiveness as a teacher is measured both by what he *makes* his choir do, and what he *allows* them to do. His effectiveness is often gauged by listing the faults which he permits to go unchecked: harsh tone, rhythmic indolence, cluttered diction, lazy breathing, meaningless phrasing, ignored expressive markings, tardiness, talking, and a whole catalogue of poor rehearsal habits. His "knowing how" involves adaptability; he can think on his feet, adapting his knowledge to the need of the moment and the crisis of the hour.

. . . . . *He shows how:* The best teaching is a fine blend of information with the appropriate technique to lead the learner to its use. In this light, conducting is teaching in its most sustained and intensive form, for knowledge and technique are wasted if the conductor cannot impel the group to put these into action — not eventually, or after due reflection, but now, at the instant of musical performance.

Conductor as interpreter

The trouble with talking about "interpreting" music is that the term has too many vague or false connotations in the public mind. A glamorized, commercial view often gives the impression that an interpretation is some magical, exciting element which is piled on the music, like whipped cream on pie. It is calculated to dazzle, stun, or overpower an audience — a whimsy of the moment, a caprice which allows the performer or conductor complete freedom to restructure the music. Many poor performances abound with just such "interpretation".

The Oxford Dictionary puts it more simply: "Rendering a musical composition according to one's idea of the author's intention." Just what "one's idea" may be is the door by which the gremlins of distortion can enter. Toscanini insisted, "It is not I ; it is the Music!", but his detractors insisted that even with him this meant "My idea of the music." The greater the integrity and skill of the conductor, the more valid those ideas become. But what of the conductor of "average" choirs? To what extent is he charged with being the Interpreter?

The act of asking singers to perform implies a request for interpretation — for "rendering a musical composition according to one's idea of the author's intention". In successful choirs this request evokes from each singer a skilled response which is molded by the conductor, using his presumably superior concepts and artistry, into a single entity, which becomes the group's "idea" about the author's intention. The dominance of the conductor's concept is essential, and ideally is a composite of his knowledge of the music, his awareness of his singers' potential, and his skill in leadership and teaching. His interpretation springs from the substance of the music and the situation and must never be thought of as an added frill; nor is it some mysterious, esoteric rite, which he alone, as an emissary of the Muse, is allowed to practice. The requirements for the conductor as *interpreter* are:

. . . . . to know the music, and be known for knowing.

. . . . . to uphold the attitude that "not as I say, but as the music says" is the basis for interpretation. Such an attitude focuses attention on the music and enables the conductor in his roles as teacher and leader to make sure that "what the music says" is a matter of common agreement, derived from accurate use of musical materials.

. . . . . to be able to discount the attitude which some singers may hold that interpretation should be flamboyant and capricious, or "glamorous".

. . . . . to foster the attitude that musical accuracy is a requisite to a sound interpretation.

. . . . . to avoid stereotyped, "juke-box" performances. Within the limits of musical accuracy as indicated by the score, the choir must feel that every performance is a new creation and that therefore new efforts must be put into recreating the music with each performance. As was observed in the "Learned-Note Level of Conducting" in Chapter 2, once music is regarded as "learned", it tends to become static, a thing accomplished, past, and not to be changed.

Conductor as counselor

Empathetic rapport between choir and conductor has been cited as a basic requisite for fluent communication. Once established, such rapport means that singers will regard the conductor as a logical, accessible source of advice, especially in musical matters. He knows about music; his efforts have stimulated in the singer interests and capabilities of which he was perhaps previously unaware, and so the singer will naturally think first of the conductor as the person to approach for answers to his musical questions.

Such questions should be regarded by the conductor as votes of confidence, for if singers held him in too great awe, they wouldn't presume to intrude; if he is only feared, they will shun him; if they doubt that he really knows, why ask? Only those conductors who combine skill, knowledge, and warm humanity will be approached by singers with questions, and such a conductor will always be willing and ready to help.

This is not to say that a conductor should become a one-man counseling service, on whose shoulders tears of personal grief may be shed. Sensitive conductors are well aware of the storms in their singers' personal lives and may occasionally extend hands of sympathy or assistance, but counseling should be confined almost entirely to the musical concerns of his choir members. Three areas in which questions are frequently asked are cited as examples:

Classifying vocal potential ■ An audition serves to assign a singer to the voice part the conductor feels is best suited to the singer's vocal potential and the needs of the choir. This is a necessary disposition, but formal, and it may not answer questions about his voice of greatest concern to the singer. In addition to learning that their voices are soprano, alto, tenor or bass, singers who have heard such terms as "lyric", "dramatic", and "coloratura" may want to know if these terms are applicable to their voices. Fundamentally, they seek some sort of reassurance that their vocal efforts have merit and in many cases would dearly love to know what the conductor — the expert — feels to be their chance for "success". This question usually comes from singers whose definition of the term is vague, but it may be that this very vagueness is what they are really asking the conductor to dispel. In responding, the conductor should realize that such an evaluation is always a risky estimate, as it must assess apparent talent, willingness to work, temperament, evident potential for growth, and a host of environmental circumstances. In spite of this jungle of intangibles through which he is asked to project clear vision, the conductor's answers must not sound like evasion or a camouflaged admission that he is ignorant.

Frequently school and church conductors have in their choirs young singers whose inherent tone quality is particularly easy and clear, and, if certain weaknesses of vocal production and personality are conveniently overlooked, seem to have an exciting potential for artistic or professional accomplishment. Doting parents and friends may have encouraged such ambitions and the longer the illusion is permitted to exist, the more confirmed the singer becomes in his unrealistic aspirations. Wise counseling which in such cases consists of truthful answers, pointing out the obstacles and the limited number of opportunities for the kind of achievement dreamed of, can save heartbreak and direct what may indeed be a valuable voice toward more attainable goals.

Unhappily, some singers are allowed to cherish their illusions of great vocal prowess into adult life, to plague church and community choirs with their frustrations and ingrown, faulty techniques. The sooner such singers can be confronted with a firm, accurate assessment of their voices by an understanding and compassionate conductor, the better chance they have to make a valuable contribution as singers. Such a confrontation should include some definition which they can understand and accept, as to the nature and extent of the disciplined work needed to raise their performance to the level they have imagined themselves to be achieving. They must, in effect, be told: "No, you do *not* sound as you think you do; and here's why: . . . . . ." This calls for tact, courage, and warm human understanding.

In his job as counselor the conductor should develop perception and tact to deal intelligently with such problems. To ignore them only leaves the singers' vocal difficulties to multiply with advancing age with a deleterious effect on group tone. As a respected musical leader, the conductor may well be in a position to give blunt but kindly advice, which the disappointed soloist would accept from no one else.

To ignore such problems can impair choir morale, for choir singers who see themselves as soloists whose talents remain unrecognized have a very different attitude about the choir from those who, while they may occasionally sing solos, have made peace with the difference between their aspiration and their potential. The frustrated soloist may regard choral singing as a necessary evil to be endured until the star of their solo career ascends, and this attitude is often openly conveyed to others. A small amount of such petulance, about which the conductor does nothing, can be most destructive.

Encouraging other musical training ■ Because he believes that choir singers' effectiveness depends on musical training beyond vocal coaching, the conductor should urge singers to develop their abilities as musicians through instrumental and theoretical studies. The inborn ease with which amateurs can often produce vocal sounds of real beauty can lull the conductor into forgetting that the value of such vocal assets is greatly diminished unless reinforced by sound musicianship. In this realm, counseling should stimulate a broader scope of musical training and experience for talented singers.

Such singers may not be sufficiently aware of their potential to ask questions about further training. In this case, the conductor may mount a subtle campaign to interest the singer in studying piano, instruments, or theory. These campaigns will be most effective when the activities of the choir have demonstrated the value of added musical skills. Singers who see that their peers are better musicians and therefore are getting more out of their choir singing, are more likely to be receptive to the conductor's suggestion of musical study.

Giving advice about general opportunities in music ■ The excitement engendered by vital choral performance often causes a few members to consider a career in choral directing, professional choral singing, or some branch of music teaching. When such persons have the potential, this is a wonderful outcome for choral music and a source of pride and satisfaction for the conductor, who should provide realistic counseling, which tempers the first flush of enthusiasm with a perspective as to what the new convert must do to achieve his goals.

Where it is apparent that the person stirred by this excitement does not have the necessary potential, an even greater wisdom as counselor is demanded of the conductor. Understanding that his example has evoked an unwise career choice, the conductor has the responsibility to prevent the damage to choral art which will result if the new devotee is allowed to continue until he is officially certificated to teach, conduct, or sing professionally. Unfortunately this happens. There are conductors and singers who are certificated and somehow find work in schools and churches whose contributions to mankind clearly would have been better made in some other realm of endeavor. The outcry of this book against lethargic, faulty conducting is in part motivated by their continued presence. Firm counseling at the outset of their careers, stressing the fact that much more than an academic degree or credential is required to be a good professional musician, might have spared the choral world the deleterious influence of these misfits.

Church conductors should not dismiss the generation of this kind of career-choosing excitement as being likely only in schools or colleges. Members of their adult choirs may have had extensive musical training which has been laid aside because of family-raising or work requirements. Such musicians can be led to undertake the responsibility of a vitally-needed children's choir or high school chorus, by the conductor's enthusiasm for the choral achievements of the adult choir. In such instances, "counseling-by-example" pays off handsomely both in terms of a stronger choral program and as a meaningful experience for the "reclaimed musician".

THE CONDUCTOR AS ORGANIZATION MANAGER

One common synonym for "choir" is "organization", which Webster defines as "an administrative and functional structure set up to . . . .arrange systematic planning and united effort." The use of the term is pertinent, and the role of the conductor is central to its effectiveness. This role starts with his "systematic planning" and reaches fruition in every phase of "united effort" he can stimulate. Much as the hard-pressed conductor might like to confine his efforts to the music alone, leaving "all that sort of thing" to someone else, he must recognize that in most American choirs the organization is very much a shadow of the conductor himself.

Certainly, a skeletal framework sustains all choirs: their church obligation, a school tradition, a written constitution that says officers shall be elected once a year, a habit of meeting one night a week to rehearse; but these are only bones. One skeleton is pretty much like another until it is fleshed out with living individuality; in the choir this is supplied by the conductor. In setting out to do so, he must bear in mind three major objectives of choir organization, stated here in order of importance.

Objectives of choir organization.

To build and maintain morale ■ The best music will be produced by a group through which a sense of oneness, an *esprit de corps,* moves strongly. The fact that choral singing relies on the inner expressiveness of each singer means that the individual expressions must all be unified and channeled in one direction. The conductor can do this fully only if there already exists within his singers an empathetic awareness of the group as an entity. Attainment of this oneness is the primary aim of organizing; it must never be thought of as an end in itself. If all details of physical and material organization have been well handled, the group is freed to work together without impediment. This is the only soil out of which true unity can grow. Habit and cold technical prowess may produce a performance of considerable polish and accuracy, but inspired, unified singing is the fruit of comprehensive organization.

To permit interpretation and creative performance ■ Effective organization allows interpretation to happen, because it establishes a framework which includes the means (the choir and the conductor), the environment (a well-structured rehearsal or performance), and the incentive (the exhilaration of starting to perform well together). The conductor who slights or wants nothing to do with organizational details should remember that he is denying himself an effective means of achieving his musical purpose with his choir.

To save time and get things done ■ The more elaborate the objectives or complex the function, the greater is the need for thorough organization. The alternatives to organization are stagnation or chaos; if the conductor is to lead the group to real accomplishment, he can afford neither.

THE A TO F OF CHOIR MANAGEMENT : *(Six Cardinal Principles)*

1. Anticipate! Plan, look forward to, and discern what will be needed. Project the actual instant of rehearsal or performance. What will be happening? What, at that moment, should already have been done? What problems should have been anticipated, and what solutions readied? What unforeseen hazards may have arisen?

Student teachers are often required to write detailed lesson plans which estimate how much time each of their activities will require during a given period or day. Some variation of such planning is valuable for the conductor, particularly the novice, or one beginning with a new choir. His plans should detail which music will be rehearsed, how long each piece will be considered, what he will tell the choir about it, what objectives he will expect them to accomplish, and what the choir's reactions will probably be. Expert planners *expect* the unexpected and anticipate that a certain percentage of their plans will not work. They provide alternatives and additional material to fill the breach. If a ninety-minute rehearsal will ordinarily touch on seven or eight anthem-length pieces, ten should be in readiness. It is far more productive to over-plan and have to omit some material than to under-plan and be caught short. The unstructured rehearsal wastes time and frays singers' nerves. The unplanned performance can be an acute embarrassment, because the lack of forethought is obvious to the people watching.

"Planning" also involves the conductor's long-range expectations for his group, such as:

.....the church choir conductor who rehearses anthems for a minimum of six to eight weeks in advance at every rehearsal.

.....the school or college conductor who plans the choir's repertoire for an entire semester or quarter and puts a printed list in each singer's hands on the first day.

.....the community choir conductor who, at the opening rehearsal of a season, not only puts such a list in singer's hands, but has already collected repertoire from which programs may be chosen for two or three seasons beyond that.

..... conductors who make a practice of putting *all* information needed by their singers into their hands in printed form well before it is needed: announcements, rule changes, rehearsal schedules, robing instructions, audition information, etc.

2. Build!

The conductor adds to the choir's framework the functions and features which will make it live. These cover many diverse activities and are successful to the extent that they involve members of the group in meaningful roles. His is the initiating responsibility to see that the following components of the organizational framework are present and functioning:

Purposes, rules, and basic procedures ▪ In Appendix II a set of By-Laws is given which was formulated by and serves as the governing instrument for, a large, active symphonic community choir. Such a document states the objectives, organization, and function of the group in a form all members have agreed upon. While some conductors may feel this to be superfluous, since their own choirs function well without it, such a formulation has proven to be the cornerstone of morale for many others. The simple fact that the codification *exists* is a confirmation of the group's entity. More complex groups also spell out rules for auditions, rehearsal and performance times, dress or robing regulations, and other matters of general concern. Frequently such information is condensed into a document of welcome to help in the orientation of new members. The reader is referred to Appendix II for further information about the construction and use of such By-Laws or constitutions.

Physical preparations ▪ Larger organizations often assign responsibility for these matters to specific officers, since these tasks can become involved and arduous. While he should welcome such helpful participation, the conductor has the final responsibility to see that these functions are carried out, some, such as the selection of music and budgeting, usually remaining his sole prerogative:

...organizing the music library and planning the distribution of music to singers and its collection from them. There should be provision for checking out of scores for individual rehearsal.

...selection, care, and distribution of robes, vestments, or other performance attire.

...planning availability and handling of performance equipment such as risers, folders, music stands, pianos, instruments, podiums, lighting, microphones.

...preparing a budget covering every phase of the choir's operation: salaries of the conductor and accompanist, music, equipment, publicity, printing, tickets, social affairs, guest artists, special events or equipment, transportation ---and, hopefully, some forecast of possible income!

...knowledge of the rehearsal and performance rooms and halls – their size, equipment, acoustics, and general suitability, including such considerations as ventilation, lighting, rest rooms, facilities, ushering, ticket management, cleanup services, etc.

. . . . . preparing printed programs: meeting necessary deadlines for printers or for inclusion in a larger publication; preparing neat, accurate copy that can be used by the typesetter; arranging for paid advertising if the program is constructed that way; selecting type, size, and stock of paper to be used; supplying pictures or cuts to be used; arranging for proofreading, and knowing how it is done; arranging for pickup or delivery of the completed programs in time for the concert.

The board of officers, and group organization ▪ Who are the officers? How are they elected? What are their strengths and foibles, and how can they contribute most to the choir? How does the choir itself regard its own officers and organization? When do the officers meet? What do they accomplish? Is their function real or artificial? How can the organizational structure meaningfully involve more members? Supplying substantial answers for these questions can be one of the conductor's most productive activities.

Scheduling procedures ▪ Are *all* the details of rehearsals, performances, and other activities taken care of? Have all the tangles of red tape been unsnarled in advance? Calendars checked and permits issued? Fees paid, equipment located and in place? Custodians and technical personnel alerted and informed? Have these jobs been allocated to involve all choir members? Has the work been coordinated with precision?

The rehearsal ▪ Before starting time, who checks to see that the room *is* open, heated, ventilated, well lighted, and all the equipment ready? Is the piano in tune, the organ free of ciphers, and the music distributed? Has the organization functioned so that the setting is conducive to prompt starting and productive work? How are announcements to be made? Roll taken? Emergencies met?

The performance ▪ Once scheduled, is the performance place ready? Has provision been made for the personal comfort of instrumentalists and guest soloists? Are the choir's seats comfortable and well spaced? Have auxiliary functions been accounted for: handling money from the box office or the offering, distributing programs, presenting flowers to soloists or conductor, recognition of visiting dignitaries, and possibly a social reception after the event? Who will take the guest artist to the airport for that late plane? If guest artists are paid, who conveys the checks to them?

Social activities ■ How is the group's natural impulse to gather socially implemented in a gracious and pleasing way? What parties, dinners, receptions, kaffee-klatches, and other social activities are planned, and how are they supported, scheduled, and carried out? Is there a coffee-break in mid-rehearsal? If so, does its reasonable ten- or fifteen-minute length usually stretch to a half hour? Does social activity enhance or tend to obscure the musical objectives of the choir?

3. Consult!

Managing a choir is successful only when it stimulates the involvement and channels the activity of *persons* — living, breathing, opinion-carrying human beings. This cannot be done at arm's length nor against a consensus of resistance. The conductor must always be aware of the tides of thought in his choir, and the fastest way to learn these is to consult the singers. Though it may be time-consuming, the act of asking opinions serves other purposes as well. It *involves* the choir members and communicates to them that the conductor invites their proprietary interest in the choir's business rather than viewing them as mere recipients of instructions. Even though the choir may have no final power of decision, consultation with the members is probably the fastest way to make decisions equably, particularly in such areas as the acceptance of extra rehearsals and performances, the color and cut of robes, whether dues are to be paid and in what amount, selection of incidental soloists in auditions, planning of social events, or methods of publicizing performances.

4. Direct! (but don't dominate)

An effective executive gets others to carry out his insights as to what needs to be done. This is a concise description of his musical conducting, and it also applies to his management of the organization. Since the final responsibility is his, he must stand ready to "do it himself" if need be, but a greater benefit to the organization will result if he uses his ability to direct the efforts of others. A board of officers is worthless unless each person is aware of his responsibility and actively working to meet it. If the conductor can discover and use the organizational talent among his singers, his organization will flourish. A cumulative sense of purpose and excitement grows when people find that they *can* function effectively and, moreover, that what they are doing is appreciated.

5. Enthuse!

The power of example is formidable. Since the conductor wants his singers to deliver a musical product infused with spirit and vitality, his best means of obtaining this result is to show them, unreservedly, that he himself is moved by that very spirit. The choir and everything about it must be important to him, and he must show this in everything he does. Even if his schedule is crowded, he must always have time for matters of concern to the choir, and members should always feel that devoting attention to choir matters is a source of pleasure and satisfaction to him. Perhaps his final triumph in this regard is to convince his choir that during a long and grueling rehearsal that their very mistakes are matters which concern him only *because* he is so enthused about their potential. If the singers believe him when he says, "I berate you only because I am so sure you are capable of doing much better!", they will accept his criticism and work for him. But if such scolding is seen as mere petulance and bitterness, he will lose them in a thickening fog of resentment.

6. Forcibly lead!

The most expensive automobile is just a mechanical trinket until it is used to take someone somewhere. Similarly, all the planning and thought put into the organization of a choir is futile unless it becomes the means of moving the group toward its goals. The conductor is the driver; he steers. His hand provides the direction, his example the acceleration. This sixth principle is addressed particularly to the conductor who may have accomplished most of the prodigies of planning and organization, but then for various reasons – weariness, lack of energy, or the deceptive hope that such an elaborately-built mechanism must surely be able to run itself – he feels he can "relax and go along" during performances.

The truly dynamic conductor confirms his status as a Renaissance man by focusing the products of his diverse activities on the moment of performance. Even for the solo artist, who must coordinate only his own physical, mental, and spiritual faculties, great performance is a difficult achievement. The conductor, however, must go well beyond this, to the coordination of his singers' efforts into a communicative unity of meaning and sound. The extent to which he accomplishes his varied preparatory tasks affects his success in transforming the moment of performance into something more than mechanical note-making. If singers have found that he is, indeed, a forceful leader in the realms discussed in this chapter and that he possesses the capacity for inspired direction in performance as well as in preparation, they will follow him joyfully onto the highest levels of artistry.

8|The Conductor's Attitudes about Styles and Repertoire

". . . . but I know what I *like!"* This patronizing refuge of the yahoo, prefaced by a completely unneeded disclaimer of knowledge ("Of course, I don't *know* anything about music . . . .") represents attitudes about styles and repertoire which are both widespread and deeply ingrained. A little reflection shows that what is really meant is: "I like what I *know,* (and that isn't much.)" Such an attitude confronts problems of diversity by wearing blinders: "So long as I can look only at what I like/know, I am secure; I just won't look at all that other stuff, and I will have no problem. It can't be very important anyway; after all, I don't like/know it, do I?"

When the conductor encounters some manifestation of this attitude it can be cause for reflection about his own criteria for choosing repertoire. If such attitudes pervade his audiences, how much must he cater to them? Should his programming be aimed at "educating" his listeners? When he looks for new music, what standards of selection shall he use? Who, or what, determines what is "good" and "bad" material for his choir's situation? Does he choose new repertoire primarily for his singers or his audiences? What is available which will fulfill his unique requirements?

Volume of new publications

Every year American publishers print thousands of new choral pieces, covering a wide range of styles and voice combinations. This swelling flood of repertoire is a factor of the conductor's environment which has assumed new importance in the last quarter-century. It reflects the American tendency to make music Big Business, and confronts the conductor with new problems as well as opportunities. The old joke that it is now possible to get an arrangement of "Old Black Joe" for three deaf-mutes and ear trumpet is only fantastic enough to underscore the reality.

The sheer volume of this production allows for wide variety. Without doubt it makes available many high-quality materials previously difficult to obtain. It also inundates the conductor with editions which upon examination prove to be unsuitable or inappropriate. They may be too hard, too easy, faddish, transitory, banal, too serious, too flippant, or too-something-else for his purposes. He may have to rummage through dozens to find one piece which is "right" for his choir.

This is no indictment of the publishers. They are deluged with manuscripts from which they can print only a small percentage. In choosing which ones, they have to ask, "If we publish this, can we sell it to somebody, somewhere, in enough volume to justify our investment?" That the answer is "Yes" in a majority of cases is proven by their continuing existence as profit-making concerns. This solvency is essential if publishers are to be able to exercise other, more altruistic and artistic motivations for publishing materials which they know at the outset will not be profitable. The conductor must realize, as he thrusts aside all those "unsuitable" pieces, that somebody probably *will* buy most of them, for there are many choirs, many conductors, diverse tastes, and numerous avenues of choral expression.

Selecting a repertoire

Valuable suggestions on program building have appeared in books about choral conducting.[1] The very diversity of these can be a problem, if they are too detailed for the conductor to adapt to his own situation or seem contradictory because they represent widely divergent backgrounds. In the final analysis, the conductor must make his own choice; *his* standards must be the effective ones in building *his* programs and repertoire. He must try all ready-made answers in the crucible of his own convictions: do they meet *his* standards?

Conductors who have attended successful choral workshops, clinics, reading sessions, and festivals have felt the tug of diverse currents of attitude about repertoire. A respected authority or persuasive demonstration can lend great weight to a particular point of view. An outstanding performance by a great choir can project a particular style or work in an aura of overwhelming attractiveness. The conductor may come away under the spell of an unrealistic motivation to change the course of his own activities in the direction of these views. Where the new ideas are relevant and provide challenge to his own choir, exhilarating growth ensues. On the other hand, confusion and frustration follow when the square peg of another choir's achievement cannot be forced into the round hole of his own group's limitations. The conductor's objective perception must determine which among alluring new ideas are actually applicable to his conditions.

Conductors hold many attitudes about repertoire use. Several examples will be projected here for examination, first as they

1 : See Appendix II for a more detailed discussion.

concern *how much* is programmed, second, as to how much *variety* is included, and third, as to *what styles* are chosen. "Programming" is used in its broadest sense, including both the construction of individual concerts or services, and selection of a group's repertoire for a normal cycle of their activity such as a church year, a semester, or a season.

How much repertoire?

The following attitudes are stated in a cause-and-effect format, in which widely-held premises are carried out to representative types of consequent action. While variations are legion, three typical examples are stated here with a hypothetical exactness, to examine in some detail a broad range of viewpoints about the question.

Attitude #1

The premises:

Because

.....my budget is limited;

.....my singers are only moderately skilled and not too enthused;

.....my rehearsal time is restricted;

.....my choir's function limits the scope and amount of repertoire they need to use;

.....my personal experience with particular works and styles has shown me that they are usable and dependable;

.....my time is too limited to do much "repertoire research";

The conclusions:

Therefore I will

.....use a small number of "old reliables" which I know can be readily learned, will work every time, and are now in my library;

.....not be too concerned with the new material coming out because I don't have the money, time, or need to use very much of it anyway;

.....rely on my choir's tradition, momentum, and enjoyment of familiar music to maintain their interest.

Attitude #2

The premises:

Because

.....my experience with certain musical styles convinces me that they are by far the most suitable ones for choral performance and for the purposes of my choir;

.....I have found that many things other choirs use are not suited to my concept of choral singing or my stylistic ideals;

.....my choir's function makes it seem advisable to limit their activities to a carefully-selected list of works or styles;

.....my budget is limited;

.....my singers seem to be interested only in certain styles and resist new works;

The conclusions:

Therefore I will

.....specialize in certain styles and composers;

.....refine and perfect a small, highly selective group of numbers in those styles, judiciously using my budget to build a small, specialized music library;

.....purchase smaller amounts of more expensive editions because of their musicological values;

.....not be concerned with the massive annual production of new choral materials, since most of it is unsuitable for my choir anyway.

Attitude #3

The premises:

Because

.....I am impressed with the vitality of the varied musical styles my singers hear from the communications media;

.....although my budget is limited, I want to use it to build an exciting and flexible library and repertoire which may prove persuasive in obtaining a larger budget;

.....I have had rewarding experiences with several musical styles in my own performances;

.....my choir's function, while limited by ritual or tradition, urgently needs the stimulus of fresh ideas;

.....although my singers' skills are limited, they quickly tire of doing the same piece over and over, and are challenged by new works;

The conclusions:

Therefore I will

.....introduce as much new music as the budget will allow, being inventive in sharing copies, borrowing from other choirs or producing my own arrangements;

.....use every work or style which is relevant to my choir's function and which they can learn to perform;

.....use a large, varied repertoire as a means of stimulating interest, challenging effort, building enthusiasm, and widening singers' musical horizons.

.....devote the time required to find fresh and effective repertoire.

These three attitudes are commonly heard in the comments or observed in the programming of conductors, modified only by the particulars of individual conditions. It is clear that these different conclusions derived from the same basic premises depend on the orientation or drive of the conductor. Attitude #3 is essentially optimistic; it makes virtue out of necessity in matters of limited budget, restrictions of choir function, inadequate singers' skills, and the time necessary for examining new repertoire. Attitudes #1 and #2 tend to regard such matters only as limitations. It is also apparent that the divergent interpretations of the premises will result in widely different amounts of musical repertoire being obtained and used, and that the nature of the choir's activity will be directly affected by this fact. Choir #1 might be characterized as complacent; #2 risks an ingrown haughtiness; #3 may embody a somewhat undisciplined excitement.

By clarifying his individual attitudes amid these extremes, the conductor equips himself to decide how many works he will ask his choir to accomplish in a normal cycle of their activity, what proportion will be new, how frequently he will repeat the most successful pieces, and other matters related to his use of quantities of material.

Church choirs are usually responsible for forty or more consecutive Sundays of regular services — anthems, responses, liturgical pieces, and special numbers. If services call for two anthems, and the choir is also expected to present seasonal concerts, problems multiply. There is always too little rehearsal time, and singers must be challenged even more forcefully to clear their minds of their daily round of activities when they begin to rehearse. School and college conductors face equally conflicting demands as they work to prepare concerts or programs while trying to teach their neophytes the fundamentals of choral singing; they too feel there is far too little time to do it all adequately.

These pressures may seem to force the conductor into Attitudes #1 or #2. An instance has been reported of a leading university choir devoting one entire quarter to a single cantata-length work of moderate difficulty, not looking at any other music at all; church choirs are known whose active yearly repertoire is limited to fifteen anthems, mechanically repeated. The choir singers who described these situations also commented on the low level of interest among choir members. It is safe to assume that with such a limited repertoire the conductor would have to be phenomenally effective in finding other means to maintain the choir's interest.

A confirmed devotee of Attitude #3, on the other hand, would try to confront the complexities of his environment with vitality and diversity. His proposed solutions might not always produce meticulously polished performance, but would stimulate great interest and enthusiastic participation. In his use of repertoire he would:

.....be sure that one-third to one-half of any cycle's repertoire consisted of new works.

.....rarely repeat an anthem within six months for a church choir, or within two years for a school or college choir.

.....create an attitude of interested anticipation about doing new works by consistently reflecting such an attitude himself.

.....be vigilant to find and select new pieces which challenge the choir's best efforts and capabilities.

.....relate new materials to the development of musicianly skills; singers learn to read by reading.

.....build group spirit and pride in their inclusive, varied repertoire.

How much variety?

Unless a choir is strictly limited by its function and purpose to the use of only one musical style, such as liturgical chant, or musical commercials, the problem of how much variety of sytle and repertoire to use must be considered by the conductor. School and college conductors make the decision each year; a majority of church choirs have enough latitude in their choice of music to make the matter relevant.

The problem would seem simple enough: many styles or few? But solutions are more complex because they spring from the particular philosophies under which choirs operate. This means that various attitudes are held about the question, and disagreement between viewpoints may be a factor with which the conductor will have to contend, because it can affect his singers' thinking about their own choir's activity. If a neighboring choir, operating under a different philosophy of repertoire, is thought by them to be more attractive or successful than their own, the problem becomes one of choir morale, and the conductor must be versatile in meeting it.

To illustrate the problem, two hypothetical, opposing, and extreme attitudes will be stated, the thinking of most conductors probably falling somewhere between them.

Attitude A : The ultimate choral virtue is to refine one style to perfection ■ Already touched upon in the discussion under Attitude #2 above, this viewpoint is seen here in its effect upon variety as well as quantity of repertoire. It consciously aims to make specialists of a choir, who will perform one style or a group of related styles, such as *a cappella* works of the 16th century, or some segment of modern popular music, or the works of Stravinsky and Ives, to the virtual exclusion of everything else. This specialization usually entails a parallel selectivity in tone quality, phrasing and expressive styling, in pursuit of performance which is "correct" in the puristic sense. If the choir achieves any tangible success or acclaim for this single-style approach, they may tend to ignore other styles as unnecessary, or, at best, perform them poorly. They may accomplish great things in their chosen style, and even become known as "experts" as long as they deal in it exclusively.

This attitude, however, risks narrowness and limited appeal. Singers and audiences who, in this age of easy communication are accustomed to hear many styles done well, may regard it as a one-sided, isolated use of the choral art. The intense concentration needed to perfect a single style may simply make it impossible to do anything else, and the result is a monotony of programming. As long as the choir performs only for an esoteric circle of devotees, the issue may not be raised. General audiences, however, will find even the most skilled performance tedious if one style is continued too long, particularly if that style is of only moderate interest to them at the outset. One Palestrina Mass, beautifully done, will move audiences who never heard of the composer. Yet, if it is followed by similar works by di Lasso and Victoria, no matter how brilliantly performed, interest is sure to lag. It is equally true that programs composed exclusively of avant-garde styles or "jazz chorals" must select their audiences with great care, or risk utter tedium.

Attitude B : Diversity is the ultimate good in programming ■ This aims at the widest possible variety of styles, both of repertoire and manner of performance. It points programming at the broadest range of audience tastes. It calls for varied tone qualities to match the requirements of successive styles and a concept of vocal production which demands more than one style. Diversity is consciously used as a means of stimulating and holding interest by trading on the excitement of the "new and different".

Almost certainly, this approach risks less-than-perfect performances of any one style, because there just isn't time for the necessary concentration. The conductor himself must be proficient in every style used, since the choir will absorb only as much as he is able to teach them. Conscientious conductors may be troubled by the possibility that this attitude only surrenders to the pervasive commercial criteria of "success" engendered by an American culture given to opulence, flamboyance, and surface values. It seems, they might add, to make musical values conditional on the whim of audience response.

Less and less can the conductor afford to ignore the issues raised by these sample attitudes. Unless his position takes full account of the unique challenges and restrictions of his situation, as well as his own idealistic constructions of what programming should include, his choir's repertoire will probably be chosen by accident or whim.

If he chooses to pursue diversity, he must be prepared to make it accurate, musically valid, rewarding, and communicative. If he is accused of merely catering to public tastes, he must make his musical product so vital that it assumes the role of taste-maker within its sphere of influence. If he chooses specialization, he must impart to it the same excitement and satisfaction-giving qualities which benefit the diverse approach. He must probably work harder to maintain the interest of singers and audiences, and must make the purity of his musical product his most attractive asset.

A few choirs in restricted environments may be able to ignore the choice. The group whose singing is limited to beer commercials may never sing Gregorian Chant, while a choir of monks won't sing Richard Rodgers. But what of choirs in between? What is the course for the school group, the college concert choir? The "45-Sundays-a-year" protestant church choir? The community chorus?

The inescapable answer seems to be that their function demands that they do *many* things, and that their success, in terms both of musical achievement and audience response, will be measured to a considerable extent by how many they do *well.* This clearly points in the direction of diversity. It remains for the conductor, in his dynamic control of the problem, to determine what forms that diversity will take in his own repertoire.

Which repertoire styles?

It has been noted that American choral music no longer has a single, generally-accepted functional justification such as produced much of the great music of past epochs. Because it has become an adjunct of many other activities and is forced to justify itself in virtually every situation, many shades of opinion are current about what styles are best, most suitable, or most popular. That very popularity can exert a formidable pressure upon the conductor's choice of music for his choir. Singers are often not at all reluctant to tell him in no uncertain terms what they feel the choir ought to sing. The conductor must have the will-power and force of leadership to be the one who establishes and maintains the group's position about the matter. He *has* to choose, if only to provide the choir with something to sing. But his choice must provide consistent quality and satisfaction or its effects will be most injurious.

When an accumulation of similar attitudes becomes strong enough in a choir, it can make a strong case for a particular style by being, apparently, the "popular", "majority", "current", "latest-thing" opinion. This may be only a vague consensus of the moment, or it may reflect a fad whose appeal is principally non-musical, but its force can be tangible. When it is strong enough to override the conductor's opinion, or happens to support some whim or predilection of his own, the whole productive image of the group can be quickly altered. Tedious, unbalanced, fad-ridden programming usually results.

The true dimensions of this problem are seen only when such terms as "popular", "current", and "latest thing" are viewed in their broadest connotations, not limited to the distinction usually made between "popular" and "classical" music. The meaning of "current, popular style" to various groups may encompass a wide variety of musical styles of sharply contrasting natures. It is a sad commentary on the current choral scene that in some extreme cases these group attitudes become fortresses, from which their devotees hurl barbs of denigrating scorn upon all outsiders who refuse to hail that bastion as the center of the choral universe. If such belligerence could always be attributed to mere ignorance, it might be overlooked; but the choice is often the conscious, patronizing weapon of persons who should know better.

When such an attitude dominates a choir with undiluted intensity, an invidious type of specialization has set in, and it should be the conductor's first purpose to combat it. It closes minds and negates creativity. It equates "popular and current" with ". . . what I *like!*", and the inevitable corollary is that the value judgments of "good" and "only acceptable style" are soon added to the equation.

Several of these attitudes about style currently afflicting the choral scene are stated here in the extreme to point up the problems they entail:

Attitude #1 : Popular music is the only really exciting music
■ If this is true, all "serious" music must be dull and stodgy.

Though this attitude is rarely encountered in pure form in school and church, the conductor should be aware that in some commercially-oriented circles, where music is regarded as a means of increasing sales or building a glamorous "image" (as in some phases of television and recording), this attitude is the prevailing sentiment. Since his singers' viewpoints are influenced to some extent by music they hear from such sources, the force of the attitude must be recognized. A college choir conductor to whose campus representatives of such attitudes have come in search of new talent, has felt the full weight of this thinking, expressed bluntly and openly to him and his students. It was couched in such questions as "Do you really want to go on bothering with that old stuff?" when referring to music by which the conductor was trying to broaden perspectives and teach technique, and which had a demonstrated durability of appeal far exceeding that which the "popular" styles have had time to achieve. If this attitude succeeds in igniting singers' excitement, the conductor's job is made more difficult. Not only are "standard" styles cast in shadow, but it becomes harder to take advantage of the unique assets of the popular styles themselves. A petulant "all-or-nothing-at-all" sentiment sows divisiveness so that virtually *no* style may be undertaken without fear of dissension.

Attitude #2 : The only great music is very old music ■ For some conductors, the isorhythmic motets of Machaut and his contemporaries constitute the entire corpus of worthwhile repertoire. The dreadful snobbery of such in-group thought concentrates on some particular composer or style, whose principal merit seems to be that it is long gone. Such purists may be very impatient with "modernists" who want to sing a little Mozart and Brahms for variety. The author has seen this attitude provide the principal motivation for musicologically-inclined groups, who nonetheless wanted to be thought of as performing choirs. Such organizations represent a small minority, but when this attitude is espoused by individual members of more generally-oriented choirs, its influence can be divisive. Even more unfortunate is the conductor who allows his own musicological-historical interests to obscure his judgment as to what is best suited to his choir. He will try to lead his singers into paths they may not wish to tread, and their mounting resistance will erode their interest, morale, and chances for productive performance.

Attitude #3 : It's good only if it's avant-garde! ■ This is Attitude #2 directed at "the latest thing". It finds its most ardent disciples in fields of dodecaphonic, chance, aleatory, and electronic music, and it maintains branch offices in certain areas of jazz. These disciples, too, are so intense that they tend to prevent the conductor from doing much with benefits such new styles may have to offer. They always demand more, usually at the expense of "all that other stuff." A group which pursues such styles as their exclusive *raison d'être* can easily become convinced that true merit attaches only to their style of performance, and that everything else must be suffered as a tedious bow to convention. There is no doubt that a truly proficient group, sincerely devoted to specialization in these styles, may be breaking paths of importance into the future of music in general, but such specialization demands a musicianship and maturity of viewpoint hardly typical of the majority of American choirs, and the conductor should carefully assess what effect the growth of this attitude might have on the musical goals of his choir.

Attitude #4 : We sing only Masterworks! ■ This viewpoint springs from the acknowledged greatness of the music itself, and is often supported by the very defendable reasoning that "since you're going to spend the time and effort rehearsing *something,* why not devote it to the very best music?" This becomes a problem only when it intensifies into snobbery, which says in effect that the *only* music worth doing at all is that qualified to stand beside Bach's *Mass in B Minor* and the Brahms *Requiem.* All else, it is implied, is dross. Valuable as the music concerned is, this view must be avoided as limiting and restricted, in contrast to that which explores the broad panoply of repertoire possibilities presently available.

Attitude #5 : Let's just sing familiar music! ■ In this view, the "successful" group sings only "music everybody knows." This usually means "music *I* know", and consists mainly of one tradition. In church choirs, this frequently means music of the gospel-hymn tradition, or anthems by late 19th-century American and English composers. In schools, the speaker refers to folk music, old-standard popular tunes, or some local style of regional popularity. Such music is promoted on grounds that it is easy to learn, and, after all, "everybody loves it!" The conductor should realize that if he succumbs to this tacit equating of "good" with "easy", he also accepts without question its opposite: "hard" equals "bad", a proposition which portends trouble.

Attitude #6 : We premiere new works! ■ This is a variant of the avant-garde attitude, broadened to include any style or work that is "new" — and laden with status. The highest good, in the view of these conductors and choirs, is for them to sing the first performance of a new work, or at least premiere it in their region. What an allure "The First West-

Coast Performance of . . . ." is thought to hold! The more prestigious the name of the composer, the greater the merit. The final accolade is to have him present to take a bow at the performance and to autograph the manuscript scores from which the performance is sung.

There is of course nothing wrong with performing new works, and composers are usually glad to have their work done, particularly (wry twist of Fate!) by choirs and conductors with established reputations as performers of new works. But for this to serve as the entire purpose of the choir's activity shuts them off from other values, and often enough leads to shallow, mechanical performances of the new works because the choir may not have acquired the breadth of experience or musical perspective to do them well.

Attitude #7 : We sing in the original language ■ This celebrates the "in-group" status which singing a work in another language is held to confer. It is often buttressed by the assertion that "you can't translate what the composer *really* wrote!", and claims that it is actually "easier" to do it in the original tongue because the musical phrasing matches the textual phrasing, and so on. It may be easier if the group is proficient in that language; otherwise it is not. The author reflected on this while attending a rehearsal of the BBC Choral Society in London, where Berlioz' *Damnation of Faust* was in preparation. The group had performed it with distinction many times, in English, but their current conductor had asked that it be sung in French. Those experienced and capable singers gave little indication that they though it "easier". However, the matter must not be summarily disposed of in favor of invariably singing in English. The conductor must decide when performing in the original language will be challenging, meaningful, and most importantly, musical. In this discussion works in Latin are not considered, as its international quality is well established. But German, French, Italian, Spanish, Russian – each calls for a separate judgment. Of all possible reasons for accepting the challenge of singing a foreign text, coveting the status of singing "in the original language" is the least impressive. Most choirs will achieve more musical results with translations, and their audiences will come closer to understanding what they are singing. The conductor should have no reluctance about admitting his choir's limitations in choosing his course of action.

No one of these seven attitudes is wholly reprehensible or faulty, nor composed of ideas which are utterly deleterious to choral music. It is only when the logic and intensity of the viewpoint is carried to the extreme of shutting out any other concept that they become unbalanced and absurd. When one of these forms of fanaticism determines the choir's purposes and dominates its activity and is generally supported by the conductor's compliance, an unproductive atmosphere results. No general panaceas are offered to correct such situations, because such corrections must be evolved from the particular nature of each environment. Rather than attempt specific solutions, yet another set of attitudes will be proposed, to outline what may be a productive outlook on the whole problem of choosing repertoire, whether it concerns quantity, variety, or style.

Some viable attitudes

Insipid music breeds vapid singing. Effective music, on the other hand, is a cornerstone of dynamic performance. The conductor's ability to tell one from the other is a valuable asset which must be cultivated at the cost of study, time, effort, and thought.

It can be shown by random samplings of concert programs, festival performances, and lists of church anthems used during an entire season, that in cases where the actual choral sound was consistently vital, meaningful, and attractive, and conveyed musical integrity, it reflected an attitude of enthusiasm for the music itself, which was implemented and enhanced by dynamic conducting. Where, on the other hand, the sound was apathetic, did not communicate to the audience anything more than a need for grim endurance, and was musically bad, the singers felt little or no regard for the music, and were simply producing notes as a mechanical exercise under the "leadership" of conducting they largely ignored.

If the conductor chose the repertoire in each of these cases, it is fair to trace at least some of the success or failure back to the nature of that choice. In either instance the choice is made on the basis of a web of attitudes he holds about repertoire and its use: the composite of knowledge, opinion, and experience which at some crucial moment leads him to take one work and reject another. Since the volume of available materials is so great and so many voices have been raised to tell him how to choose, he faces confusion. The inability of any authoritative guide to fully encompass all the requirements of his situation means that he must formulate his own comprehensive viewpoint as the starting point for his choices. Applied with vigor, persisted in with courage, and mellowed by experience, this will make his repertoire choice increasingly consistent and effective.

It is ironic that, once he has acquired this facility, he probably won't be able to pass it on to others. Many outstanding conductors and writers have gone through the process, and have published lists of principles and criteria based on the most deeply-felt and experience-proven convictions. Valuable as these may be as suggestions, they cannot take the place of a choice evolved from the conductor's own experience. This is because, like decisions made in the heat of performance, such choices represent the instantaneous bringing-to-bear of accumulated thought, experience, attitude, and force of personality. Since all of these represent him as he uniquely *is,* no one can make the choice for him.

With this basic disclaimer recorded, it is the purpose here to suggest some dimensions of attitude which should frame his choosing. These state some characteristics of effective programming in terms of what singers, audiences, and the conductor himself will think of, react to, value, or feel and remember about a particular musical work. Each of these statements in some degree provides an attitudinal measurement of its effectiveness. No one of them clearly defines the "ideal piece", nor is the complete lack of any one of these utterly fatal. These and all other criteria will remain only bookish value judgments until the conductor finds out for himself whether they are valid for his choir.

Attitude #1 : Effective repertoire has recognizable vitality ■ Webster defines "vital" as "existing as a manifestation of life; full of vigor." Measured by this definition, the statement of this attitude may not be quite as self-evident as it seems at first. Not only must the music contain life; the fact must emanate and be recognized. It is simply a fact that a great deal of music has no such tangible vital spark. It is either a mechanical academic exercise or a commercial product whose tenuous life expired with the passing of the particular non-musical conditions which brought it into being. Merely assembling notes doesn't make vital music.

The trouble with vitality is that, because of its nature, no formulas can encompass it. It is *there,* — an essence, a soul, an inner spirit which can be felt to breathe through the sounds — or it is *not.* About all the composer can do is to capture the pattern of notes and words in which he senses it, putting them down in the hope that others will be able to recreate the sounds which will make it live again. If in looking at the music the conductor is perceptive enough to see the possibility of its existence in those note patterns, the decision is successfully made.. If the composer was only partially successful, and the conductor's estimate is hit-or-miss, the result may be only a musical corpse, propped up in public view. This spirit of vitality is essential; it is the Grail toward which the conductor's search must constantly aspire. But here, words end; he must go on alone.

Attitude #2 : Effective repertoire is communicative ■ The most effective piece speaks meaningfully to audiences, if only because it has already spoken clearly to the singers. This is an obvious characteristic of any style of music that has ever enjoyed lasting influence. It can be equally true of the greatest classic and latest popular hit, even though the styles and the audiences are worlds apart. The successful work conveys its vitality and musical content in the act of being accurately performed.

Many programs, unfortunately, are *not* communicative. They are tedious obituaries, celebrating either the composer's failure to capture life in his notes or the conductor's inability to tell vital music from dead. Or perhaps nothing has been communicated to the singers, who therefore produce nothing vital.

In virtually every musical style there is a mountain of dull, mechanical, content-less sound which has nothing to say to anyone save the most impassioned devotee. Most "great" composers wrote voluminously, and it is logical to assume that not all of it was inspired. The urge of the musicologist and publisher to capitalize on the success of those composers' more inspired works has brought into print much sheer junk that should have been left to gather dust in manuscript. Popular styles of the present, while often bursting with energy and immediate impact, contain many pieces that will be gone tomorrow, and should be; if it takes the choir until day after tomorrow to learn them, they are already voiceless corpses before they are accomplished in sound. Avant-garde styles, some of which may well be shaping the course of future music, contain much that is so experimental that even its originators can point to no communicative content beyond mere novelty. Even the masterworks can be faulted for dull moments – passages created for a specific time and occasion, which speak the musical language of a particular era too exclusively to be relevant to modern ears.

The difficulty deepens when the need for communication conflicts directly with the need for breadth and scope in programming. An entire program of musical lollipops, whose only virtue is their instant communication, can be a vitiating experience, for it demands nothing of the listener's attention. A work of more austere nature, whose full message must be wooed by attention, would be eliminated in constructing such a program, and that very act would be one of the principal reasons the program was weak. On the other hand, the mere fact that a work is by Victoria, Bach, Brahms, Stravinsky or Rodgers is no assurance at all that it will have anything to say to *this* audience when performed by *this* choir. The conductor must bring to bear a piercing objectivity to find whether the work, stripped of all its status and non-musical accoutrements, really has anything to say.

Repertoire which does not actually communicate does choral music a real disservice, no matter how well intended. It perpetuates in the minds of listeners already disposed to question the relevance of choral singing an attitude that *this* style is something you bear with, or just ignore, for it doesn't say anything. This is far more fundamental than the rebuttal sometimes advanced, that to be bound by a need to communicate is only an attempt to curry popular favor. An avant-garde composer remarked to the author, "I really could not care less if people don't listen to or enjoy my music! The creation of it is the only important thing!". Another says, "If you enjoy anything in my music, I have failed, for you enjoy only what you have heard before, and I wanted to write something new." In such views communication has no place.

Yet, if choral music is to continue to have any viable social impact beyond what it does for the singer himself, it must speak to its auditors. Such speaking need not be restricted to terms they already know and like. The very greatest choral styles have always been distinguished by the fact that what they had to say was of such trenchant meaning that it demanded, and received, attention from those to whom it was addressed.

Attitude #3 : Effective repertoire makes its musical values manifest ▪ A fundamental question the conductor needs to ask is, "Will this piece emerge from my choir's performance as a truly *musical* entity?" Applied rigorously to many actual programs, this measurement would be devastating. No matter how strong or lofty the musicological, social, commercial, dramatic, or textual reasons which urge that a work be performed, unless its actual realization in sound conveys inner musical integrity, all other motives for its use are suspect. All of the conductor's prowess as a musician is needed to discern this in a new work, and correctly estimate his choir's chances of conveying it. Is it, in itself, a *musical* construction, or simply an assemblage of music-like sounds wrapped around a non-musical idea? Is the construction solid, the style valid? Are musical materials used with meaning and quickened by the breath of vitality? If these must be anwered with "No", or these qualities are so covered over with gimmicks and "effects" that they will not be noticed, the value of the work is very limited.

Attitude #4 : Effective repertoire is achievable ■ A clear distinction must be drawn by the conductor between that which will challenge and lead his choir to successful performance and that which, though undeniably challenging, is simply beyond their ability. This is not always merely a matter of complexity or technical difficulty. It includes the choir's ability to comprehend idiom and style, taking account of their experience and general orientation.

Unless a piece is done right, it usually fails dismally; there is very little middle ground. When it does fail, the illustrious names studding the program become mere bids for status; mishandled popular styles are viewed as the awkward contortions of "squares"; faltering attempts at the avant-garde merely sound wrong; and the masterwork which is obviously beyond the powers of the choir suggests pygmies trying to move a mountain, one stone at a time.

A conductor who allows his musical eyes to exceed the capacity of his choir's musical stomach leads them poorly. He should ask himself whether greater value lies in unsuccessfully attempting music of complex meaning and great status, or in producing great musical sound with materials of simple meaning but less acclaim value. On his answer to this question and the accuracy of his estimate of his choir's abilities, the wisdom of his repertoire choices hangs. Prepared lists of criteria become only marginal commentaries on it.

Attitude #5 : Effective programming is diversified ■ In his search for the qualities outlined in the first four Attitudes, the conductor's chances for success will be enhanced by exploring many styles and epochs. His singers are reared on an opulent diversity of things, ideas, and communication, and will respond to repertoire which shows a similar variety. The wide availability of styles and materials makes it theoretically possible to build programs, or even entire seasons, exclusively out of materials which are the most vital, communicative, musical and achievable works representing several successful choral eras. Even the partial realization of such an objective will strengthen and invigorate a choir's whole program.

The conductor must decide which of the widely-used methods of program building best suit his purposes. Shall they be chronological, or grouped by styles? Will "serious" pieces alternate with "light"? Will he open with his most demanding works, on the theory that the audience's attention span is greater at the outset, as some authorities claim, or will he catch their attention with a "throw-away" piece of great impact but little weight, as others advise? What is the best way to approach *this* particular audience? Will a theme be useful? How much variety and what styles will make the strongest program?

The church conductor must choose the format by which he will plan music for his church year. Methods are many and varied: relate music to sermon topics, when the minister can be induced to plan *his* work at least eight weeks in advance; alternate accompanied with unaccompanied pieces, Sunday by Sunday; designate one Sunday a month as "New Music Sunday", or "Hymn-of-the-Month Sunday"; incorporate works with instrumental accompaniments; concentrate on one style or composer for a given service or season; use multiple choir works which bring together adult and children's groups, or include visiting choirs; plan attendance at festivals and use that repertoire in regular services. The more completely these plans are incorporated into the year's structure at the outset, the more diverse and interesting that structure becomes.[1]

SEVEN QUICK QUESTIONS FOR SCREENING REPERTOIRE

In order to see these five Attitudes in a practical perspective, the following questions give them a form which the conductor can apply directly to each work as he starts through the latest stack of new pieces. He must weigh and balance. A work studded with affirmative answers to most of these questions will probably be an asset to his repertoire. Too many negative answers, or the presence of one or two glaringly insurmountable barriers, probably tell him to leave the work alone.

1. Has it discernible quality?

Does it contain discernible strength of melody, logic and richness of harmony, vitality and coherence of rhythm, and logic of form? If it is a "new" style, does it successfully convey the new musical concept it embodies? Does it seem to have the musical potential to endure beyond the status of a fad? Does its effectiveness spring from integrity of structure and substance, or from its surface, associative, momentary impact?

2. Is it written chorally?

Is it music that was clearly written to be sung by a group, or as a solo or instrumental piece? Does its effectiveness rest squarely on things that only combined voices can achieve, or is it an attempt to force voices into some other mold? Are such adaptations of function obvious or hidden? Do they manage to solve the problems they raise? What use is made

1 : See Appendix II for a detailed discussion of program construction.

of non-choral "effects" and "gimmicks"? Do the lines lie naturally in the voice, or are they built-in non-vocal shapes?

3. Does the text make sense?

Are the words understandable and of value or significance to the singers who will use them? If they will be obscure at the outset, can their meaning be clarified without an effort disproportionate to their value? When they have been clarified, will they say anything worth bothering with? Do the words contribute a meaningful element to the performance which will enhance the choir's expressiveness and assist the audience's understanding? Do they have independent merit as poetry, prose, or thought content? Are difficulties of language (foreign or phonetic) solvable within the rehearsal time and frame of attitude in which the singers encounter them?

4. What will it communicate?

Will the piece speak to singers in a way which will stimulate a vital performance by this choir in this situation? Will it convey to the audience that it is a relevant, expressive entity of tangible worth? Will it convince singers that it is worth doing at once, or after reasonable rehearsal? Is what it communicates primarily musical? Does it have real vitality, and can this quality be conveyed by performing it?

5. Which objectives does it serve?

Is its principal value musical, liturgical, commercial, or social? Does it principally enhance musical accomplishment, status, public image, social acceptability, or performance prowess? Is it being used in response to pressures of momentary fads? Does it serve to build up, or simply trade upon, the musicianly skills and understandings of the choir? Is its attraction found more in its inspirational qualities or its practical usability?

6. Does it fit the total repertoire?

Will its presence add a new dimension or call for a new skill? Will it merely add to an already-long list of pieces of the same general style and content? Is it being considered *only* to enhance status, or because it seems to be a worthy contribution to the musical growth of the choir? What specific performance settings will it be used for? Why?

7. Is the edition asset or liability?

Is the print clear and understandable, or cluttered and forbidding? Is it edited to be understandable at the level of this choir? How much time will be needed to explain its technical requirements or shortcomings, or correct its errors? Is its cost within reason as far as my budget is concerned? Has the price been inflated to account for non-musical frills such as unnecessarily heavy, glossy paper, multi-color printing, ornate art work, page space wasted by overly-large notation and excessive "white space", or several pages devoted to advertising other works in the publisher's catalogue? Are other editions of the same work available from another publisher, in a better format? Is the edition itself readily available, or will it take weeks or months to receive it?

Lists of suggestions and admonitions come and go, and the tide of new materials flows on. Dynamic conductors long ago learned to accept that their job includes hours of repertoire research to find exactly the "right" music for their choirs. Other conductors seem content to let chance govern the choice, or simply to imitate the programming of someone else who has put in the time and thought required. Programming of stifling mediocrity and dullness abounds even in the face of plenty. Only when enough conductors are fired with conviction as to the real advantages of dynamic, vital repertoire will the fullest benefits of the modern cornucopia be realized.

9|The Impact of the Conductor's Image

What composite image of its conductor does a choir see? What impact does it have upon their response to him? How does it shape his total effectiveness as a conductor?

It is usual to "re-touch" portrait negatives to "improve" them; that is, make the final pictures conform as much as possible to the subject's mental image of himself. In the process, assets are pointed up and deficiencies are softened. In trying to define a choir's enduring picture of its conductor such kindly treatment is not always possible, for by the nature of his job he stands constantly before them in full view, so that they see him as he is, un-retouched.

The importance of image

If "one picture is worth a thousand words", the cumulative impact of what they see can be of basic importance to his continuing success. It can be the fundamental ingredient of a choir's morale. It can condition their pride and enthusiasm or their willingness to undertake the purposeful activity which must precede effective performance. It sums up their total impressions of what he is, what he knows and can do, and his direct relation to them as leader, teacher, and mentor. It is a far deeper, more substantial entity than that implied by Madison Avenue's use of "image", which is a false front meant to convey a predetermined and basically deceptive impression. Such an impression, indeed, embodies a drastic re-touching of reality, and is exactly the opposite of the honest image a choir receives of its conductor.

Modern man, nonetheless, is thoroughly accustomed to think in terms of "image". He is inundated with advertising which impresses "images" of the false-front variety on his mind to influence his buying. He accepts the "star system" in the media and athletics, which focuses his attention on the person who presents the most graphically individualized image. Politicians and public figures come to him on television trying to impress him with the reality of their images as genuine persons. It is reasonable to assume that when he comes to the choir rehearsal and observes his choir leader, he brings along the habits of thought to which these conditions have accustomed him.

Appraising its qualities

What are the components of a conductor's image, and what can he do about them? Earlier chapters of this book have dealt with many of them in detail, and this chapter will try to summarize them into a usable concept which will be helpful to the conductor's self-evaluation. It is assumed that the conscientious conductor will perennially re-examine his own image, as it is reflected in his choir's responses. Since this is an intensely personal matter, touching on deeply-rooted habits and characteristics, he must do it for himself and should limit his concern to those facets of the image which he can control or change.

Elaborate surveys have been devised which seek to measure every aspect of the conductor's function and to create "precise" instruments of rating or evaluation. These may have limited value in specific situations, but generally the results do not justify the effort. Many of the most crucial factors they seek to gauge are too fleeting for precise measurement, and their impact depends upon the unique components of the moment.

A more meaningful appraisal of the choir's image of its conductor may be obtained by sampling reactions to his activity through broadly inclusive questions such as those listed below. No valid statistical results can be expected, for these questions deal with transitory impressions, moods, and attitudes of the conductor's environment. A characteristic strength of the dynamic conductor is that he develops a sensitive, empathetic awareness of currents moving in the atmosphere of that environment, and so is able to derive meaningful answers to questions of this sort, finding in them reliable indications of his image and impact. Compressing several matters already discussed at length into the implications of a single terse question in effect imitates the demands which conducting itself places upon the conductor. To perform well, he must compress all his knowledge, skill, and insight into the instant. The responses given in that instant answer many questions about him and his relation to the music.

1. Is he dynamic or passive?

Is he live, or taped? Is what they see of him infused with reality, presence, honesty, and vitality, or is it a static, distant, rule-bound, habit-motivated automaton? Does he emanate positive assurance or timidity?

2. Is he an original or a copy?

Is he unique, and therefore of special value and interest? Does he exhibit true originality and individuality? These demand initiative, purpose, and courage, — the marks of true leadership. Great choirs are not led by consensus any more than Toscanini was a committee.

3. Does he really know, or is he faking?

Is there any reason to doubt that he knows music, conducting, and people? Can his word be depended upon for accuracy, relevancy, and timeliness? Is his knowledge a mere compilation of statistics, or does it show broad comprehension?

4. What is he "known for"?

With what requirements has he structured the choir's working environment? What is he respected for? Notorious for? Given adulation because of? What accomplishments of learning, habit, skill, personal discipline, satisfaction, and artistic expression result from what he does?

5. What has the choir learned to ignore?

To which ideals and "requirements" do they know he pays only lip-service? What do they politely overlook while waiting for more positive, productive things to happen again? Which personal idiosyncrasies have they forgiven him?

6. Is he poised or uneasy?

Does he emanate equanimity, or do his frustrations show? Is he resilient in the face of inevitable disappointment, or is his boiling point low? Can he hold on to his sense of humor? Can he think – and act – on his feet? Does he reflect the sureness of great humanity, or the petulance of mere smallness?

7. Does he really lead?

Singers expect him to; does he? Has he both the ability and the courage to move people, even against their initial will or inertia? Can he relinquish for the moment his human desire to be liked, and risk active resistance in pursuit of his vision of what must be done? Can he successfully overcome the normal lethargy of his singers, and motivate their diverse efforts into a single productive channel?

Great conductors' images

Great conductors with legendary reputations typify vivid images. These reputations distill the ideas people hold about them and produce an aura which represents their style, individuality, accomplishment, and total impact on public consciousness. It connotes their way of doing things and establishes them as points of reference for others. People form their images of leadership from observing such conductors because of their demonstrated ability to *lead.*

Average conductors, who may never attain broad acclaim or reputation, still have a certain kinship with these great images. *Their* choirs look to *them* for leadership, and within their more limited sphere, they too are seen as leader-images. Their choirs' attainments will depend on how forcefully that leadership-image makes its impact upon their minds. For a choir of beginners, a weak image will preclude their producing a beautiful, satisfying tone, and thus even their limited expectations will be disappointed. Before a choir of professional singers a blurred conductor-image may mean a masterwork performed shoddily, and so their *broader* potential has been wasted. Vague, uncertain conducting in school and church choirs often serves to turn away from further choral singing potentially skilled beginners. In an era which increasingly calls upon choral music to justify its relevance such an influence is more harmful to the long-term health of the choral art than an occasional indifferent performance by a usually fine conductor and choir.

Controllable elements of the image

To some extent a conductor's image results from inherent characteristics he cannot change. Other facets of it, however, result from training, conscious thought, or accumulated experience, which may be re-shaped by the conductor. Since many of these have been dealt with in earlier chapters, here they will be summarized. Others, which represent the combination of several elements, will be discussed more fully. No meaningful order of priority can be assigned, for individual circumstances may raise any one of these facets to primary urgency, and their final impact depends squarely on what the conductor does with them.

His facade of personality

What kind of person is he? What kind of person do his singers *think* him to be? How different are the two? How can his immediate and lasting impact on others be described?

A sensitive conductor is aware of the impression he makes, and this is an important aspect of the non-verbal communication discussed in Chapter 3. It is a two-way traffic in impressions, reactions, and mutual understandings. Its nature can be delineated by sets of terms which contrast extremes of various character traits about which his singers invariably form their own judgments. If the conductor is aware of a catalogue of such terms and the reactions they evoke from his singers, he may be led to sudden insights as to his choir's feelings about him. Such revelations, direct and non-verbal, may be the fastest means to the conductor's self-improvement, because the changes involved must begin as inner-directed activities. To confront within one's self irrefutable evidence that respectable segments of choir opinion consider him to be mean, petty, inefficient, or whatever, will give the conscientious conductor real cause for reflection.

The following lists of terms contrast the "dynamic" conductor with one who is weak and inept. Each pair of terms offers a continuum along which a conductor may locate his position in the minds of the choir. Charting his placement between each pair of extremes should make up a revealing and instructive profile of his total impact as a person. If it is true that what people *think* is true often has as great an influence on events as what actually *is,* his choir's composite opinion is of continuing importance to him.

THE COMPLETELY DYNAMIC CONDUCTOR IS:	THE COMPLETELY INEPT CONDUCTOR IS:
Prepared	Unprepared
Knowledgeable	Ignorant, given to "faking"
Efficient, well-paced	Disorganized, fumbling, wasteful
Confident, outgoing	Timid, unsure, apologetic
Courteous and considerate	Rude and thoughtless
Forceful, motivating	Weak
Interesting	Dull
Communicative	Hard to understand, obscure
Pleasant, attractive	Forbidding, abrupt, sarcastic
Dedicated, inspiring	Indifferent, deadening
Enthusiastic	Lethargic
Accurate, precise	Wrong or vague
Tolerant	Bigoted
Original, inventive, versatile	Pedantic, strictly imitative
Intriguingly unpredictable	Ploddingly predictable
Idealistically practical	Cynically unreasonable
Neat, appropriately groomed	Sloppy, careless, eccentric in dress
Poised, resilient	Nervous, easily rattled
Leavened by a sense of humor	Grim, severe, humorless
Patiently persistent	Temperamentally tantrum-ridden
Consistent	Erratic

It is important that the conductor not confuse the choir's impression of him as a musical director with his image as a person. While singers *may* forgive grave sins in the latter if they are sufficiently impressed with the former, it is very risky for the average conductor to expect that they necessarily *will.* When a conflict of this sort confuses the choir's reactions the conductor may find himself being feared, hated, or simply ignored. While music of some sort can be produced even under such handicaps, it calls for singers with expert, independent musicianship, whose personal musical integrity will not allow them to be deterred by their contradictory reactions. If the conductor is respected and liked as a person as well as highly regarded for his musical accomplishments, he and the choir will produce more satisfying, artistic musical results. Sensitivity to his singers' reactions in terms such as those listed above helps the conductor avoid such conflicts.

His depth of preparation

Modern stress on speed learning and condensation cannot alter the fact that choral performance is an involved and detailed artistic discipline. Its essential requirements cannot be met with gimmicks, popularization, and "personality" alone, for basic musical components are involved which are technical in nature: rhythm, melody, interval, intonation, harmony, use of voice, and mechanics of expression. A conductor whose training has not adequately prepared him to deal wisely with these essentials will gloss them over, or apologetically try to camouflage them in "fun", and thus fail to insist that his singers accomplish these absolutely fundamental objectives. Choirs are not slow to sense this deficiency of training, particularly when it results in tedious rehearsals and limited accomplishment. Below are listed four areas of conducting skill on which a choir will judge the conductor; each has been discussed in detail in the chapters indicated.

a. *His musicianship (See Chapter 6)* ■ Choral singing's richest rewards come to singers who achieve the most completely *musical* performances. One of the conductor's most pressing mandates is that he lead his choir to realize its ultimate potential in musicianly work. The intensity of his allegiance to this obligation becomes increasingly apparent to his singers and strongly colors their picture of his effectiveness. If he lets them get away with unmusical singing, they will experience little of the intense satisfaction which results from a really musical performance, and will quickly come to view the conductor's work — as well as the entire choir activity — as routines of only moderate interest and importance in their lives. Where dynamic conducting achieves truly musical results, that satisfaction is so intense that singers cherish singing with the choir among their most invigorating and memorable experiences.

As suggested in Chapter 6, his musicianship must have a comprehensiveness which permits him to convey musical habits to his singers as an interesting part of what they are doing. He must not force "musicianship" onto them as required doses of dullness, a price they must pay for getting on to the fun of singing. If he himself works in musicianly ways, they will find it normal to give musicianly responses. His leadership image should stand for the attitude that musicianly skills, which must be learned and drilled, are actually of the same substance as artistic performance, which is appreciated and enjoyed.

b. *His teaching and conducting skills (See Chapters 2, 3, and 7)* ■ As a leader, the conductor is presumed to be skilled, knowledgeable, and musically well prepared. But can he convey the fruits of these attributes to his singers? Does his preparation include learning means of communicating his craft to others? It has been noted in many ways that modern society places a premium on being able to communicate readily and well. This undoubtedly increases the singer's sensitivity to this quality in his conductor, and contributes measureably to the over-all impression of the conductor's strength of leadership.

c. *His knowledge of vocal techniques (See Chapter 5)* ■ The choral singer's reliance upon his conductor as a principal source of vocal guidance has been examined at length. If singers find that what he tells them actually works, they view him as a reliable authority. If his directions are unreasonable, unvocal, or simply do not correspond to what they find their own voices will do, his image is blurred. This forces them to seek more competent advice elsewhere, or, as happens in a majority of cases, they just ignore their vocal potential altogether and continue to sing in a haphazard, unmusical way.

d. *The effectiveness of his repertoire (See Chapter 8)* ■ A choir's "favorite" works generally prove to be those which have demanded the most from them in time, effort, and devotion. This is because the intensity of those demands forces singers to learn the work thoroughly. Works of quality stand up to such searching attention and repay effort with rewards of satisfaction. If the conductor has chosen wisely, that is, he has discerned in the work the potential for just such satisfaction, the wisdom of his choice will not be lost on the choir. Conductors whose repertoire, year in and year out, is rich and varied, rejoice in having singers thank them, even years later, for having exposed them to such treasured musical experiences. Both the quality and diversity of programming the conductor chooses for his choir quickly become prominent features of what they think of him.

The quality of product

In its most inclusive view, the choir's image of its conductor reflects what he produces, or, more accurately, what he leads *them* to produce. This is a composite of many things, some of which have already been elaborated on. This product is probably a sum greater than the total of its parts. No simple adding-up of technical accomplishments can fully account for the electric force of a fully vital choral performance, and it is precisely the dynamic quality which the conductor alone can supply that gives it final coordination and impact. Once a choir experiences this, their image of their conductor takes on strong overtones of awe and adulation. Some of the more definable elements contributing to a fine choral product are:

a. *An organized sense of purpose and accomplishment (See Chapter 7)* ▪ Several of the conductor's reponsibilities for structuring a choir's activities have been discussed in detail. The outcome of such organization is that the entire momentum of the group, in rehearsal and performance, becomes a concerted, disciplined effort, taking full advantage of the capabilities of the singers and the potential of the music. Singers come to value this ability highly, as any one of them will quickly attest who has moved from a well-organized to a poorly-coordinated group.

b. *A rich and expressive choral tone (See Chapter 4)* ▪ More than any other tangible product of a choir's effort, the quality of its composite tone results directly from what the conductor has done or failed to do to shape it. Ranging from the meticulous precision of pitch and color sought by the St. Olaf philosophy, to the raw, unmodulated noises made by poorly trained choirs — for which the sarcastic epithet "early accidental" is most apt — choral tone displays graphically to the world just what the conductor thinks and does about one of the most crucial fundamentals of the choral art.

The human voice is capable of a vast spectrum of sounds. To hope that somehow the simultaneous productions of many voices will magically produce a unified whole stretches credulity. The conductor must confront the raw tonal combinations presented to him much as the sculptor regards new clay: as material to be molded into consciously-chosen shapes and meanings. In this effort the first step is often the drastic one of merely stopping the noises being made so that singers may become aware of a better concept. It is unfortunately too possible to hear groups in concert, festival, school, and church who have evidently never enjoyed the purging of this primary discipline, for the sounds they make are insipid, uncontrolled, colorless, out of tune, and even blatantly hideous. Where such a tonal product reveals a conductor who *allows* his singers to go on committing such mortal choral sins, his image as a leader is a fuzzy one. He has not impressed his singers with a leadership forceful enough to take them out of their grievous ways.

The rich tonal palette heard in recordings by professional choirs bears this out by its extreme contrast. Naturally the voices of such groups are highly trained, carefully chosen, and skilled far beyond those of amateur choirs. The fact that the tone is the most impressive feature of many such recordings, however, only confirms the primacy of tone in all choral singing, for it illustrates that the most effective performance of a work depends directly on the presence of a rich and flexible tone. It would seem that an obvious aid for many conductors would be to play such recordings in rehearsals, to expose their singers to non-verbal concepts of tone production which may be new to them.

The non-professional's impulse to dismiss this comparison as unfair to his choir is refuted by the work of many leading college, high school, and church choirs who *do* produce ethereally beautiful tonal results. For every such choir that can be named there are, unfortunately, many, many more in virtually the same environment, whose singers come from comparable backgrounds of interest, experience, and training, whose tonal product is pure cacophony. *The one identifiable difference is the conductor.*

c. *Artistic, expressive performance (See Chapter 7)* ■ Since participation in the choir is the only experience with artistic music-making many singers will ever have, the conductor's influence in defining "artistic" and "expressive" is of crucial importance. Their image of his role in this depends on his being able to show them in their own performance what the difference is between sounds that are merely mechanical and meaningless, and those that convey feeling, expression, and inspiration. This is summed up in their understanding of his role as Interpreter, and the more convincingly he fills that role, the more complete will be their understanding and use of their capacities for expressive singing.

d. *The conductor's recognized identification with music* ■ It would have been ludicrous to picture Toscanini as a week-end musician who earned most of his living doing something else. Like every eminent conductor, he was a living embodiment of music within his cultural milieu — which in his case was virtually the entire world. School and church conductors rarely achieve such complete identification, for it is characteristic of the modern scene that much choral music is produced by avocational effort or professional work which occupies only part of the conductor's time. Few situations financially support a conductor on the basis of choral work alone.

It is nonetheless true that dynamic school and church conductors *do* become living symbols of music within their more limited environments, and that this very image can be an important cornerstone of their effectiveness. To some extent this can result from the momentum of circumstances, if the natural course of their lives has always directed them toward music. But to a considerable degree it reflects a conscious choice to accept the status of "choir director" as their way of life, fully appreciating its particular rewards, limitations, challenges, trials, and privileges. The more positive and complete the decision, the more the conductor's leadership will emanate confident assurance and infectious enthusiasm. If the matter remains in doubt in his own mind, his actions and demeanor will leave lingering aftertastes of uncertainty, lack of direction, and vaguely apologetic apathy.

Leadership by dynamic conductors is the fundamental condition for continuing success in choral enterprises. Modern conditions add special urgency to the need, but as yet nothing has altered the fact that singers continue to respond with joy and alacrity to the conductor whose training, knowledge, personality and leadership truly qualify him as "dynamic".

APPENDIX

I. Practical Projects

II. Practical Answers
to Recurring Problems

APPENDIX I : PRACTICAL PROJECTS

Each project outlined below draws on concepts in one or more chapters of this book, and is designed to place the conductor in practical situations related to those concepts. These projects have proved useful as bases for specific assignments in conducting classes. The individual conductor should also find them instructive means of exploring his own difficulties and challenges.

Their usefulness will vary with the degree of involvement on the conductor's part. If done as mechanical exercises, they will be of limited value. Each project is constructed to force the conductor into contact with the realities and implications of a live situation, which are too detailed or tenuous to list, and which in any event can be understood fully only by personal contact. A starting point for each project can be the discussion of concepts and devices in the chapter cited as being relevant. In every case these must be enlarged upon by the conductor in terms of his actual situation.

Several projects suggest the use of actual choirs; the value of doing this cannot be over-emphasized. For working conductors, this means simply the adaptation of their regular schedules to allow for the project – in itself a worthwhile exercise in organization and choir management. For new, aspiring conductors who do not yet have their own choirs, early negotiations for a position as assistant or volunteer helper in some established choir are urged. Ultimately, conducting must be learned by *conducting.* One rarely becomes a swimmer without getting wet!

These are projects for *doing,* and not simply for study. The more directly they can be tried in the fires of actual practice, the greater will be their value.

Project 1 : A Survey of Choral Experiences
(Refer to Chapters 1, 8, & 9)

Over a period of at least two weeks make a list of every instance in your normal schedule when you hear any sort of music which employs voices in groups of more than two singers. Devise your own format for recording the information,

Project 1: Choral survey

but include provision for at least the following kinds of information or statistics:

Source or location:	Live performance, church service, radio, television, rehearsal, recordings, motion picture, public event, background, etc.
Musical style:	Folk, pop, jazz, sacred, concert, symphonic, oratorio, school music, commercial, etc.
Type of group:	Professional choir, commercial group, pop, rock, or jazz combo, church choir, symphonic chorus, school or college group, madrigal singers, etc.
Size of group:	Approximate figures are sufficient.
Title of music:	List composer also, if available.
Quality of the performance:	State in as much detail as you wish the prominent features of the performance; list glaring faults and principal assets.
Audience reaction, if observable:	If it is music played as a background, this in itself defines a certain expected reaction.

Remember that *all* music involving groups of voices qualifies. To summarize the project, prepare a report which might be delivered to a class, a choir, or interested laymen, compiling the accumulated data and drawing summary conclusions about the following:

1. The over-all amount of chorally-oriented sound you have heard in the given time-span. In that time, how much more do you think you missed, heard subconsciously, or failed to tabulate?

2. The variety of styles you heard, which ones you heard most, which ones caught your attention most forcefully, and why.

3. Some estimate of the impact of what you heard on your reactions to other music, to the choir music you normally hear or work with. In short, try to summarize the impact of this environmentally-received choral sound upon your association with the choral music you are either singing and/or conducting. Examine the psychological bases and implications of your conclusions.

PROJECT 2 : A PROFILE OF A WORKING CHOIR (Chapters 1 & 2)

Construct an analytical profile of a specific choir by use of an information-survey form as suggested below. Any regularly working choir is suitable; your own is preferable, but it should be one with which you can work closely for extended periods of time. If someone else directs, prepare the survey form and approach him with the suggestion that the results will be valuable to him as well as to you; ask his help in refining it so that his choir members will cooperate. When results have been tabulated, provide him and his singers with copies. Frame all questions to be answered anonymously. Modify the following questions to fit the circumstances, but include at least these areas.

1. The singer's age, sex, marital status, and educational achievement.

2. Occupation or profession; if a student, specify the major subject or vocational objective.

3. Extent and nature of musical training: Formal instruction in class or solo, instrumental, vocal, theoretical, or "appreciation". How recent? Phrase questions to draw out as much detail as possible.

4. Formulate several questions such as the following designed to record shadings of opinion about music and the choir held by individual singers:

   a. List your "favorite" television and radio programs, (musical and non-musical); also recording artists and public entertainment figures. List any motion picture you have seen in the past year in which you remember specifically hearing the choral music of the sound track.

   b. List at least one musical commercial of which you can sing or recall the tune immediately. Does it involve voices?

   c. Disregarding choral music, what is your favorite style of music? Check any of the following that apply, and double check those you favor most strongly:

popular ballad	symphony	folk music solo
rock and roll	concerto	exotic: Indian, etc
jazz combo	concert band	military band
big band sound	piano alone	________________
musical comedy	chamber music	________________
musical commercials	folk music groups	

d. Please feel free to answer the following question honestly and completely: If you could improve this choir in just one specific way what would that way be?: ------------------------------------
----

e. Please check one: I think the over-all functioning of this choir is
- ☐ Tremendously successful
- ☐ Quite successful
- ☐ Only moderately successful
- ☐ Not really successful at all

f. Check any of the following you consider a contributing reason for your being a member of this choir. Check primary reasons twice.

----I enjoy singing choral music.
----It gives me a chance to serve the (church, school, community).
----It's where my friends are.
----The group is congenial and friendly.
----I'm getting a grade or academic credit for it.
----There's status involved in being a member.
----I like the conductor personally.
----The conductor produces inspiring music with his choirs.
----It's a good recreational activity.
----The group is well known.
----I've sung for years and I want to go on with it.
----Just curiosity; people told me I'd like it, so I had to find out.
----Music is my major interest (vocation, hobby).
----It is an important part of my music program.
----My wife/husband likes it, so I come along.
----This choir sings exciting music I want to perform.
Etc. etc., to match local situation.

Compiling the results:

In compiling results, assemble statistical results in one section, then construct a short profile, probably in prose rather than outline, which draws conclusions in the following areas:

1. What kind of people make up the choir? Who are they, what do they do? What are their interests? What is their general educational-social-economic level?

2. What are their musical preferences? What other artistic or cultural interests are implied?

3. Why are they taking part here? What do they want? How do they regard this choir and its activities? What are their views about the purposes of the choir?

PROJECT 3 : ANALYSIS OF COMMUNICATIVE TECHNIQUES (Chapters 2, 3, & 9)

With advance permission from each, observe two different conductors in at least two rehearsals each. When all observations have been completed, write a confidential summary analysis of the following:

1. For each conductor list the principal verbal and non-verbal techniques of communication you could identify in his work. Starting with those discussed in chapters 2 and 3, make a point of identifying others they may use. Note cases where such communicative techniques were particularly effective, or unsuccessful; if reasons for these reactions are apparent include them.

2. In a separate statement for each conductor, estimate from your observation what were his strongest means of communication, and which his weakest, and what, if anything, hampered his attempts at communication more than anything else. If you are fortunate enough to have observed an accomplished master at conducting, it is important that this fact itself be recognized in your summary.

3. Finally, write a comparative summation of the effectiveness of the two. Include in this at least the following areas:

   a. Over-all control of the rehearsal situation.

   b. What musical accomplishments of the rehearsal you feel were most directly related to the conductor's communicative prowess, or its lack.

   c. An estimate of the image of the conductor held by each choir. How do they respond to this image? Can you gauge the leadership of each, and draw meaningful comparisons between them based primarily on their ability to communicate?

   d. An estimate of the relative chances for successful performance by each conductor, based on what you saw, giving reasons for your statements.

Reports should be written in a "Conductor A – Conductor B" format, and no names used. Maximum value to the project will be added by choosing conductors whose work and reputation is unknown to you in advance.

Project 4 : Planning Tonal Devices for another Conductor's Choir (Chapter 4)

Plan in written detail a rehearsal with a hypothetical choir to which you have been invited to come as guest conductor. Specify exactly the level and nature of the group on which the project is based: high school, adult, college, church or school, community, etc. Add the following difficulties at the outset: Since you have heard the choir perform, you know that their usual tone is flat or harsh, with a persistent blatancy, yet you have been asked to conduct them in works of a quiet *a cappella* style. To further complicate matters, it is apparent to you that the choir's tonal problems spring largely from faulty or inadequate training provided by the regular conductor.

Choose two or three specific pieces suited to the interests and ability level of the choir, and list in rather thorough detail the devices or techniques you plan to use in a two-hour rehearsal. Show how these devices will attempt to deal with the following objectives:

1. Materially change, at least for this rehearsal, the fundamental tone production of the choir.

2. Use such changed tone to begin to reveal to the singers the potential beauty of the work being sung.

3. Avoid casting reflections on the regular conductor or in any way damaging his image in their minds.

4. Insure that the choir will make at least a few exciting, intensely rich quiet tones during the course of the rehearsal. Use music such as *Jesu dulcis memoria,* by Victoria, *Call to Remembrance,* by Farrant, *The Eyes of All,* by Berger, or *The Silver Swan,* by Gibbons.

For maximum value to the exercise, arrange to put as many of your plans as possible into action with a live choir. Trade rehearsals with another conductor, even though the tonal problems of his choir may not be exactly those you have specified; this will only force you to adapt your plans in the course of the rehearsal. An interesting variant for more advanced conductors is to take on a rehearsal knowing only the titles of the music to be rehearsed and the general nature of the choir membership, but with no prior experience with their tone.

If no complete rehearsal is available to you, but you can try one or more of the techniques you planned using a class or demonstration choir, write a brief summary of the following after the event:

1. How well the device worked in accomplishing its aims.
2. Its principal weaknesses and whatever reasons you can discern for them.
3. Your own effectiveness as a conductor in using the device.
4. Any reflections of your image in the group's estimation which you may be able to observe.

PROJECT 5 : PLANNING A GROUP VOICE TRAINING DEVICE OR LESSON
(Chapters 5, 7, 2, 3)

Plan in detail, and deliver to a live group if possible, either one single lesson, or a group of shorter lesson-segments or devices, designed to help a specific group with particular problems of personal vocal production. For purposes of the project, write every phase of the preparation out, even though when it is used with a choir, it should be done with a minimal reference to notes or outlines. In this written planning, make provision for the following matters:

1. State the nature, size, and composition of the choir involved: their age level, experience with singing, and with music generally. Note the strength of the organizational morale which characterizes the group.
2. Determine how many singers have had, or are now taking, private voice lessons. This information will materially affect the nature of your planning.
3. Plan the exact relationship of the lesson(s) to the continuing work of the group: A separate lesson, or part of a rehearsal? How much time will it take, and where will it be inserted? Will it be a series of short devices, or a sin-

gle concept which is reviewed in future lessons? If so, how?

4. What are the specific vocal objectives of the lesson(s)? What are you trying to teach them? Is the concept clear in your own mind, in detail? Why does *this* choir need *this* lesson?

5. What, exactly will you *do,* and ask the singers to do? Is each phase pre-timed? What will you do if you have misjudged their reactions? Do you have alternative material ready?

6. What musical materials will you need? Can the lesson be related to music being rehearsed? What provisions have you made for actually supplying needed materials?

7. What means have you provided for measuring the positive achievements of the lesson? What benefit has come to the *group,* as contrasted with its individual members?

Project 6 : Planning Devices or Lessons in musicianship (Chapters 6, 2, 3)

Following roughly the same format used in Project 5, develop specific devices or lessons designed to teach a particular musicianly skill to a pre-selected choir. This selection is crucial, as the nature of the skill to be taught will be pretty well determined by what they don't know. To add practicality, design these as "Capsule Concepts", "Limited Lessons", or even "Mini-Minute Marvels", restricting each to no more than nine minutes. Focus each one on a single concept or skill; use the discussion of Chapter 6 as a basis. Provide in your planning for necessary follow-up and review.

Project 7 : Organizing a New Choir (Chapters 7, 4, 5, 6)

Prepare a complete, written prospectus for a new choral group to be organized within an existing institution such as a school, church, college, or community. If it is possible actually to set up such a group, use your plans as guidelines, keeping running accounts of their effectiveness. If this is not possible, engage the assistance of an experienced conductor in evaluating your plans. Structure your prospectus according

New choir

to the way in which you think it would be introduced: to "sell" the idea to a committee or an administrator, or to publicize it to the public, seeking members, or in some other way which your unique situation may dictate. Make all the plans detailed and specific. The following areas must be represented:

1. A statement of the need or opportunity for the group: what public or institutional interest is present? Under whose auspices will it function? For what purpose? Where and when will it perform? Why? Whose support will be needed to further the organizational plans?

2. Nature and composition of the group: type of individuals involved, their age level, amount of experience with singing, and preferences as to kinds of music; expected working size of the group.

3. When, where, how often, and for how long the group will rehearse and perform.

4. What music will they sing? How will it be obtained, processed, stored, and distributed? How many copies of each number will you plan to purchase: one for every singer, one-to-two, or? Add a list of twenty-five specific pieces, listed by title, composer, arranger, publisher, edition number, and price, with which you propose to start their music library.

5. What kind of accompaniment will the group need? Who will provide it?

6. What budget will be needed for the first fiscal year? See Chapter 7 for budget categories to be included. Be sure to state any possible sources of income (ticket sales, donations, social events, etc).

7. Outline the choir's organization, including all officers and functions; use Chapter 7 as a guide.

8. Project the number and nature of performances, indicating the location, supplies, and specific equipment that will be needed.

9. How will the choir dress for performance? How will such garments be financed and obtained? Outline specific plans, including present market prices of the kind of garment or vestment you propose.

10. What provision is necessary for publicity, to secure members, announce auditions, for concerts and ticket sales?

How will this be handled, and by whom? If the group is not the sort usually associated with "publicity", are there nevertheless ways in which a little appropriate public notice can be used to enhance the image of the choir in the member's eyes?

11. Lay specific lesson plans for the first two or three rehearsals. What will be your "opening approach"? What objectives of tone and musical skill will be sought after first? How soon after the first rehearsal will you plan a performance, and why?

12. What will be your policy about attendance and promptness at rehearsal? How will this be implemented?

13. What provision have you made for social activities of the organization? How will these relate to the objectives of the group? How will they be financed and managed? Who will do it?

PROJECT 8 : PLANNING A FESTIVAL CONCERT (Chapters 7, 2, 3)

Assume that your church, school, or college choir will be host to a combined-choir and orchestra festival concert five months from the beginning of the project. It is one of a continuing series of festivals, and will include performances by each participating choir, singing up to twelve minutes of music of its own choosing, and a combined performance with orchestra of a work about of the length and difficulty of the Kodaly *Te Deum.* Individual choir performances will be adjudicated; you are to decide whether this adjudication is to be in the form of competitive ratings or merely critical commentary. Registration fees of $1 per singer support the event, except that your own institution supplies the performance hall and utilities without charge. With this basic information in mind, write a detailed plan for the festival, showing how each of the following matters will be met and disposed of:

1. Date, time, place of the festival concert(s).

2. Who will adjudicate the choirs' performances, and conduct the combined number? How will he be contracted, transported, paid, and returned?

3. A complete master schedule, showing all planning events, rehearsal, publicity, and performance deadlines.

4. What orchestra will be used? Who will rehearse them? When? Will there be an orchestra rehearsal before the combined rehearsal? Will they be paid? If so, are available funds sufficient? If not, what do you plan to do?

5. In what ways will the members of your choir act as hosts? (Meeting and guiding visiting choirs, ushering, providing equipment, staffing committees, providing refreshments and receptions, assistance in robing and seating.)

6. What auxiliary organizations will be needed to help? P.T.A.? Women's Association? Civic League? In what ways will their help be meaningful, and what specific persons should be approached?

7. Who assembles program materials, gets them to the printer, proof-reads the copy, picks up the finished programs — and pays for the job? How many copies of the program will be printed?

8. How will publicity for the event be handled? Who is in charge of securing information from the groups involved, writing up the story, and getting it to all the media outlets in the proper format?

9. Who will be in charge of contacting participating choirs with details of organization, scheduling, registrations, fee-collecting, etc?

10. What printed adjudication form will be needed? Who prepares and supplies it? Will the adjudicator be provided with a secretary, or tape recorder? How will the results be announced?

11. In what ways will the elected officers of your own choir be involved in positions of responsibility? Who will serve as master of ceremonies at the concert programs, if one is needed?

12. What dignitaries will be involved in the program? Why? What will they be expected to do or say? Who actually invites them? How?

13. What provisions for emergencies have been made? A nurse? Doctor? First aid room?

14. If other choirs bring buses, where will they park? Will the cooperation of the local police department be needed to handle traffic?

15. Will there be a dinner or banquet involved? If so, who is in charge, who cooks or caters the meal, how is the cost determined, and how are the funds collected? What happens if those who made reservations don't show up, or many who have no reservations do? Is the available space actually sufficient to handle the event as planned? Will the total time schedule allow the event to happen easily and graciously, and yet not waste time?

16. If no formal meal is planned, what happens at intermissions, or at meal time if the festival is long? Will there be refreshments? Are there adequate eating places nearby? Can a snack service be supplied at cost?

17. Who handles tickets for the public? Who gets them printed, sorted, numbered, and distributed? What method of accounting for the funds have you set up? Can a realistic estimate be made of what this will add to the total budget?

18. In the midst of all this, what music will YOUR choir sing, and how will rehearsing it be fitted into your other musical obligations? List your repertoire, timed to twelve minutes.

Project 9 : Repertoire Planning (Chapter 8)

Specify a choral group with which you are acquainted. List its size, nature, and general function ("An adult church choir, Protestant, 35 members"). Indicate the frequency of their performance, and something of the size of their repertoire, or the demands which their environment places on them to produce particular amounts and kinds of music.

Select *one piece from each of twenty-five different publishers* which you feel is suited to the group's needs and capabilities. Be sure that each piece is currently available on the market, and if possible, purchase a copy for yourself. The surest means of accomplishing this research is to visit the showrooms of major music retailers in large cities, where the works of many publishers will be on display. If this is not possible, find out the name of such a store in the large city nearest you, and correspond with them about sending materials on approval for your examination.

For this project, list each work you select by title, composer, arranger, publisher, edition number, voicing, and current price. After thorough study of each work, list the following:

1. Reasons you found this piece attractive or potentially useful for the group you have designated. Be as specific as possible.

2. Obvious problems which the music is likely to pose for rehearsal or performance: vocal, rhythmic textual, harmonic, or others. Remember that if a work looks completely free of problems, that may be a problem in itself: a simple lack of challenge.

3. What type(s) of program it is best suited for. What audience will it appeal to?

For maximum benefit, try to avoid too much repetition of answers in moving from piece to piece. Some will be inevitable, but the more the information reflects the unique nature of the piece, the more valid the judgement.

PROJECT 10 : PROGRAM BUILDING
(Chapter 8 and Appendix II)

Using the materials of Project 9, or other materials chosen by different means, prepare two different programs for the choir designated. Each should last 45 minutes, and use only materials from the Project list if possible. Solo or ensemble numbers using other music may account for no more than eight minutes of the total.

Include, in the total project of planning both programs, overall contrast, variety, and balance of styles. If a theme is possible, include it in at least one of the programs. Strive for continuity, and take into account the choral, vocal, and musical satisfaction of singers and audience. If you have chosen pieces which include incidental solos, use at least one on each program. Check your timing carefully, allowing time for what will actually go on between numbers.

In a commentary which accompanies the program formats, defend in some detail how you feel the program will be vital, possible, challenging, and satisfying to the specific group for which you designed it. Point out the reasons in the music itself why you think it fulfills these requirements. Relate these reasons to your knowledge of the group's capabilities and limitations . . . . . *and* interests.

Designate the nature of the audience to which this choir might sing each of these programs, and estimate what you think the reactions of those audiences would be.

Include numbers which might be used as encores. Specify whether the music is to be memorized or sung from copies.

Project 11 : Constructing An Image Profile (Chapter 9)

Using the materials of Chapter 9, construct a written image-profile of a particular conductor after extended study and observation of his work. For working conductors, this will be most valuable if it concerns their own work, even though such an exercise requires courage and determination. For those without choirs, permission to make such a study should be obtained in advance, after a consultation which explains the purposes and outcomes being sought. The results must be kept completely confidential, and all observations should be made in the most unobtrusive manner possible.

This is an advanced project, and must be handled with the greatest care and sensitivity. Its survey instruments must be designed to sample choir members' reactions without in any way influencing them. The person doing the project must remember at all times that its most urgent objective is simply to *make him aware of the currents of opinion and reaction which are flowing within a given environment.* Much of this is done without ever asking anyone anything, but simply by sensitive observation. This limits the validity of surveys and questionaires, although informal personal interviews are probably advisable.

The final form of the profile can be worked out by the person doing the project. It can, very meaningfully, be simply a concise prose statement of the salient features of the choir's mental image of their conductor. If added details increase the statement's validity, they should be included. The writer of this profile should remember that, while it is important to write it out, by the time he is ready to do the writing, the major values of the project have been accomplished. The profile should include the following areas:

1. An objective attempt to compress into words the consensus of non-verbal opinions about the conductor held by the choir members. Use the image facets discussed in Chapter 9 as points of reference. Sample opinions heard from the choir members which represent widely-held reactions should be quoted verbatim as examples.

2. Either as part of the above or separately, try to isolate what the choir holds to be the outstanding strengths and pronounced shortcomings of the conductor. These are bound to be tenuous; it should be remembered that what is sought is a consensus of the *choir's* views, and *not* the reactions of the observer, whose observations are necessarily of shorter duration and less depth.

3. Finally, some estimate should be made of the relation between the image projected by this profile and the total effectiveness of the conductor as demonstrated by the musical quality of his performances, his reputation in the community and the profession, and his general recognition as a leader-figure. Every scrap of objective evidence, such as newspaper reviews, his inclusion on committees and commissions, and his activity in clinics and festivals, which can be adduced should be cited.

Remember: This profile is intended to delineate what *is,* as distinct from what you think *should be.* To draw this fine line may seem virtually impossible at times, but every effort must be made to make all comments in light of the former.

APPENDIX II

PRACTICAL ANSWERS TO RECURRING PROBLEMS

Problem A:
Should an instrument play along with a choir on an *a cappella* piece if the singers feel insecure?

An accompaniment should never be used as a crutch. Music conceived for voice alone should be sung that way. Singers achieve the most satisfying and accurate performance when they are led to learn they *can* sing independently and with assurance without the "help" of an instrument playing their notes.

While this may seem to be a big step for some groups, the problem is usually the conductor's timidity more than the singers' lack of ability. Use of an accompanying instrument to bolster voices is aesthetically objectionable because the instrument does *not* make the "same" sound as voices. The pitch and duration may be the same, but everything else about the tone is different. This means that the singers must adjust their vocal sound to those differences, and the result often robs choral sound of its unique character. The conductor and his singers may initially feel insecure without an instrument to provide pitch and rhythm in troublesome passages, but as long as they continue to rely on the instrument, they will never learn the music for themselves and will continue to have the same trouble.

This applies to intonation problems as well as to wrong notes and rhythms. To expect the mere presence of an instrument to correct sagging pitch is a forlorn hope if nothing is done to attack the vocal causes of the problem. It is more likely that the continual contrast between instrumental accuracy and vocal deficiency will simply be another agonizing feature of the choir's performance. If a flatting problem has not been solved before performance time, it may be better to remove the instrument and let the choir flat, rather than constantly remind them and the audience that all is not well. Such problems can be corrected *only* by improving the capability of the voices themselves, and this can be more readily accomplished if instrumental tone is not present to confuse the matter.

Even beginners can be led to sing rounds without accompaniment — literally, *a cappella*. Initial hesitation about singing more sophisticated music without accompaniment can be quickly overcome by the dynamic conductor, who with assurance and cheerful leadership, shows his singers that what they do in a simple round can help them conquer more difficult music. He also helps them experience the incomparable satisfaction of an accurate, well-produced, and expressive choral sound, which needs no instrumental "help".

The establishment of assurance in singing unaccompanied choral sound is an essential step toward being able to sing accompanied styles well. When instrumental parts add a complementary musical element to what the voice sings, the choir members are not called upon to match tones and qualities exactly with the instruments but to carry on a type of dialogue. If they can be trained to regard their parts as a rich *a cappella* texture, sung with the vocal integrity and control which unaccompanied singing demands, the choral and instrumental parts will be heard as equal, but contrasting, textures. This will help to make sure that the choral sound is not overwhelmed by instrumental sound, and it will forestall the need to weaken instrumental tone to the point of distortion so the choir may be heard. If the choir has developed confidence in singing a rich tone without accompaniment, the conductor's whimsical reference to singing an accompanied piece "*a cappella* with instruments" often produces the desired tone and balance almost at once.

PROBLEM B:

How valuable are "warm-up" exercises for a choir? What kinds are best? When should they be used? (See Chapters 3, 4, and 6)

Chapter 3 suggested that "warm-up" exercises, used merely for their own sake, are a nuisance. If allowed to become mechanical routines which appear on schedule and require no thought, they waste time, do little for the voices, and bear no relation to the rest of the rehearsal. Yet some activity, at least partly vocal, is a valuable physical and psychological preparation for serious music making. Thoughtfully devised and wisely used, such activity focuses group attention on singing, on the music at hand, and prepares the entire physical-mental-vocal complex to perform flexibly. On such a broad base, "warm-up exercises" may include:

1. Rhythmic drills (See Chapters 4 and 6) ▪ Improvised stamp-clap devices, preferably related to a work in rehearsal, will involve singers physically and mentally at once, and while the voice itself is not given "warm-up" in the usual sense, the general muscle tone of the body is improved, and breathing often deepens.

2. Octave and unison tunings (See Chapter 4) ■ Sing well-tuned octaves with each part in a comfortable range. When accurately done in a reasonably resonant room this produces audible overtones of the 5th which singers can hear and recognize. It can be pointed out that such overtones are heard because of the accuracy of pitch and the resonance of tone being sung; further, that the overtones tend to disappear when octaves go out of tune or the tone becomes unresonant. When a choir can consistently sing octaves up and down scale passages without losing the overtones, they will have accomplished tangible progress both vocally and musically.

3. Musicianship devices (See Chapter 6) ■ Singing scales in the key of the first work to be undertaken in the rehearsal, using syllables, numbers, letter names, or neutral vowels, focuses attention on musical materials, clears the vocal apparatus, and demands immediate concentration. The conductor must be versatile in this area, rarely using the same device twice, and expanding the process to include drill in a variety of musicianly skills his choir needs, such as interval-size recognition, discernment of harmonic textures, contrapuntal devices, and so on. Such devices should not be followed by vocalises designed only to "warm up the voice", in the mistaken belief that singing muscianship drills does nothing for the voice.

4. Immediate concentration on the problems of a specific work ■ Under the right circumstances, this is the most completely effective "warm-up" device possible. If the preceding rehearsal of a given work has left a problem unresolved, immediate attack upon it in the fresh energy of a new rehearsal may solve it quickly. This method accomplishes such diverse side-effects as reminding singers of on-going objectives, demanding immediate involvement with a familiar problem, allowing for vocal limbering up, and providing the most relevant impetus for the beginning of the rehearsal. If, in addition, fatigue and frustration had led the conductor to "blow his top" about the problem at the previous rehearsal, this method allows him to return naturally and with humor to the good graces of his group and may actually enhance their image of him as a human and competent leader.

5. Vowel-color and blending devices (See Chapter 4) ■ These, too, are most valuable when they spring from a work in preparation. Immediate concentration on the vowel color involved in a troublesome passage serves most of the objectives of "warm-ups" very well. Use of the "Tonal Continuum" technique to demonstrate the many alternative possibilities of tone and color usually proves most productive.

6. Peremptorily re-seat the choir ■ An apathetic or disinterested group can be stimulated immediately by the wise use of this device. It must be handled with good humor and an attitude of "Let's try this for a while to see what happens", with a deft, light sparring defense in response to the inevitable grumbling. It shakes up singers a bit to remove the crutch of hearing the same voices on left and right and to be confronted with not only other voices but other parts as well. After the initial reluctance and confusion singers will begin to hear new things in the music, and probably improve their blend, balance, and overall tone quality. They should be asked to sing familiar music to begin with, and only gradually work to music demanding greater independence. Many groups come to request seating in vocal quartets because they find that this is the surest way they can participate in and control their choral sound. A variant of this device is to move whole sections to distant corners of the room or auditorium and have the entire choir try to sing a piece together. While the resulting performance may be disjointed, this forces each singer to listen to the group's production from a radically changed perspective, and many non-verbal choral values are underscored.

7. Start the rehearsal with a quiet, legato, rich-harmony piece ■ A usual justification for "warm-ups" is that the voice is supposedly not ready to sing without them. Yet the first activity undertaken is singing — of exercises! If this effort can be directed to a musical work in rehearsal, which is not excessively demanding but provides a rich harmonic and melodic texture, interest is captured, time is saved, and musicianly preparation begins immediately.

8. Use any device that demands the unexpected (See Chapters 3 and 7) ■ Any device which can be shown to be relevant, which singers can understand, and which galvanizes attention, involves participation, and challenges ability in a fresh and interesting way, qualifies as a "warm-up". The conductor's capacity as a leader will suggest such devices to him and remind him that they should rarely be repeated in the same form. Their novelty is their strongest asset, for they confirm the choir's belief that their conductor is a leader they can depend on to keep them working in an interesting manner. This is a priceless asset in itself.

PROBLEM C:

What are some effective principles to be used in building smooth, effective choral programs and concerts? (See Chapter 8 and Appendix I).

When repertoire has been chosen, the conductor must still decide which specific pieces he will use in a given program or concert and plan their order and manner of presentation. These choices should reflect the conductor's individual style and take full account of the particular characteristics of the choir and audience involved. The following principles have been found relevant to a wide range of choirs, and can be adapted to program-building in school, college, church, and community organizations.

PRINCIPLE 1: *Know your choir's ability.*
What can they do well? What do they like to do? What can they NOT do? How far toward perfection can you actually take them by the time of the program or concert? How willingly and well do they take on new styles or works? These questions demand honest answers, not tainted by either wishful thinking or false modesty. Effective programming builds on the confidence which singers develop in their own capability. If too great a portion of a program is approached by singers in fear and trembling — AND insecure technique — disaster is virtually inevitable. It is better to perform a simple piece to perfection than to destroy a work which is obviously impossible for the choir. Yet a program offering no challenge to the choir will bore them and the audience. As pointed out in Chapter 8, one of the conductor's most basic responsibilities is to pick repertoire which will vigorously challenge his singers, but not lead them into a morass of difficulties beyond their ability to solve; to choose his programs at just the right level of difficulty, a conductor must know his choir very well.

PRINCIPLE 2: *Know your audience and your relation to them.*
Who are they? Why will they be present? What will they expect of you and your choir? What music are they prepared to accept? What music will they openly reject, and why? Is there something special about this concert or program which may alter the nature, interests, or receptivity of the audience? Are they *your* audience, or merely captive? Are you trying to educate, inspire, reform, or entertain them? Or some combination of these? How much will the reaction of this audience affect your choir's morale?

A 30-minute performance of monophonic Gregorian Chant at the Fourth of July Picnic of the Rotary Club would be a guaranteed catastrophe even if it were sung by a choir of angels. If the archangel conductor would have answered honestly such questions as those above about the nature of his audience and its situation, such catastrophes would be avoided. Failure to take account of these matters can negate the value of much fine preparation and erode choir morale. Today *all* audiences, from service clubs to church congregations, are television and recording oriented, which means, whether the conductor likes it or not, that their tastes and receptivity have been to some considerable extent pre-structured. Searching application of the questions given above will materially affect both the structure of programs and the effectiveness of performance.

PRINCIPLE 3: *Choose and develop a program format.*
This format is simply a consistent organizing principle which supplies cohesiveness to the whole. Many different types and combinations are possible, among which the following are most common and workable:

a. The theme format ■ Establish a specific theme or motive, musical or extra-musical, around which all the music on the program can be logically assembled. This is such a popular method that care must be taken to avoid having the chosen theme appear too hackneyed or simply a poor imitation. Christmas, Easter, patriotic holidays and events, the seasons of the church calendar, and many other events supply built-in themes, and in many of these applicable music is plentiful. More general concerts frequently benefit from a theme, particularly if the music used appears to fit without unnatural strain. The conductor's ingenuity and scholarship can well be used to devise purely musical themes for his more sophisticated audiences. Examples might include a program of choral works related to German Chorales, using works of Hassler, J.S. Bach, Mendelssohn, and Distler; or settings of the Dies Irae from Gregorian Chant to Maurice Duruflé; or the evolution and uses of a famous folk-melody such as "Greensleeves"; and so on.

b. The contrast format ■ Here the aim is to build in sharp contrasts of style, texture, idiom, dynamics or tempo in a manner which holds the audience's attention and interest. The development of contrast within unity is one of the most basic concepts of all programming, and successful conductors know that the surest way to hold an audience is to present well-timed changes of pace. A successful example of this format in operation was a concert by the author's college choir, the De Anza Chorale, of De Anza College in Cupertino, California. A Spring Concert had an announced theme of "Spring Lovesong", in which a tongue-in-cheek tone was adopted for the program notes, which suggested that since "Love makes the world go around", the program would bring music inspired by many kinds of Love. The entire program is listed below, with many of the program notes. The sharp, angular contrasts of style, mood, and tempo are obvious. What cannot be reproduced here is the instant and continuing enthusiasm with which audiences greeted the concert. Many individual members of the two different houses to which the concert played, representing both younger and older generations, made a point of congratulating the conductor and the choir on the program's contrast and variety.

FOR OPENERS .... A bright medley about Love's many moods

What the World Needs Now .... Bacharach

Love, Your Magic Spell .... Goulding

What Now, My Love? .... Becaud

Aquarius (from "Hair") .... MacDermot

The Chorale, with the Rock Band "Red Witch"

AND NEXT .... Love in the old Romantic vein

Ten Lovesong Waltzes (Op. 52) .... Brahms

The Vintage Singers (28-voice specialty group, with 4-hand piano accompaniment. Some staging and dancing by the singers was involved.)

THEN, FOR VARIETY .... Improvisation

Our Guests, "Red Witch" (A five-piece Rock Band)

NOW, FOR CONTRAST. Music inspired by the love of God and noble things

The Song of Fate (Schicksalslied) .... Brahms

The Chorale, with String Quartet and Piano

Exsultate Justi .... Viadana

Ave Maris Stella .... Grieg

All Breathing Life (from Motet #1) .... J.S. Bach

A BRIEF INTERMISSION .... in which you can comment to your neighbor about how LOVE-ly this all is!

HERE WE GO AGAIN! .... A potpourri of this and that about Love Painfully Enjoyed, Whimscally Viewed, Moodily Unrequited, and even Countrified! If we haven't hit your particular favorite style yet, this ought to do it!

Ten Thousand Miles .... arr. Ringwald

I'll Not Complain .... Schumann

The Chorale

A Piano Solo: Original improvisation on a motion picture theme

(played by a member of the Chorale)

Home Life: A Whimsical Satire .... Stanton

Written for the Chorale, based on an American Folk-song.

A Comedy Quartet

Three men and a girl; Barbershop Quartet style.

Waters Ripple and Flow .... arr. Deems Taylor

O No, John! .... arr. Miller

The Vintage Singers

Softly, As I Leave You .... deVita

Sweet Evalina .... Stanton

The Chorale

Encores:	The Impossible Dream	Leigh-Ringwald
	Frere Jacques	arr. Terri
	Fall, Leaves, Fall	Bright
	Take My Heart	di Lasso

A change of pace should characterize even the segments of a program, so that one number flows into and contrasts with the next. Different kinds of contrast are possible: alternating fast with slow, accompanied with unaccompanied, entire choir with ensembles or solos, bright mood with dark, loud with soft, secular with sacred, men's voices with women's, and so on. Nor should the matter of key relationships be overlooked. If the change is too distant a musical modulation or intervening announcement to distract attention from the previous key is wise.

c. The chronological format ■ This is primarily a musical arrangement which places the numbers on the program according to the date of their composer's birth. Many feel that this isn't really a format at all, but only a tradition which is perpetuated in place of more inventive thought. However, it often places the least-familiar works early in the program, when theoretically the attention-span of the audience is longest, and if well used, does put the most familiar music last, which tends to leave a good impression with the audience. A truly dynamic conductor will soon find that this approach rarely meets his needs.

d. The "heavy-works-first" format ■ This format begins with an estimate as to when the audience will be best prepared to listen to the most demanding music on the program. It is usually assumed that since the listeners come in interested, this music should be first, and there is considerable experience to show that this assumption is valid. The "demands" of such music may be measured in terms of complexity, unfamiliarity of style, emotional intensity, or simply duration. This format principle is especially valid for the presentation of completely new works or styles, when such works are balanced later with familiar, easily-received styles and works.

e. The "happy-overture" format ■ Usually this is only a modification of the "Heavy-Works-First" approach. It suggests, in effect, that if the program is to present demanding styles or works it should insure first that the attention of the audience has been fully engaged. To do this, a bright, familiar opener is scheduled first, which will please the audience and put them in a receptive frame of mind for what follows. To be effective, the opener must be well performed, and not give any impression of "talking down" to the audience. This technique may be extended to more than one number, as illustrated in the complete program given above. Arrangement of the remaining music on the program must be done with care to avoid a letdown of enthusiasm after a particularly effective opening number. The most effective techniques of contrast are called for.

f. The eclectic format ▪ Various combinations of the first five formats are not only possible, but usually desirable. As suggested above, programming should reflect individual style and the conductor's ability to manipulate program materials in a creative way. If he can use elements of these formats and principles in some new combination which is effective and attractive, his audiences will be enthusiastic.

PRINCIPLE 4: *Be concise and direct, and plan for effect.* How long shall the program be? How much music is actually possible? Do the circumstances of the program dictate inclusiveness or exclusiveness as far as repertoire is concerned? How accurately can actual audience reaction be predicted? Will some of the music be more effective if "staged" or "dressed up" with some visual effects? What possibility for conveying boredom is contained in initial plans? How can this be corrected? What proposed material should be cut from the final program list?

These are some of the most difficult yet crucial questions of program planning. Conductors who do not face them squarely risk programs that are tedious or unbalanced, and almost certain to bring apathetic audience response. It is a cliché of show business that one should "leave 'em wanting more!"; in choral programming this requires the ability to predict when they will stop "wanting more", and to stop the program before that point is reached. If encores are appropriate to the situation they should be planned as carefully as the rest of the program, the number depending on the conductor's judgment as to when the applause turns from enthusiastic to polite.

Farsighted planning, as suggested in Chapter 8, will have projected more numbers than the choir will use, so that in the final stages of program preparation the conductor may cut away works which haven't developed as planned, leaving on the program only those with a good chance of success. This principle applies to performances of major works also. If certain sections of an oratorio or cantata prove to be more than the choir can accomplish, they should be cut. Doing possible things well, rather than impossible things poorly, will reflect more credit on the conductor and choir, even though a cut presentation results, than an obviously poor performance, which only advertises the fact that the choir and conductor got in over their heads.

PROBLEM D:

When a choir has to sing in a strange hall, or outdoors, or in a gymnasium, what will help them overcome the acoustical problems?

Many choirs are asked to sing in acoustical conditions which are basically wrong for choral singing. While many conductors simply refuse to expose their singers to such hazards, there are times when most choirs, to fulfill the objectives of their organization, must face the problem. The conductor must do everything in his power to reduce the difficulties of the situation, and he must also prepare his singers' attitudes so that acoustical problems will not be able to disrupt the choir's performance. No one of the following suggestions will completely solve these problems, and specific situations may make one or more of them completely impossible, but every possible avenue should be explored. Perhaps the most fundamental understanding the singers must have is that they will NOT have the same sound amid the problem situation which they know from their accustomed environment, and that they should be mentally prepared to perform well anyway. Having impressed this on his singers, the conductor should also:

1. Form the choir as near as possible to some flat surface: a wall, side of a building, or, if physically possible, a performance shell. Adamant insistence upon this is only sensible, for this is the only way to be sure the choir will be heard at all.

2. Have the choir in as nearly circular a formation as possible, so that in effect they sing at each other. A variant of this is the position used by church choirs singing in divided chancels. It must be recognized by all concerned that solving the problems of sound inherent in certain settings must be given priority over the choir's visual appearance.

3. Place outside voices of the harmony (bass-soprano, or alto-soprano, or 2nd bass-1st tenor) so that they can hear each other easily.

4. Insist that each row of singers be on a different elevation. Tone produced by singers directly behind others on the same level is wasted. A difference of eight inches is a minimum, and sixteen inches is preferable.

5. Insist on multiple microphones if amplification is to be used. One or two microphones placed vaguely in front of a group will inevitably produce distortion, giving the audience a faulty impression and working adversely on the singers' morale. If it is possible to be heard without amplification, a more musical result will be obtained unless sophisticated amplification equipment is present, managed by skilled operators. In performances without amplification what is lost in dynamics and resonance is usually gained back in balance and musical quality.

6. Caution the choir to sing *under* the dynamic levels indicated until the group has established its blend and balance. In reaction to the dramatic loss of resonance or changed reverberation of the new location, their first impulse will be to shout everything. The conductor must convince his singers that the only way they can produce *and hear* a choral sound is to avoid shouting altogether.

7. Insist on time and opportunity to work out a balance between the choral tone and any instrumental tone which accompanies it. A piano will sound strange and stringy outdoors and will echo in most gymnasiums. A band or wind ensemble can easily overpower the most forceful chorus unless schooled to play at soft dynamics. The conductor must use every means to insure that his choir's tone is heard in balance and must insist that planning for the event takes this need into account.

PROBLEM E:
Are auditions valuable for the average choir?

The better a choir wants to be, the more important auditions become. To be most effective, the audition must be regarded as a means by which the group itself helps build its own efficiency and maintain its standards, rather than as a means of exclusion. While there are values in a "come-one-come-all" approach to chorus building, skillful choral performance is generally not one of them. Real choral achievement requires a tangible contribution from every singer, and the audition should be seen not only as a means of assuring that those who join are potentially able to make that contribution, but also as a way to diagnose and perhaps remedy shortcomings. When well handled on this basis, the mere fact that auditions are required can be one of the choir's strongest assets. Periodic reaudition, devoid of any threat of loss of membership but rather seen as a means whereby the conductor can give personal assistance to individual singers, can also work to the choir's advantage.

Some conductors with new volunteer choirs, where additional members are hard to come by, feel strongly that to require auditions would be suicidal because it would discourage timid prospective members. Yet is has been found in such situations that the absence of an audition served to turn away capable singers who would have valued the standard implied by its presence. In these cases some form of deferred audition has been effective, allowing new members to begin singing with the group at once in a probationary status. Only after a specified time in this status are they asked to audition for full membership. If this probationary period has had the dynamic quality it should, new members will not regard the audition as a threat.

An audition should be based on the following generally-understood aims:

1. It is a component of the group's desire to achieve high standards, and thus it applies equally to all. It is "something we do". While it involves each individual, it must never be seen as a personal singling-out or a punitive threat.

2. The conductor should see the audition as a chance to get to know the auditioner as a person, a specific vocal sound, and a potential performer. To neglect any of these areas reduces the value of the audition in that it limits the conductor's ability to be helpful to the singer and to establish a close rapport with him.

3. The exact nature of the audition should be understood beforehand. Any mystery or doubt about it should be dispelled in advance. Exact details of what will happen during the audition, what will be expected of the singer, what preparation would be useful, who will be present, how soon and by what means results will be announced, and any other pertinent matters concerning the audition should be thoroughly publicized. Perceptive conductors see that the first singers auditioned are those whose success is assured, taking great pains to make the experience pleasant and relaxed. Word gets around quickly that auditioning is not a forbidding thing, and if the conductor succeeds at the same time in relating the audition to the developing objectives of the choir it takes on an increasingly positive aspect in everyone's mind.

4. The form of the audition must make it a pleasant experience. The auditioner will be nervous and should be put at ease by being asked at first to do what he can do easily, and only gradually led into more challenging areas. A perceptive conductor learns as much from what the singer does easily and well as from what he cannot do.

An audition should have the following elements, structured according to the choir's objectives and the conductor's mode of operation:

a. Singing a familiar song, hymn, folksong, or even popular song. The aim is twofold: to reassure the singer by asking him to begin with something familiar and to hear the voice as naturally as possible.

b. Exploration of the resources and limitations of the voice: extremes of range, comfortable tessituras, specific vocal faults or mannerisms, power, intonation, and support. Exercises graded from easy to difficult to test these matters should be conducted in a polite, friendly atmosphere, the conductor noting problems mentally without making them issues of conversation at the moment. For him to make notations after each vocalise or exercise can be regarded by the singer as an ominous act, which may increase his tension.

c. Examination of the singer's choral skills: rhythmic acuity, ability to hear intervals separately and as parts of a chord, ability to maintain one part against another, and so on. For complete beginners this may be confined to singing simple scales accurately and imitating specific intervals.

d. Determination of the singer's ability to use notation and his reaction to an unfamiliar score. This can range from asking him to follow his part while the entire song is played, to actual sight-reading without accompaniment. The conductor needs to observe what the singer does with the score from the outset: Does he reject it with a nervous "Oh, I don't read music!", have trouble locating his line, begin to count but quickly lose the beat, follow his part by ear if it is played for him, or actually read the notation? For beginners this should be done in an apparently off-hand way, the conductor lending encouragement by stressing those things about the score which can be easily seen, such as the words, the movement of the melody, and so on.

e. Observation of the singer's reactions under stress. This permits the conductor to form a preliminary estimate as to how the singer will fit into the choir. Does his nervousness spring from ignorance or from a perfectionist desire to excel? Is he apathetic, vital, or high strung? What personal defense mechanisms does he use to cover his insecurity?

PROBLEM F:

How does the conductor maintain the best relations with accompanists and organists?

Very often the success of a performance depends as much on the skill of his accompanist as on that of the conductor. The art of successful accompanying is a difficult and sensitive one. The dynamic conductor takes great care to secure the best talent available, and then sees that the accompanist's task is pleasant, rewarding, and secure. Even with student accompanists, whose skills are less than the conductor might wish, he tries to take advantage of their capabilities without making their shortcomings the issue of open conflict. The accompanist must never have to serve as a whipping-boy for the conductor's faults or poor preparation.

The following principles have demonstrated their value in successful conductor-accompanist relationships. They might be termed "The Accompanist's Bill of Rights".

1. *The accompanist will be respected by all as a person and a musician.* He will be appreciated for his skills and his qualities as an individual, and even overt shortcomings and mistakes will be dealt with politely and objectively, in the assumption that he is trying to do his best. If there is evidence that he is not trying, or that he is simply not competent, his services should be discontinued, but never in a way to cause him embarrassment.

2. *The conductor will always give the accompanist clear, complete, musically precise, easily understandable directions.* The accompanist will not be expected to read the conductor's mind, or perform impossible feats of musicianship or technique.

3. *The accompanist will be informed ahead of rehearsal time what music will be used.* He will be given the scores in time to rehearse them beforehand, whenever this is physically possible, and in any case will not be asked to read a new score at sight unless he has agreed in advance that he is willing to do so.

4. *The accompanist is expected to be prepared when he comes to rehearsal.* This includes personal examination and practice of the music which the conductor has supplied, as well as consultation with the conductor about any special problems.

5. *The accompanist and the conductor mutually agree that the conductor is in charge.* The accompanist will not try to

"take over", offer advice that is not asked for, or make derogatory comments in the rehearsal. The conductor will exercise his authority politely, engaging the accompanist's cooperation rather than commanding it.

6. *The conductor will take care to see that program credits given to the accompanist are thorough and accurate.*

7. *The accompanist will not ordinarily be asked to conduct the choir in the absence of the conductor.* Unless such an arrangement is agreed to and thoroughly understood by all, in advance, the accompanist should not be an assistant or emergency conductor. The converse of this is also true: The conductor should ordinarily not accompany the choir if the accompanist is present, even though more than one instrument is available.

PROBLEM G:
How can the conductor determine the "right" or "appropriate" tempo when the music contains no metronome marking?

A great deal of music is marked with only the vaguest indications of tempo. Even such standard terms as *allegro, andante,* and *largo* are relative and allow wide latitude. Metronome markings added by editors only supply an educated guess as to the composer's intention and may not be possible or appropriate for a particular choir's performance. The conductor must study the music in light of his choir's ability and the conditions under which it will be performed in order to establish a tempo which will do the music and his choir full justice. He should take note of the following:

1. *The shortest note-values in the vocal parts:* A usable rule-of-thumb is: The metric beat should be at the fastest tempo in which short-note passages can be sung cleanly, accurately, and with vitality. If these notes can't be sung because the chosen tempo doesn't allow time for the tone or consonants to be clearly formed, the tempo is too fast. If the tempo is slowed so that those short notes sound sluggish or labored, it is too slow.

2. *The prevailing mood in a given performance:* When a choir knows a work thoroughly and is highly skilled in technical matters, they are often able in performance to project a mood which will actually alter the tempo. In exceptional cases, when they "catch fire", it may be wise to sacrifice some clarity or precision in the interest of conveying mood values. This calls for a high degree of coordination between choir

and conductor, and the most dynamic, accurate conducting techniques. A notable example was a performance of the *Missa Solemnis* under Toscanini. Even the highly proficient Robert Shaw Chorale is pushed beyond its ability to sing runs clearly in Toscanini's driving, exciting tempos in the *Credo,* but the performance is generally regarded as exceptionally effective.

3. The built-in difficulties of the music: Tongue-twisting word or consonant combinations, unusually difficult interval progressions, rhythmic complexities, or unusual relations between voices and accompaniment are but a few of the considerations which affect the tempo chosen for a given piece.

The conductor's ability to anticipate these problems may save him from a disastrous rehearsal or performance. If he fails to anticipate the problems and asks his choir to sing such a line as "Through the clouds th'angelic hosts thrice shone" at a fast, light tempo, he will be in for trouble!

4. The acoustics of the hall: Fast tempos in halls with long reverberation times tend to blur into tonal mud. On the other hand, very dead halls often call for faster tempos to overcome the devitalization and listlessness of the sound. Excellent acoustics can pose a problem even more crucial: without acoustical faults behind which to take refuge, the conductor's tempos must be accurate and musical or they are glaringly exposed. The wise conductor does his best to adjust his tempos to the requirements of the hall and to the actual sounds his choir makes in that hall when the audience is present. He chooses tempos which are "appropriate" in terms of musical meaning rather than those which merely conform to printed instructions.

5. The morale of the choir at the moment of performance: A recording or juke-box perpetuates one tempo forever, but it can be argued that the competent, expressive choir should *never* use the same tempo in a given work twice in succession. If they are elated and sharp at the moment of performance, as suggested above, they can be led to mold tempo to expressive ends very readily. If they are psychologically depressed as a performance begins, adjustments of tempo can often overcome the depression and lead them to a far better performance. The conductor's perception of the non-verbal means of communication discussed in Chapter 4 will open to him many avenues of control in this realm.

PROBLEM H:
How important is the stage appearance and deportment of a choir?

In a word: Vitally! Our television-oriented culture inclines audiences to "hear with their eyes". If a group looks sharp and attractive they will be more likely to be heard as sounding right. If they are sloppy in appearance, their performance may be heard by many as unimpressive. Nor is this an audience reaction alone; the confidence and group spirit developed among singers who know that they "look sharp" can be a tangible base for fine performance. This is illustrated in many choral festivals in the sharp contrast between groups for whom appearance has a high priority and those who have evidently given the matter little thought. Church choirs also illustrate the importance of group appearance when their service reflects little understanding of the choir's key role in controlling the mood and dignity of worship through its visible as well as audible actions. The conductor's responsibility here is inescapable; while he may delegate some details to officers or committees, it is *his* choir that performs. What they do, how they look, and what they communicate all reflect what he has done, thought about, and held to be important.

A check-list of questions about details of appearance and deportment has proven valuable to conductors in making their plans in this area. The dynamic conductor will add his own questions to the following list:

1. Is every singer's robe or uniform adequately and comfortably fitted? What effort has been expended to see that all robes or uniforms are the same? Are robe-lengths matched, so that the hem-line of every row forms a straight line when the choir stands? Are hoods, collars, stoles, or other special elements of the total apparel in good repair, clean, and easily available? Does every singer know how they are to be worn?

2. What dress regulations are enforced? Do singers understand that such regulations apply absolutely, or do they feel they may be regarded lightly? Do they understand the reasons for the conductor's insistence upon uniformity? (See the sample Dress Regulations for Robed Choirs suggested below.)

3. What pride do the singers feel in their robes or uniforms? What has the conductor done to instill such pride from the outset? Do singers regard dress regulations as tedious rules they must obey, or as a positive aspect of "how we do things"? Has the conductor made it clear that wrinkled, dirty, or inappropriate uniforms or robes will simply not be allowed in performance, so that singers as a matter of course come properly prepared? Does singers' pride in their uniform or robe lead them to be careful about what they do while wearing it, so that they refrain from smoking or engaging in horseplay while wearing robes, and do not stand around with the robe or uniform in obvious disarray in view of potential audience members?

4. Are rituals and movements of worship performed with skill, accuracy, and coordination? Do they reflect dignity and conviction? Are hymnbooks and folders held at uniform heights and angles? Are folders the same color and size, and not stuffed with personal junk? Have singers learned to stand, sit, kneel, and turn in a unified and dignified manner? If there is a Processional in the service, has the choir learned to walk with poise, natural spacing, and a sense of purpose that communicates to the congregation? Have they disciplined themselves to sit still and avoid whispering or note-passing during those parts of the service which do not involve them directly?

5. Have performance disciplines been thoroughly learned? Can the choir walk into place smoothly, get on and off risers with dignity, hold music or folders naturally, and avoid unnecessary movement of the body while singing? Have they learned the importance of keeping the hands unobtrusive during a performance? Do they watch the conductor and sing to the audience, or bury their heads in the music? Have they learned to acknowledge applause without becoming badly disorganized as a group?

Dress Regulations For Robed Choirs

Women:

Black shoes with solid toes and moderately low heels.

No clothing visible at hem, neck, or sleeves of the robe.

No webbed, colored, or patterned hosiery.

No jewelry: bracelets, necklaces, earrings, hair clips, or headbands.

Men:

Dark trousers (preferably black)

Black sox and shoes

White shirts (no stripes, no colors)

Dark, solid-color tie

(If collars or hoods are worn, men may omit the shirt and tie, wearing a T-shirt under the robe).

PROBLEM I:
Should a choir have a constitution, by-laws, and formal organization?

Some choirs function well with no formal organization. If their responsibilities structure their activities rather completely, as might be the case in some church situations, an organizational structure might be redundant. Larger, more diverse groups usually find it to their advantage to establish an organizational structure which defines and establishes guidelines for the most efficient operation. A current set of By-Laws for an active organization of large scope is given below. This shows how one group has been organized and how they have chosen to formulate their rules of operation. In the development of these By-Laws the following principles were clearly in operation:

1. *Organization follows action:* The most efficient organization serves explicit goals, expedites established functions, or systematizes activity already begun. Building an elaborate organizational plan first, in hopes that it will be fleshed out by future activity, probably falls into the category of busywork in the average choir situation.

2. *Organization must reflect the actual objectives of the choir involved:* What is *this* choir organized to do? How will *this* organization implement those aims? What officers, rules, plans, and agreements are *necessary* to help this group achieve what it is supposed to? What things are *not* needed? Has the choir's experience shown that the existence of officers and written rules actually does facilitate the group's function?

3. *Choir members must be involved in building the organizational plan:* That plan, after all, concerns them as individuals. Even if the resulting format looks much like those of other choirs, the crucial decision is that the members themselves have decided that it is specifically suited to their needs.

4. The plan must provide for recurrent re-examination of its own validity: What works now may seem rigid or outmoded in five years. The philosophy of organization must flexibly respond to changed conditions. Choir members should regard their organization as the living embodiment of their own needs and habits, and not as a cold holdover of tradition.

The By-Laws of The Schola Cantorum of the Foothill College District of Cupertino, California resulted from the operation of these principles in a group of 150 highly talented adults in this symphonic choir. Organized in 1964, the choir sang with the San Francisco Symphony under Josef Krips and the Peninsula Symphony under Aaron Sten during its first concert season. After personal auditions in which 250 applicants were heard and 125 selected as charter members, the group began rehearsing. The size and logistical demands of the Schola made it obvious at once that an organizational structure was required, and a committee of the membership was formed to establish By-Laws. These were written with a view to the brief experience already obtained and a projection of the course of events for the coming few years. They were adopted by the entire membership after due consideration.

At the onset of the Sixth Concert Season in 1969, the Executive Board felt the need for a thorough revision of the By-Laws, and appointed a committee for that purpose. The committee was instructed to produce a set of By-Laws which reflected the habits of operation acquired by the group, and to set forth clear and workable rules for operation in such areas as membership and attendance requirements, dues, and the functions of the various officers. After thorough, extended deliberations, the following revised By-Laws were adopted by the group early in 1970.

The Schola Cantorum is a community choir sponsored by the Office of Community Services of the Foothill Junior College District, involving both DeAnza and Foothill Colleges. Its membership is largely adult, with strong representation from various professional and occupational areas typical of the cultural community on the peninsula south of San Francisco. Many of the members have sung with leading professional, semi-professional, and university choirs throughout the United States. Membership is by personal audition, and during its entire history a waiting list of qualified applicants has been maintained. Auditions are held once each year.

While a community choir of this size and scope probably calls for more detailed organization than some church or school choirs, this format may prove instructive because it represents the operation of the principles stated above, and because it presents a specific solution to organizational problems common to many choirs.

BY-LAWS

ARTICLE I : NAME AND AFFILIATION

Sec. 1 *Name:* The name of this organization is THE SCHOLA CANTORUM.

Sec. 2 *Affiliation:* The Schola Cantorum is a function of the Office of Community Services of the Foothill Junior College District, in cooperation with the Fine Arts Division of De Anza College in Cupertino, California. The College District will provide facilities for rehearsal and performance, as well as basic financial support and supervision. It is the intent of these By-Laws that The Schola Cantorum shall be a self-governing organization operating within the framework of the Foothill College District Community Services Policies, pursuant to Sections 6368-73 of the California State Education Code. As such it will assist in its own financial support through assessment of dues and concert box-office receipts.

ARTICLE II : PURPOSES

Sec. 1 The objectives of The Schola Cantorum are:

a. to establish and maintain a tradition of choral excellence.

b. to present fine performances of major choral literature, accompanied and unaccompanied, secular and sacred, from all musical eras.

c. to develop channels for performance with various symphony orchestras in the Bay Area.

d. to exert a positive influence on choral performance standards throughout the Peninsula and the Bay Area.

e. to stimulate and commission new choral writing by major composers for premiere performance by the organization.

ARTICLE III : MEMBERSHIP

Sec. 1 *Who may join:* The Schola Cantorum is a symphonic choir of competent adult singers. All persons beyond high school age who demonstrate proper qualifications in audition with the Music Director are eligible to join.

Sec. 2 *Requirements for continued membership:* Retention of membership is contingent upon consistent attendance at rehearsals and concerts as defined in Section 3 below, regular payment of dues as defined in Article IV, and upon continued vocal and musical proficiency as determined by the Musical Director through periodic re-audition.

Sec. 3 *Rehearsals and concerts and absences therefrom:* The concert season begins in September and ends in June. Rehearsals and concerts shall be held at times and places to be designated by the Music Director. In addition to regular weekly rehearsals, special rehearsals may be held prior to concerts; when the schedule of such rehearsals is announced to the members three or more weeks beforehand, attendance will be required for the maintenance of membership.

a. *Excused absence:* If a member must miss a rehearsal or performance or any part thereof, he shall notify his Section Leader beforehand in order to qualify the absence as excused.

b. *Unexcused absence:* An unexcused absence is defined as one for which prior notification and a valid reason is not given to the Section Leader or for which the member fails to present to the Membership Committee satisfactory evidence of extenuating circumstances.

c. *Repeated absence or tardiness:* Continued absence or tardiness for any reason shall call for review and such action as the Membership Committee may consider appropriate.

Sec. 4. *Reasons and procedures for suspension:* A member may be suspended for the duration of one concert period at the discretion of the Membership Committee if for any reason he misses, arrives late at, or leaves early from a total of more than three rehearsals for that concert; if he is unexcusedly absent from any of the four rehearsals immediately preceding that concert or if for any reason he misses more than one of those rehearsals.

Sec. 5 *Reasons and procedures for dismissal:* A member may be dismissed from The Schola by a majority vote of the Executive Board for any of the following reasons:

a. *Unexcused absences:* Two unexcused absences during a concert season shall be cause for dismissal.

b. *Repeated suspension:* Provocation of a second suspension shall be considered as evidence of unsuitability for membership and cause for dismissal.

c. *Other reasons:* A member shall be subject to dismissal, at the discretion of the Executive Board, for failure to abide by the rules and By-Laws of The Schola Cantorum, or for conduct not in keeping with the nature and goals of the organization.

Sec. 6 *Leaves of absence:* If, for personal or business reasons, a member wants a temporary leave of absence from the choir, he shall submit to his Section Leader a completed "Request for Leave of Absence" form stating the duration for which the leave is required and the reasons for it. The request shall be considered by the Membership Committee and shall not be considered to have been granted until agreed to by that committee. Absences not covered by such action shall be considered unexcused.

A member wanting an extension of a leave shall apply for same to the Membership Committee. If a leave is not extended it will be ended, and if the member does not return it shall be considered that he has resigned.

Return to membership after a leave of absence shall be subject to the availability of an opening in the section concerned. While every effort will be made to reinstate the member on leave, such reinstatement will not be allowed to affect adversely the balance of voices.

Sec. 7 *Readmission:*

a. *After suspension:* In the absence of any special conditions requiring the action of the Executive Board, a suspended member will be reinstated at the beginning of rehearsals for the concert following his suspension.

b. *After dismissal:* A dismissed member may be readmitted upon presentation of satisfactory evidence of extenuating circumstances. Such readmission shall require the concurrence of the Executive Board and the Music Director.

ARTICLE IV : DUES

Sec. 1 Members shall pay annual dues in an amount and at a time to be determined by the Finance Committee. These dues, once determined, shall not be changed during the concert season for which they are specified.

Sec. 2 Monies collected from dues shall be handled as Foothill District Income, credited to The Schola Cantorum.

Sec. 3 Acceptance of membership in The Schola Cantorum under these By-Laws implies agreement that, upon resignation, suspension, or dismissal, no member shall be entitled to any refund of dues paid.

ARTICLE V : EXECUTIVE BOARD

Sec. 1 *Composition:* The Executive Board shall consist of the officers specified in Article VI, the Music Director ex officio, and the Section Leaders.

Sec. 2 *Responsibility:* All affairs of The Schola Cantorum, except where provided otherwise in these By-Laws, shall be conducted by the Executive Board, whose authority shall be final, except where modified by policies of the Foothill College District, the California Education Code, or the Community Services Office. Issues shall be decided by a simple majority; each member shall have one vote.

Sec. 3 *Meetings:* The Executive Board shall meet at least four times during each concert season. Further meetings may be held at the discretion of the President or the Music Director, or when asked for by the written request of two or more Board members.

Sec. 4 *Duties:* The Executive Board is charged with:

a. holding meetings at such times and places as are deemed necessary.
b. conducting the business of The Schola Cantorum, and formulating policies except as specifically delegated to the Music Director in Article X Section 3.
c. advising and planning for the annual budget, and assisting in promotion of such money-raising activities as may be thought advisable.
d. making final decisions about the suspension, dismissal, readmission, and reinstatement of members.
e. appointing committees, carrying on correspondence and communication, employing agents or assistants, establishing policy and direction, and otherwise revising and carrying into execution activities deemed proper and constructive for the objectives of The Schola Cantorum and the welfare of its members.

Sec. 5 *Line of authority:*

a. The President is the principal executive officer, and shall preside at all meetings.
b. The Vice-President shall preside in the absence of the President.
c. In the absence of the President and the Vice-President, authority shall continue in the following order:
    1. Business Manager
    2. Treasurer
    3. Secretary
    4. Assistant Business Manager

Sec. 6 *Resignation:* A member of the Executive Board may resign at any time by giving written notice to the President or Vice-President. Such resignation shall take effect at the time stipulated in the notice, and, unless otherwise stipulated, acceptance of such resignation shall be automatic.

Sec. 7 *Vacancies:* When a vacancy occurs on the Executive Board it shall be filled without undue delay by a majority vote of the remaining members of the Board at a special meeting called for that purpose. Such elections must be held within thirty days from the date of the vacancy. Board members thus chosen will hold office for the balance of the current concert season, or until replaced as provided elsewhere in these By-Laws.

ARTICLE VI : OFFICERS

Sec. 1 *Titles, Qualifications, Duties, and Terms of Office:* The officers of The Schola Cantorum shall be President, Vice-President, Business Manager, Treasurer, Secretary, and Assistant Business Manager. Officers shall be active members of The Schola Cantorum in good standing. They shall serve without remuneration for one year and be eligible for re-election; continuation in office shall be contingent upon satisfactory performance of the duties of the office, subject to the discretion of a majority of the Executive Board.

Sec. 2 *The Music Director* shall be an officer ex officio, and shall be the official representative of the Office of Community Services and the Foothill College District.

Sec. 3 *President:* The President shall be the chief executive officer of The Schola Cantorum and shall exercise general management of its business and supervise the functions of its other officers. The President shall preside over all meetings of the Executive Board and over all meetings of The Schola Cantorum. He shall be a member ex officio of all operating committees of the organization. He shall serve as liaison between the Music Director, the Executive Board, and the general membership. He shall compile and present at the Annual Meeting the annual report on the transactions and condition of the organization.

Sec. 4 *Vice-President:* The Vice-President shall assume the responsibilities and carry out the duties of the President in the President's absence. He shall also serve as Chairman of the Membership and Nominating Committees. It is assumed that under normal circumstances the Vice-President will succeed to the Presidency upon expiration of his term as Vice-President.

Sec. 5 *Business Manager:* The Business Manager shall serve as Chairman of the Concert Committee and as Member ex officio of the Promotion Committee. He shall be responsible for the following:

a. all physical arrangements within the rehearsal and concert halls.
b. storage and maintenance of all property belonging to the organization, including appointment of the Librarian and distribution of music.
c. programs and literature for the use of the organization in connection with its performances.
d. maintenance of standards and mode of dress for concerts as agreed upon by the Executive Board and the Music Director.
e. providing and managing ushers for concerts as needed.

Sec. 6 *Treasurer:* The Treasurer shall collect all monies acquired by The Schola Cantorum, except where provided otherwise in these By-Laws or by vote of a majority of the Executive Board. He shall deposit such funds in the name of the organization according to procedures established by the Foothill College District. He shall render a statement of the condition of such funds to the members of the Executive Board whenever so requested. He shall give and receive receipts for money and other property due and payable to The Schola Cantorum from any source. He shall serve as Chairman of the Finance Committee. He shall, in cooperation with the members of the Finance Committee and the Music Director, assist and advise in the preparation of the annual budget. He shall perform any other duties incidental to his office as may be directed by the Executive Board.

Sec. 7 *Secretary:* The Secretary shall record the proceedings of the meetings of The Schola Cantorum and of the Executive Board in books kept for that purpose and belonging to the organization. He shall maintain a file of the organization's business records and correspondence. He shall have charge of the correspondence of The Schola Cantorum. He shall in addition perform such other duties as may be assigned by the Executive Board.

Sec. 8 *Assistant Business Manager:* The Assistant Business Manager shall help the Business Manager in the performance of his duties. He shall serve as Chairman of the Promotion Committee and with the assistance of this committee and its subcommittees, he shall be responsible for:

a. publicizing and advertising The Schola Cantorum and its performances.
b. the printing, distribution and sale of tickets for all performances.
c. the production and sale of recordings.

It is assumed that under normal circumstances the Assistant Business Manager will become the Business Manager upon expiration of his term as Assistant Business Manager.

Sec. 9 *Other Officers:* The Executive Board may appoint such other officers and agents for such periods and with such authority as it shall deem necessary; however, if positions thus created are to continue beyond the concert season in which such appointments are made, they shall be supported by appropriate amendments to these By-Laws in accordance with Article XII.

ARTICLE VII : MEETINGS

Sec. 1 *Annual Meeting:* The Annual Meeting of The Schola Cantorum for election of officers and for the transaction of such other business as may properly come before the meeting shall be held on the final Monday in May of each year, unless such day is a legal holiday or the Executive Board designates otherwise.

Sec. 2 *Special Meetings:* Special Meetings of The Schola Cantorum may be held from time to time upon call from the President or any two Board members, or upon petition of at least thirty members of The Schola, at such time and place as may be designated in the call for the meeting.

Sec. 3 *Notice of Meetings:* Notice of each meeting of The Schola Cantorum, whether Annual or Special, shall be given to the membership at a previous rehearsal at least seven days before the meeting; members not present at that rehearsal shall be notified by mail. Such notice shall state the purpose for which the meeting is to be held and the time and the place of the meeting.

Sec. 4 *Quorum:* Seventy-five percent of the members of The Schola Cantorum qualifying under Article III Section 2 of these By-Laws shall constitute a quorum at any meeting, unless otherwise stated in these By-Laws.

Sec. 5 *Voting:* Every member of The Schola Cantorum qualifying under Article III Section 2 of these By-Laws shall be entitled to one vote at every meeting of the organization. Absent members shall not be entitled to vote by proxy. At all meetings of The Schola all matters shall be decided by simple majority vote, provided that a quorum is present, excepting those matters required in these By-Laws or by statute to be decided otherwise.

Sec. 6 *Conduct of Meetings:* Annual and Special meetings of The Schola Cantorum shall be conducted by the presiding officer in such a manner as to conform to proper parliamentary procedure.

ARTICLE VIII : NOMINATIONS AND ELECTIONS OF OFFICERS

Sec. 1 *Nominations:* The Nominating Committee, having deliberated as stated in these By-Laws, shall report all nominations to the Executive Board at least two weeks prior to the date of the Annual (or as applicable Special) Meeting, and the nominations contained in the slate drawn up by the Nominating Committee shall be presented to the membership of The Schola Cantorum in writing at least one week prior to the Annual or Special Meeting. Further nominations will be accepted at the Annual (or Special) Meeting.

Sec. 2 *Elections:* Elections shall be conducted as follows:

a. The Secretary of The Schola shall read to those present the slate prepared by the Nominating Committee. The President shall then open the meeting for nominations from the floor, per Section 1 above.
b. In the event that no nominations are presented from the floor the President shall entertain a motion and voice vote to instruct the Secretary to cast one official ballot for the entire slate drawn up by the Nomination Committee, and these persons shall be announced as elected.
c. If any office is contested, ballots shall be distributed to all members present for the purpose of recording the vote.
d. Official ballots cast shall be collected and counted immediately by tellers appointed by the President, and the result then shall be announced by the Secretary.
e. Written notice of the result of any election shall be posted for the members of The Schola Cantorum as soon as possible thereafter.

ARTICLE IX : COMMITTEES

Sec. 1 The permanent committees and subcommittees of The Schola Cantorum shall be as follows:

- Membership Committee
  - Section Leaders
  - Hospitality Subcommittee
  - Historian Subcommittee
- Nominating Committee
- Finance Committee
- Concert Committee
  - Arrangements Subcommittee
  - Concert Dress Subcommittee
  - Library Subcommittee
  - Ushering Subcommittee
- Promotion Committee
  - Program Subcommittee
  - Publicity Subcommittee
  - Tickets Subcommittee
  - Recording Subcommittee

In addition, the President may, with the approval of the Executive Board, appoint such other incidental working committees as deemed necessary.

Sec. 2 *General Duties and Responsibilities:* Each committee and subcommittee of The Schola Cantorum shall, through its chairman and the officers of the organization, be responsible to the Executive Board, and shall implement the programs and policies of the Board as the Board may direct. Each committee chairman shall prepare and submit to the President an annual written report at least one month prior to the Annual Meeting.

Sec. 3 *Membership Committee:* The Membership Committee shall be comprised of the eight Section Leaders and the Music Director with the Vice-President of The Schola Cantorum serving as Committee chairman; for consideration of the attendance record of a particular member and the action required thereto the responsibilities and powers of the committee shall be delegated to a subcommittee consisting of the Music Director, the Vice-President and the Section Leader of the member concerned. The Committee shall be responsible for maintaining an accurate record of members and attendance. It shall suspend members in accordance with the provisions of Article III, Sec. 4 and report thereon to the Executive Board. It shall also report excessive absence to the Executive Board for its consideration and appropriate action in accordance with the provisions of Article III, Sec. 5 The members of this Committee shall serve as liaison between individual members of The Schola Cantorum and the Executive Board.

a. *Section Leaders:* Section Leaders shall be elected by the members of their respective sections at the first rehearsal for the third regularly scheduled concert of the season. If a vacancy occurs during the year, the section shall elect a successor at the second rehearsal following the occurrence of such vacancy.

b. *Hospitality Subcommittee:* The Hospitality Subcommittee shall be appointed by the Membership Chairman, and shall use every means at its disposal to promote a friendly atmosphere within the membership of The Schola Cantorum including serving refreshments at rehearsals.

Sec. 4 *Nominating Committee:* The Nominating Committee shall be appointed by the Executive Board in September. It shall be composed of a chairman and one member from each section of The Schola Cantorum. The Vice-President of The Schola shall serve as chairman of the committee. At least six weeks prior to the Annual Meeting, the Chairman shall notify the members of The Schola that suggestions for nominations for officers are to be received. The committee shall accept such suggestions from any member of the organization, provided that the individuals suggested are eligible to serve according to these By-Laws. It shall consider the qualifications of these candidates and shall determine their willingness to serve in the capacities for which they have been suggested. From these candidates the committee shall select a slate of nominees, and the Chairman shall then report to the Executive Board, as stated in Article VIII Section 1 of these By-Laws. The members of the Nominating Committee shall be committed to use discretion with respect to the deliberations of the committee until such deliberations have been presented to the Executive Board.

Sec. 5 *Finance Committee:* The Finance Committee shall be composed of the Treasurer as chairman, the Business Manager, and one other member of the Executive Board appointed by the President. It shall be the duty of this committee to assist the Music Director in formulating the budget for The Schola Cantorum for submission through the Executive Board to the Office of Community Services.

Sec. 6 *Concert Committee:* The Concert Committee shall be responsible for all physical arrangements within the rehearsal and concert halls and for the storage, and Manager of The Schola shall serve as chairman of this committee. He shall appoint the subcommittees listed below, and the chairmen of these subcommittees shall comprise the Concert Committee. In addition, the Business Manager, with the approval of the Executive Board, may appoint such other incidental working subcommittees as may be deemed necessary. The composition of the several subcommittees shall be left to the discretion of the subcommittee chairmen and the Business Manager.

a. *Arrangements Subcommittee:* The Arrangements Subcommittee shall be responsible for the physical arrangements within the rehearsal and concert halls.
b. *Concert Dress Subcommittee:* The Concert Dress Subcommittee shall be responsible for maintenance of the standards and mode of dress for concerts agreed upon by the Executive Board and the Music Director.
c. *Library Subcommittee:* The Library Subcommittee shall be responsible for the control and distribution of music belonging to The Schola Cantorum.
d. *Ushering Subcommittee:* The Ushering Subcommittee shall be responsible for providing and managing ushers for concerts as needed.

Sec. 7 *Promotion Committee:* The Assistant Business Manager of The Schola Cantorum shall serve as Chairman of the Promotion Committee with the Business Manager serving as a member ex offico.

a. *Program Subcommittee:* The Program Subcommittee shall be responsible for the preparation of all programs and literature intended for use by The Schola Cantorum in connection with its performances.
b. *Publicity Subcommittee:* The Publicity Subcommittee shall be responsible for devising and preparing materials for publicizing and advertising The Schola Cantorum and its performances, using the facilities and personnel of the Foothill College District as needed.
c. *Tickets Subcommittee:* The Tickets Subcommittee shall be responsible for preparing tickets, distributing them to the membership of The Schola and to public outlets for sale, accounting for tickets sold and returned, and for devising means for the sale of the greatest possible number of tickets. The scale of prices to be charged for these tickets shall be determined by the Executive Board.
d. *Recording Subcommittee:* The Recording Subcommittee shall be responsible for arranging for the recording of concerts, selecting and editing portions suitable for duplication, and arranging for pressing and sale of recordings. They shall obtain prior permission to record in cases of copyrighted works. Proceeds of recording sales and costs of recording shall be handled through The Schola Cantorum Trust Fund.

ARTICLE X : MUSIC DIRECTOR

Sec. 1 *Selection:* The position of Music Director for The Schola Cantorum will normally be filled by a choral director of the Foothill College District or by a qualified individual otherwise associated with the De Anza or Foothill College Divisions of Fine Arts. In the event that such individual cannot or does not elect to serve as Music Director of The Schola, the Executive Board shall select a Music Director acceptable to themselves and to the Foothill College District Office of Community Services.

Sec. 2 *Salary:* The Music Director of The Schola Cantorum shall be paid a salary to be determined by the Office of Community Services with the advice of the Executive Board.

Sec. 3 *Function:* The Music Director's province shall encompass all matters of a musical nature relative to The Schola. It shall include, but not be restricted to, the following:

a. the audition and selection of members;
b. the programming of concerts, and the selection and ordering of music;
c. the selection of soloists, either professional or from within The Schola;
d. the selection of accompanists and orchestral groups to assist in preparation for, and performance of concerts;
e. the conducting and scheduling of all rehearsals, unless otherwise delegated by him, and of all performances. During the first six months that any person holds the office of Music Director the selection of and allocation of funds for the payment of professional accompanists, soloists and orchestral groups shall be subject to the approval of the Executive Board. The Board may waive this right of approval at any time before the expiration of the six-month period.

ARTICLE XI : AUDIT

Sec. 1 Auditing of all funds shall be performed as part of the annual Foothill College District audit.

ARTICLE XII : AMENDMENTS TO THE BY-LAWS

Sec. 1 Petition for amendments to the By-Laws of The Schola Cantorum will be accepted by the Executive Board at any time. A petition by thirty or more members or action by the Board shall be cause for convening a Special Meeting of the membership for the purpose of considering and voting upon the proposed amendments. Otherwise, proposed amendments shall be considered and voted upon at the next Annual Meeting of The Schola. A copy of all proposed amendments shall be circulated to the membership of the organization at least two weeks prior to the meeting at which they are to be considered. The approval of any amendment requires a two-thirds majority of those voting, provided that a quorum is present at the meeting in accordance with Article VII Section 4. Any amendment adopted shall be posted for the members of The Schola Cantorum as soon as possible after its adoption.

ARTICLE XIII : DISSOLUTION

Sec. 1 In the event of the final dissolution of The Schola Cantorum, its assets shall in no wise be deemed property of the members but shall revert to the possession of the Foothill College District.

Revised: March, 1970

OTHER ORGANIZATIONAL PUBLICATIONS

A useful device popular with large, highly-organized groups is an orientation folder or pamphlet to be handed to incoming members. This serves several functions which are important to the entire organization as well as to new members. It welcomes the new person and informs him of the operating rules, traditions, and obligations of his membership. It formally confirms his acceptance into membership in a tangible way. For the newcomer to the group, such a folder symbolizes a well-functioning organization, and for old members it may serve as a reminder of things they may tend to forget. The conductor should encourage members of the organization to draw up and produce the folder, to insure that it includes all the matters which members themselves think important and wish they had been told when they entered the choir.

The following pamphlet (a simple four-page folder, reproduced flat below) was prepared by a committee of The Schola Cantorum.

(Outside)

DRESS FOR CONCERTS

In order to present a professional appearance at concerts, the following dress regulations have been adopted by The Schola, and are mandatory for participation:

FOR MEN: Black suit (NOT charcoal, dark blue, brown, pin-stripe, etc., and no tuxedos), white shirt (plain: no lace or ruffles), black shoes, black sox, black bow tie.

FOR WOMEN: Black floor-length dress; separate skirt and top are acceptable. Gown must be sleeveless, but no narrower than two inches at the shoulders; no extreme necklines, front or back; no noticeable trim such as ruffles or lace; no sequins or shiny buttons. Black dress shoes. a minimum amount of conservative jewelry. No dangling earrings, no rhinestones or other jewelry which catch or reflect light. If in doubt, do not wear it.

Further questions about dress should be discussed with your Section Leader or a member of the Concert Dress Committee.

REHEARSALS AND PERFORMANCES

Rehearsals are held Monday evenings from 7:15 until 10:00 p.m. in the Choral Room (A-11) at De Anza College, unless designated otherwise.

Ordinary seasons contain four principal concerts, although some of these are given twice, frequently in different locations. Music is rarely, if ever, performed from memory.

April, 1970

YOUR INTRODUCTION TO

The SCHOLA CANTORUM

Your name ____________________

Your voice ____________________

Your Section Leader ____________________

His/Her home phone ____________________

His/Her business phone ____________________

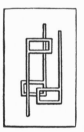

(Inside)

Welcome to membership in
THE SCHOLA CANTORUM

Here is information which you will need as a member. Please read it carefully, since it answers questions which are frequently asked by incoming members.

In addition, we ask that you read the By-laws, which contain detailed information about the Schola and the policies which govern it. If you have questions about any of these materials, please consult your Section Leader, or any of the other officers.

MEMBERSHIP

The Schola Cantorum is a symphonic choir of competent adult singers. It is sponsored and supported by the Office of Community Services of the Foothill College District, and is open to all adults who qualify by personal audition.

Retention of membership is contingent upon regular attendance at rehearsals and concerts, payment of dues, and continued vocal-musical proficiency as determined by the Music Director in periodic re-auditions.

In addition to regular weekly rehearsals, special rehearsals may be held prior to concerts. When the schedule of such rehearsals is announced to the members three or more weeks in advance, attendance will be required for the maintenance of membership.

ATTENDANCE

The musical quality of our performances and the morale of the organization depend upon regular attendance at rehearsals by all members.

Absence from rehearsals or concerts is classified as excused or unexcused. For an absence to be excused you must contact your Section Leader BEFORE the rehearsal, and provide an acceptable reason for the absence.

According to the By-Laws, if for any reason you are absent from, arrive late at, or leave early from more than three rehearsals for any one concert you will be suspended for the remainder of that concert period.

Two or more unexcused absences from rehearsals in one concert season may lead to dismissal from The Schola.

While every effort will be made to be reasonable about unavoidable absence, it must be clearly understood that members do not automatically "get" any specific number of absences. We trust that you will value your membership sufficiently to understand the wisdom of firm attendance policies.

DUES

The By-Laws provide that members shall pay dues in an amount and at a time to be determined by the Finance Committee. Currently these are $10 per year, payable in early fall. For members entering late it is the custom to prorate dues according to the date of entry.

Monies collected from dues shall be handled as Foothill District income, credited to The Schola. Acceptance of membership in the organization is an implied agreement that, upon resignation, suspension, or dismissal, no member shall be entitled to any refund of dues paid.

MUSIC

Much of the music used will be provided by the Music Library of The Schola Cantorum. However, many members find it advantageous to purchase their own copies. In these cases, and in situations where available funds cannot supply all the music, the De Anza College Bookstore will have copies available for purchase in the evenings prior to rehearsal.

BIBLIOGRAPHY

Conducting Techniques:

Coward, Henry *Choral Technique and Interpretation* – London: Novello & Co., 1914

Davison, Archibald T. *Choral Conducting* – Cambridge: Harvard University Press, 1940

Ehmann, Wilhelm *Choral Directing* – Minneapolis: Augsburg Publishing House, 1968

Ehret, Walter *The Choral Conductor's Handbook* – New York: Edward B. Marks Music Corp., 1959

Garretson, Robert L. *Conducting Choral Music* (2nd edition) – Boston; Allyn and Bacon, Inc., 1965

Howerton, George *Technique and Style in Choral Singing* – New York: Carl Fischer, 1958

Jones, Archie N. *Techniques in Choral Conducting* – New York: Carl Fischer, Inc., 1948

Korthkamp, Ivan *The Advanced Choir* – Tower, Minn.: Mohawk Publishing Co., 1969

Krone, Max T. *The Chorus and Its Conductor* – Park Ridge, Illinois: Neil A. Kjos, 1945

- - - - - - - *Expressive Conducting* – Chicago, Illinois: Neil A. Kjos, Inc. 1949

Neidig, Kenneth L., and Jennings, John W. *Choral Director's Guide* – West Nyack, N.Y.: Parker Publishing Company, 1967

Sunderman, Lloyd *Some Techniques for Choral Success* – Rockville Center, N.Y.: Belwin, 1952

Young, Percy M. *A Handbook of Choral Technique* – London: Dennis Dobson, Ltd., 1953

Voice Training:

Appelman, D. Ralph *The Science of Vocal Pedagogy* (with album of recorded examples) – Bloomington: Indiana University Press, 1967

Christy, Van *Expressive Singing* (Two volumes) – Dubuque: Wm. C. Brown, 1961

Klein, Joseph J. *Singing Technique* – Princeton: D. Van Nostrand Company, 1967

Peterson, Paul W. *Natural Singing and Expressive Conducting* – Winston-Salem, N.C.: John F. Blair, 1966

Reid, Cornelius L. *Bel Canto Principles and Practices* – New York: Coleman-Ross Company, 1950

------- *The Free Voice* – New York: Coleman-Ross Company, 1965

Stanton, Royal *Steps to Singing* – Belmont, Calif.: Wadsworth Publishing Company, 1971.

General:

Ades, Hawley *Choral Arranging* – Delaware Water Gap, Pa.: Shawnee Press, Inc. 1966

Adler, Kurt *Phonetics and Diction in Singing: Italian, French, Spanish German* – Minneapolis; University of Minnesota Press, 1967

Bamberger, Carl (ed.) *The Conductor's Art* – New York: McGraw Hill Book Company, 1965

Dart, Thurston *The Interpretation of Music* – New York: Harper Colophon Books, 1963

de Angelis, Michael (ed. Nicola Montani) *The Correct Pronunciation of Latin According to Roman Usage* – Philadelphia: St. Gregory Guild, 1937

Graham, Floyd F. *Public Relations in Music Education* – New York: Exposition Press, 1954

Grant, Parks *Handbook of Music Terms* – Metuchen, N.J.: The Scarecrow Press, 1967

Jacobs, Arthur (ed.) *Choral Music* – Baltimore, Md.: Penguin Books, 1963

Roe, Paul F. *Choral Music Education* – Englewood Cliffs, New Jersey: Prentice-Hall, 1970

Roth, Ernest *The Business of Music* New York: Oxford University Press, 1969

Schonberg, Harold C. *The Great Conductors* – London: Victor Gollancz, Ltd., 1968

Sunderman, Lloyd F. *Choral Organization and Administration* – Rockville Centre, L.I., N.Y.: Belwin, Inc., 1954

Waring, Fred *Tone Syllables* – Delaware Water Gap, Pa.: Shawnee Press, 1945

Wright, Gene, and Lambson, Arthur R. *The Staged Choral Concert* – Delaware Water Gap, Pa.: Shawnee Press, 1957